A Danger Which We Do Not Know

A Danger Which We Do Not Know

A Philosophical Journey into Anxiety

DAVID RONDEL

OXFORD
UNIVERSITY PRESS

Oxford University Press is a department of the University of Oxford.
It furthers the University's objective of excellence in research, scholarship,
and education by publishing worldwide. Oxford is a registered trade mark of
Oxford University Press in the UK and in certain other countries.

Published in the United States of America by Oxford University Press
198 Madison Avenue, New York, NY 10016, United States of America.

© Oxford University Press 2024

All rights reserved. No part of this publication may be reproduced, stored in
a retrieval system, or transmitted, in any form or by any means, without the prior
permission in writing of Oxford University Press, or as expressly permitted
by law, by license or under terms agreed with the appropriate reprographics
rights organization. Inquiries concerning reproduction outside the scope of the
above should be sent to the Rights Department, Oxford University Press, at the
address above.

You must not circulate this work in any other form
and you must impose this same condition on any acquirer

CIP data is on file at the Library of Congress

ISBN 9780197767245

DOI: 10.1093/9780197767276.001.0001

Printed by Integrated Books International, United States of America

To my students

Docendo discimus

A real danger is a danger which we know, a true anxiety, the anxiety in regard to such a known danger. Neurotic anxiety is anxiety in regard to a danger which we do not know... There are cases in which the attributes of true and of neurotic anxiety are intermingled. The danger is known and of the real type, but the anxiety in regard to it is disproportionately great, greater than in our judgment it ought to be. It is by this excess that the neurotic element stands revealed.

Sigmund Freud, *The Problem of Anxiety* (1936)

Contents

Acknowledgments ix
Preface xi

Introduction 1

1. The Dizziness of Freedom 16
2. When Something Bitter Rises Up 46
3. Anxiety Reveals the Nothing 71
4. A New Lap in the Race 98
5. To Clear Our Minds of Selfish Care 127
6. Never Let the Future Disturb You 154

Notes 183
Bibliography 197
Index 213

Acknowledgments

I have accumulated many debts in writing this book. Let me begin by registering heartfelt thanks to numerous colleagues, friends, and boosters, for help and encouragement, in ways big and small: Awais Aftab, Barry Allen, Tom Angier, David Antonuccio, Ethan Bair, Nadya Bair, James Bondarchuck, Devin Code, Ryan Doody, Dennis Dworkin, Jason Fisette, Katherine Fusco, Tim Gibson, Jonathan Gingerich, Simone Gubler, Steven Hayes, Colin Koopman, Carlos Mariscal, Cara Nine, Meredith Oda, Stephen Pasqualina, Susan Pittenger, Bretton Rodriguez, Lisa Schramm Gibson, Katharine Schweitzer, Suzanne Silverman, Chris Stancil, Jared Stanley, Ravi Thakral, Krista Thomason, Blake Watson, Christopher Williams, and Benjamin Young.

Embarking on this project required that I become much better versed in a new (to me) area of philosophical research. Numerous people were extremely helpful to me to that end. Thanks to Lucy Prior at the University of Birmingham, who organized an online reading group on the philosophy of anxiety, and also a stimulating conference on the subject. Working as editor on another volume about the moral psychology of anxiety was also immensely beneficial. Thanks to Mark Alfano, editor of Rowman & Littlefield's wonderful book series on the moral psychology of the emotions, for his belief in that project, and to my co-editor, Samir Chopra, for his wisdom, generosity of spirit, and many stimulating conversations. I also want to acknowledge the contributors to *The Moral Psychology of Anxiety* (Michael S. Brady, Deborah Brown, Ian Dowbiggin, Leah Kalmanson, Charlie Kurth, Michelle Maiese, Massimo Pigliucci, Jesse Prinz, Mauro Rossi, Christine Tappolet, and Juliette Vazard), from whom I learned so much.

Two public talks I gave while I held the Joe Crowley Distinguished Professorship in the Humanities at the University of Nevada gave me the opportunity to test out some new material that would eventually find its way into the book. Another presentation at the *Nevada Humanities Literary Crawl* and a colloquium talk to the philosophy department at the University of Cape Town, South Africa, also helped me sharpen some of the book's arguments. I'm grateful to all of those audience members for their questions and proddings.

Rob Sternberg, my dear friend of many years, deserves a huge debt of thanks for reading an early draft of the entire manuscript and for offering invaluable comments and suggestions—both substantive and stylistic. Lucy Randall at Oxford University Press is a paragon of publishing professionalism and skill. I'm grateful for her amazing patience, wisdom, and kindness. Thanks are also due to Lauralee Yeary at OUP, who became involved in the project at a crucial stage, and to Theodore Reiner, who helped see the book across the finish line. The painting featured on the book's cover is Christopher Pratt's *Solstice Drive to St. Anthony* (2008). Sincere thanks to Anne Pratt, the Christopher Pratt estate, and Mira Godard Gallery for permission to use it.

As always, my greatest debt is to my family—my wife, Stephanie, and children, Beatrice and Nathaniel. I love you more than you can imagine.

Preface

> What is the use of studying philosophy if all that it does for you is enable you to talk with some plausibility about some abstruse questions of logic, etc., and if it does not improve your thinking about the important questions of everyday life...?
> —Ludwig Wittgenstein, "Letter to Norman Malcolm" (November 16, 1944)

Where does the impulse to philosophize come from? What is it that prompts so many people to ask philosophical questions and think philosophical thoughts? The intellectual tradition that is dearest to my own heart—the tradition of American Pragmatism—tells an interesting story about philosophy's sources. According to this story, human beings philosophize in response to genuinely felt "problems." Problems disrupt the normal flow of experience when they arise, provoking reflection on behavior, beliefs, habits, and feelings about which we have become unreflective. When genuine problems show up on the scene, it's no longer feasible to carry on as usual.

I didn't recognize it clearly at the time, but anxiety was the main "problem" that first lured me toward the study of philosophy, and eventually to a career as a philosophy professor. Anxiety has been prominent in my experience as far back as memory takes me. Excessive, irrational worry was pretty much my default state as a child. Beginning around the age of nine or ten, I also began suffering with panic attacks. These episodes were utterly horrifying, as anyone who has endured the nightmare of a panic attack can attest. Because I lacked the language to label or understand them, the attacks were also bewildering. I had no idea what these terrible feelings that would bubble up seemingly at random even were, let alone that they might be managed or treated somehow. (I think I vaguely assumed that everyone's experience was like mine and that navigating occasional bouts of escalating terror was just an unfortunate fact about how human lives happened to be.)

People can become enthralled with philosophy for different reasons. But it's hard to deny that psychic pain is one of philosophy's most powerful contexts and catalysts, and that the field has a corresponding propensity to attract suffering people. It's often in times of anguish and despair that we feel compelled to ask those timeless philosophical questions about the self and the nature of mind; about knowledge, freedom, and ethical responsibility; about the meaning of life and the prospect of death. It's often in times of emotional struggle—when we find ourselves contending with darkness and fear, pain and loss, the unsettling sense of life's shortness and insignificance—that such questions are most salient for us.

This is basically how things went for me. I became obsessed with philosophy as soon as I encountered it (in 1997, as a freshman at the University of Western Ontario), and studying philosophy offered my anxious mind a strange kind of relief in turn. Something about philosophy's abstractness and imaginativeness, about the deep, momentous questions it considered, about the precision and clarity it tried to achieve, delivered a temporary peace from the pain of anxiety. Doing philosophy felt (and still sometimes feels) like a little vacation from the anxiety of everyday life.

I wrote this book in homage to my personal experience and trajectory. I dedicate it to my students (many of whom, I have a hunch, were drawn to the study of philosophy for more or less the same reasons as me).

Reno, Nevada. Summer 2023.

Introduction

> The source of philosophy is anxiety. . . . Religions are attempts to make an inhuman universe humanly habitable. Philosophers have often dismissed these faiths as being far beneath their own metaphysical speculations, but religion and philosophy serve the same need. Both try to fend off the abiding disquiet that goes with being human. . . . Philosophy testifies to the frailty of the human mind. Humans philosophize for the same reason they pray. They know the meaning they have fashioned in their lives is fragile and live in dread of its breaking down.
> —John Gray, *Feline Philosophy*

Anxiety is one of the main contexts in which the inclination to philosophize arises. We humans are fearful, worrying creatures. Seeking out knowledge is a natural response to being afraid. And so, occasionally, when anxiety rises up, we instinctively go hunting for answers. Having more information sometimes helps to quell the fear. Thomas Hobbes wrote in 1651 that "anxiety for the future time, disposeth men to enquire into the causes of things" (Hobbes 1991, 74). Friedrich Nietzsche similarly claimed that it is our innate "instinct of fear" that ultimately "bids us to know."

> And isn't our need for knowledge precisely this need for the familiar, the will to uncover among everything strange, unusual, and doubtful something which no longer unsettles us? Is it not the *instinct of fear* that bids us to know? And isn't the rejoicing of

the person who attains knowledge just rejoicing from a regained sense of security? (Nietzsche 2001, 214)

Hobbes and Nietzsche seem to agree that we philosophize because we are anxious. The experience of anxiety prompts us to reflect and inquire, drawing us toward perennial philosophical questions about the nature of reality and knowledge, freedom and morality, the meaning of life and the prospect of death. And turning to philosophy sometimes offers relief. Because of the precision and clarity of thinking it helps us achieve. Because reason can sometimes be deployed as a weapon against fear. Because highly abstract thought can serve as a form of escapism, a happy diversion from the anxiety of everyday life. Because philosophy itself has a long and illustrious history as a form of therapy.

It's difficult to imagine that there would be anything like the strange and beautiful activity we call philosophy if there was no anxiety in the world, if these kinds of disquieting thoughts and feelings just happened not to arise for human beings. But even if philosophy would have emerged unfazed in that kind of anxiety-free world (maybe Plato and Aristotle were right that it is in wonder, not fear, where philosophy's original spark is to be found), many of us know firsthand that the experience of anxiety can prompt us to ask philosophical questions that we otherwise might not have asked, to see those questions in a new light, or to consider them with a new intensity. Anxiety can give these questions fresh urgency, can make them vivid and momentous in ways they otherwise might not be.[1]

A Danger Which We Do Not Know comprises six vignette-like chapters that, taken as an ensemble, tell a story about how philosophy and anxiety are joined at the hip. The chapters themselves offer a mixture of different things: a dose of argument, a serving of personal musing, a pinch of self-help, tidbits of wisdom about the nature and experience of anxiety handed down to us from great philosophers throughout the ages. There are also occasional splashes of memoir, which I desperately hope don't come across as excessively whiny or self-important. I include some of this more personal material not because I think my own struggle with anxiety is unique or noteworthy in some way. Quite the contrary. I now judge it as completely unexceptional—mundane even—and the hope is that these snippets about my personal experience might resonate with some readers as a result.

The chapters in this book cover a lot of ground, historically and thematically, and together provide something like a philosophical guide to anxiety. Each one focuses on the work of a particular philosopher or philosophical tradition with an eye toward showing how their ideas help us better understand anxiety's nature and meaning. The chapters overlap with one another in various ways and build up to some larger arguments, but each one is written to be able to stand on its own. The chapters also bounce around a lot, chronologically speaking. Our journey begins in nineteenth-century Copenhagen, with Søren Kierkegaard's account of existential anxiety as "the dizziness of freedom" and ends in second-century Rome, with an inventory of anti-anxiety techniques and strategies promulgated by the great Stoic philosophers of that period. Along the way, visits are paid to Cambridge, Massachusetts (home of William James), in chapter 2, and Oxford, England (home of Iris Murdoch), in chapter 5. There are also excursions to Hamburg and Berlin, in chapter 4, where we consider some of Arthur Schopenhauer's ideas about why anxiety might arise and what it feels like when we're in its grip, and to a little wooden hut in the Black Forest Mountains, where we contend with Martin Heidegger's thinking about the connections between anxiety and death, in chapter 3.

No book of this kind could possibly have aspired to cover everything. Unavoidably, there are omissions. There is no chapter on Hindu or Buddhist thinking about anxiety, for instance, although there are a few sideward glances toward some of this material in chapter 4. Similarly, the philosophy of Epicureanism does not receive its own chapter, but there is some discussion of Epicurus's and

Lucretius's famous arguments against the fear of death in chapter 3. Allusions to Sigmund Freud are sprinkled throughout—and the book's title, *A Danger Which We Do Not Know*, is taken from one of his famous characterizations of anxiety—but there is no chapter dedicated to his groundbreaking work. Jean-Paul Sartre's seminal work on existential anxiety is referenced in a few places here and there, but a different pair of existentialist thinkers (Kierkegaard and Heidegger) occupy a more prominent place, in chapters 1 and 3, respectively. The point is that different thinkers and traditions might have easily found their way into the chapters of this book, either in place of or alongside those who are already here. Whether I have curated well will have to be for others to decide.

Two large ideas animate and give this book its shape. One has to do with anxiety's amazing variety and heterogeneity. To get a sense for this, consider the following handful of characterizations from philosophers and psychologists. Anxiety, we're told, is:

- "one of the fundamental emotions, as central a part of what it means to be human as happiness, sadness, or anger." (Freeman and Freeman 2012, xiii)
- "an all-encompassing attitude toward the world." (Solomon 1993, 229–230)
- "the philosophical mood *par excellence.*" (Trigg 2017, xxxi)
- "a unique and coherent cognitive-affective structure within our defensive motivational system" (Barlow 2000, 1249) and a "*future oriented* mood state in which one is ready or prepared to attempt to cope with upcoming negative events." (Barlow 2004, 64)
- "fear about future outcomes." (Prinz 2012, 275)
- "an emotion similar to fear, but arising without any objective source of danger." (Marks 1987, 5)
- "an affective state . . . a combination of certain feelings in the pleasure-unpleasure series with the corresponding innervations of discharge and a perception of them." (Freud

1989, 774) More formally put, anxiety involves three essential features: "(1) a specific character of unpleasure, (2) acts of discharge and (3) perceptions of those acts." (Freud 1959, 61)
- "a form of affective anticipation, something that is inextricable from how one's current surroundings appear salient." (Ratcliffe 2017, 72)
- "a negatively valenced affective state" and an "aversive emotional response to problematic uncertainty." (Kurth 2018, 7)
- "the apprehensive anticipation of future danger or misfortune accompanied by a feeling of worry, distress, and/or somatic symptoms of tension." (DSM-V, American Psychiatric Association 2013, 818)
- "the most prevalent mental health problem around the globe." (2002 World Mental Health Survey, cited at Dowbiggin 2011, 184)

There are characterizations of anxiety here as an emotion, a mood, a feeling (or cluster of feelings), an attitude, an affect or affective state, and a more generalized state of "aversion," "apprehension," "anticipation," or "worry." We're told that anxiety is both "a central part of what it means to be human" but no less the name of an extremely prevalent kind of mental disorder (of which there are numerous and multifarious diagnostic varieties).[2] Anxiety is variously depicted as a "trait" and a "state"—a vague but stable aspect of a person's character or personality, on the one hand, and as something more fleeting and situationally specific, on the other. Depending on its severity and the context in which it occurs, anxiety can be both helpful and harmful, evolutionarily beneficial in some instances and maladaptive in others. Under the right conditions, anxiety can make us keener and more vigilant, possibly even more virtuous.[3] But it can also be the cause of terrible pain and suffering.

Anxiety is sometimes described as a philosophical mood or attunement, in which deep truths about human existence are disclosed. It's also commonly described as something more primitive and biological: as a part of the cognitive-affective structure that explains how organisms defend themselves against dangerous threats. We also deploy the concept when we're thinking of a more amorphous cultural condition, the sort of thing W.H. Auden was trying to put his finger on when he wrote in his Pulitzer Prize-winning poem about, "that anxiety about himself and his future, which haunts, like a bad smell, the minds of most young men" (Auden 1976, 451). There is also the pervasive colloquial usage, in which "anxiety" is flung around more or less interchangeably with a cluster of other nearby emotional-mental states (dread, disquiet, apprehension, worry, panic, unease, anguish, trepidation, angst, and so on).

What does all of this suggest about the kind of thing anxiety is? Highbrow metaphysics about natural kinds is not my particular cup of philosophical tea. But given the wide array of different uses of the term, I think it's plausible to conclude that anxiety is a heterogeneous category (Baumeister and Tice 1990, 166). There is disagreement about what it would mean for an emotion like anxiety to represent a natural or unified kind. Traditionally in the history of philosophy, pronouncements about natural kinds have been taken to imply a realist metaphysics, according to which natural kinds are presumed to accurately map a mind- and language-independent reality. On this more traditional view, natural kinds indicate "where the natural joints are," as Socrates unforgettably put it in the *Phaedrus* (265e). To say that anxiety is a natural kind, then, is to say that anxiety has a unifying essence. But it's also possible to conceive of natural kinds independently from any project in realist metaphysics, to think of them only in terms of the role they can or might play in scientific explanation (Boyd 1991; Machery 2009). On this kind of view, natural kinds indicate nothing more grandiose than "categories about which we can make scientific discoveries" (Griffiths 2004, 235). If an account of anxiety as a unified or natural kind is in the offing, the latter (scientific) path strikes me as much more promising than the former (realist metaphysical) one, but that's a discussion for another time and place.[4]

The thesis about anxiety's heterogeneity isn't confined only to recondite metaphysical and scientific debates about kinds and categories. It can be extended to cover questions about anxiety's phenomenology (*What does it feel like to be anxious? Is anxiety object-directed or more diffuse? What are its symptoms? How and in response to what does anxiety arise?*) and its normativity (*Is anxiety an appropriate or "fitting" emotion? Is its presence or absence always consistent with a person's evaluative judgment about the anxiety-worthiness of some situation?*), and so on. As we'll see, answers to these sorts of questions are diverse and wide-ranging.

Anxiety is everywhere we look. Millions of us (probably billions) are running scared. And yet, the experience of anxiety is far from monolithic. Anxiety can strike anyone, at any time, and it can arise in response to literally anything. People have anxiety about driving a car and riding in an elevator; about death, public speaking, or the presence of a spider in a room; about getting cancer, falling asleep, and attending a party. Some people feel anxious when they are in large groups of people. Others are afraid to be alone. For some people, anxiety is triggered by small or confined spaces. For others (like me), a wide-open landscape will make their bodies tremble with agoraphobic fear. Anxiety is often experienced as something predominantly cognitive and cerebral: intrusive thoughts, the concoction of improbable scenarios, interminable worry about this or that, are the telltale characteristics. But sometimes, for some people, a hyper-awareness of anxiety's bodily sensations (racing heart, churning stomach, dry mouth, dizziness, tightness in the chest, etc.) are the principal and most disturbing symptoms.

Anxiety is mostly experienced as something unpleasant and unwanted. Anxiety tends to be a "blight on our daily existence when it occurs," as Michael S. Brady nicely puts it. But even here there are exceptions to the rule. As Brady argues, the fact that we sometimes intentionally seek out situations that make us highly anxious (in our playing and spectating of sports, for instance, but also in literature, films, and music) confirms that anxiety can sometimes enjoy a certain "allure" (Brady 2024, 198). Ronald de Sousa similarly notes that, "Some people report finding anxiety or fear to enhance sexual excitement" and occasionally seek it out on that basis (de Sousa 2004, 71).

The experience of anxiety also admits of strikingly different levels of belief-dependence. Some emotions seem to be founded completely on beliefs. To change these emotions, it's sufficient to change the belief or beliefs on which they depend. Embarrassment and grief are examples of emotions that are heavily (if not wholly) belief-dependent. "For my embarrassment to vanish," de Sousa writes, "it is sufficient that I should find out either that no one was watching my faux-pas or that I did not in fact commit one. Grief can be stopped with a word" (de Sousa 1987, 137). But other emotions seem not to be founded on beliefs at all. Worry and hope are examples of emotions in this class, since there is no belief that is either necessary or sufficient to induce them.

Placing anxiety on this continuum—from strict belief-dependence on one end to full belief-imperviousness on the other—is far from straightforward. This is because, as de Sousa correctly says, "Some forms of anxiety are quite resistant to reason; others can be dispelled by the appropriate piece of news" (de Sousa 1987, 137). Sometimes anxiety is responsive to new information about the world. My anxiety about the class I'm scheduled to teach tomorrow can be dispelled by the freshly acquired knowledge that, thanks to heavy snowfall overnight perhaps, the class has been cancelled. But sometimes anxiety seems impervious to new information. If I wake up in the middle of the night for no clear reason—anxious, heart racing, tightness in the chest, body whirring with nervous adrenaline—there is no uniquely placed piece of news that will drive these feelings away. Robert C. Solomon puts a more general version of the argument like this:

If fear is always about the world, then it is a matter of considerable interest and concern that fear is sometimes immune to the relevant information about the world, namely, that the object of fear is really not dangerous. Accordingly, irrational fears can be notoriously difficult to eradicate, even in the presence of the relevant knowledge. We say (unsympathetically) to a friend: "how can you still have a fear of flying when you know that it is statistically much safer than driving to the airport?" or "how can you be afraid of that itsy-bitsy spider, when you know that it will not bite and wants nothing more than to get away from you?" How does the fear, which is about the world, get disengaged from the very information that it is supposedly about? . . . It becomes increasingly evident that fear is not just about the world but involves something else as well. (Solomon 2007, 33)

Sometimes anxiety is experienced as sharp and episodic, sometimes more like a dull and continuous buzz. On many occasions, the object of anxiety is specific and clear: *I'm feeling anxious because I hate being in this tightly packed subway car. I wish I could flee.* On other occasions, anxiety is experienced as a generalized and diffuse state of unease: *I feel jumpy and uncomfortable but there is no specific object or state of affairs to which these feelings correspond.* In the latter kinds of cases, anxiety is experienced more like a "gut feeling" than something translatable into overt belief (de Sousa 1987, 198). In short and to sum up, some episodes of anxiety are object-specific, others are not. And there is good reason to expect that these differences will correspond to different degrees of belief-dependence.[5]

There are many instances in which a person feels anxious about X despite their considered evaluative judgment that there is nothing genuinely anxiety-worthy about X. In such cases, anxiety is what philosophers call a "recalcitrant" emotion—an emotion that persists "despite the agent's making a judgment that is in tension with it." A recalcitrant bout of fear or anxiety, for example, would be one where an agent feels frightened or anxious about something "despite believing that it poses little or no danger" (D'Arms and Jacobson 2003, 129). Much of the garden variety anxiety people suffer with is recalcitrant in this way. But sometimes there is no mismatch between a person's anxiety and their considered evaluative judgment. Think of a surgeon who is feeling anxious about a long and complicated operation they're scheduled to perform. It's easy to imagine that the surgeon would reflectively endorse the anxiety they were experiencing (provided it wasn't excessive and incapacitating), judging it a proper emotional match with the seriousness of the situation at hand. Having no anxiety in a situation like this would be, given the difficulty of the assignment and the life-or-death stakes, incautious and cavalier.[6]

Recalcitrant emotions indicate an *internal* dissonance, *viz.*, an agent continues to have a certain kind of emotional experience despite their belief or considered judgment that conflicts with it. But we can also ask how well our emotions fit with the *external* world itself. An emotion is said to be appropriate or "fitting" when it correctly represents its object.[7] "Everyone agrees," writes Alex Grzankowski, "that fearing that which is not dangerous is unfitting or inappropriate" and that a person "in some sense, ought not fear such things" (Grzankowski 2020, 512). (The reverse side of the same coin, of course, is that having no fear in the face of a genuinely dangerous situation is equally inappropriate or unfitting.) Many of us frequently feel anxiety about happenings and possibilities that, as a matter of fact, we shouldn't feel anxious about. Anxiety is inappropriate or unfitting in such cases. But sometimes anxiety is apposite and proportional to its object. Modern life is teeming with worrisome, genuinely anxiety-worthy prospects. As Charlie Kurth helpfully explains, feeling anxious in such contexts is apt and makes sense:

> Some situations we face are clearly safe, others clearly dangerous; but there are a range of cases in between where the nature of the

threat is uncertain. It's in situations like these that anxiety is fitting ... walking through the streets of an unfamiliar city late at night; negotiating a conversation with someone you want to impress; and needing to make a novel or difficult decision (e.g., get a PhD in philosophy or head to law school). In situations like these, one faces problematic uncertainty. So these are situations where ... anxiety is fitting. It is fitting because given the uncertainty and the stakes, these situations really are worrisome—they are situations where it's fitting to feel anxious. (Kurth 2018, 108)

In short, depending on the context in which it arises, anxiety can be both appropriate or inappropriate, fitting in some instances and unfitting in others.

It should be clear by now that there is a huge range and diversity of experience associated with anxiety. Anxiety arises in different ways, for different reasons, with different profiles of symptoms and different degrees of belief-dependence. Depending on the context, human beings both recoil from anxiety and actively seek it out. Anxiety can be episodic or more continuous, object-directed or more nebulous, recalcitrant or reflectively endorsed, appropriate to its object in some circumstances and inappropriate in others. And so on.

An appreciation for its incredible diversity and heterogeneity makes anxiety ripe for philosophical exploration, a point which brings another animating impetus for this book into focus. I maintain that there is a uniquely *philosophical* perspective from which to consider anxiety, which is not reducible to scientific, evolutionary, historical, or medical approaches to the subject, but which nevertheless draws on knowledge and insight from those other perspectives. There is of course nothing novel about this suggestion. Philosophers from all over the world have been thinking and writing about anxiety since time immemorial, even if nowadays scientific and medical or psychiatric approaches are the dominant players in the field. As Rollo May rightly reminds us in his influential study, before the coming of Freud and other psychologists, the problem of anxiety "lay in the provinces of philosophy" (May 1977, 19).

There are obviously many perspectives from which something as vast and consequential as anxiety can be approached. Most of these are valid and illuminating in their own way. As always, choosing the optimal perspective will depend on what one is trying to find out, on the specific task or inquiry one has in mind. A physician prescribing medicine, a neuroscientist conducting research on brain circuitry and neurochemicals, a metaphysician trying to figure out whether "anxiety" picks out a natural or unified kind, a cultural historian tracing how attitudes about mental health and illness are subject to change over time and place, an evolutionary biologist investigating the nature of the human "alarm response," a legislator trying to understand how a government might fund a certain kind of pharmaceutical research, and a clinician contributing to the next edition of the *DSM*, will all approach the subject of anxiety from different angles. Properly so. I'm not suggesting that the philosophical perspective adopted in this book is the optimal one, the "one true account" of anxiety to which other approaches must for that reason give way. But we also do ourselves a disservice if we try to subsume all philosophical efforts into a coldly reductionist scientific vocabulary. Or so I contend.

Anxiety is much more than simple, blood-pumping fear. The human experience of anxiety has a distinctively evaluative and interpretive element. It's bound up with our capacity to *reflect* on sensations of fear, to *anticipate* and *interpret* them, and to have such thoughts and feelings (themselves always mediated by language and culture) shape how we see the world and ourselves in it. As philosopher Samir Chopra beautifully explains, anxiety is a "colouration that grants the sufferer's experiences their distinctive hue." It is a "hermeneutical relationship with the world whose text now gets read in a very peculiar way by this anxiety-laden vision," Chopra continues. "Things and persons and events fall into focus depending on their interactions with our anxieties: that man in the corner becomes threatening, this chair becomes unstable and unbalanced, that food becomes the agent of a fatal illness" (Chopra 2018). Suffering with anxiety is never simply a colorless fact, but an experience that must be understood in light of what matters to us, in light of who we are and what we care about (Häggland 2019, 177). Something biological and physical is happening here, of course. No one is doubting the reality of what Scott Stossel calls the "brute biological factness of anxiety" (Stossel 2013, 30). But anxiety is not equivalent or reducible to any biological or physiological symptom or function. Bluntly put, there is no set of physical facts that will provide a complete account of anxiety and its meaning.

It's hard to take issue with Freud's famous (1924) characterization of anxiety as "something felt." But it would be a mistake to say that anxiety is nothing more than a series of bodily feelings and sensations. Consider Richard Sorabji's example about people "who have and feel the physical reactions characteristic of anxiety, but who have become accustomed to the idea that there is nothing to be anxious about and behave perfectly calmly. We may think of them as having only feelings of anxiety, not as being anxious" (Sorabji 2000, 150). The suggestion is that for a person genuinely to "be anxious," the physical feelings have to register in a certain way. They need to strike as disconcerting, unsettling, a cause for concern. Something meriting nervousness and worry.[8] In short, we can agree with Freud that anxiety has a "marked character of unpleasure," but crucially, what counts as an instance of "unpleasure" cannot be explained merely by appealing to the physical symptoms themselves (Freud 1959, 60). After all, nothing in the nature of things tells us that a little bit of tightness in the chest needs to be interpreted as a medical emergency. There is nothing intrinsic to the feeling of a sudden stab of panic that tells us we really must flee the party or pull the car over to the side of the highway. It's possible for a person to experience the physical sensations of anxiety, to handle or process them in a certain way, and then to more or less move on from them.

Adopting a philosophical perspective doesn't require disavowing anything that scientists might tell us about the nature of anxiety: about what's occurring in the brain when anxiety strikes; about anxiety's physical properties or physiological causes; about its bodily symptoms and evolutionary history. A philosophical perspective on anxiety is not in zero-sum competition with other approaches. The argument is not that philosophy somehow gets right what science gets wrong. It's that questions having to do with anxiety's *meaning* and *value* (about what the experience of anxiety is like and how it can change us, for better and for worse; about the philosophical wisdom that might follow from the fact of anxious suffering) belong to a kind of broadly humanistic inquiry that, while certainly not opposed to scientific or medical approaches, is nevertheless distinct from and non-reducible to them. As the young Wittgenstein dramatically put a version of the same point in the *Tractatus*: "even if *all possible* scientific questions be answered, the problems of life have still not been touched at all" (Wittgenstein 1999, 107). The qualification "at all" at the end of Wittgenstein's passage is probably too resolute, but the important anti-reductionist objection is sustained. If the main thrust of this book is on the right track, there is more to be learned about anxiety than what empirical science alone is capable of teaching us.[9]

This book is not argumentative in the conventional way philosophy books typically are. There is no comprehensive, systematic *theory* on which the chapters that follow converge. Instead, I seek out stories, examples, images, explanations of what this or that philosopher had to say about anxiety. Wanting to make everything conceptually neat and precise is a laudable philosophical instinct. But I try to adopt a looser, more easygoing attitude. To embrace the blurrier side of things. To proceed in the spirit of the great Frank Ramsey, who wrote in 1929 that, "The chief danger to our philosophy, apart from laziness and woolliness, is *scholasticism*, the essence of which is treating what is vague as if it were precise and trying to fit it into an exact logical category" (Ramsey 1990, 7), In something like this Ramseyan spirit, I ask readers not to quibble too much about where various lines are properly drawn (between the ordinary and the pathological; between anxiety understood as a "normal" human emotion, a mental disorder, a spiritual-philosophical condition, or a more nebulous aspect of culture; between the varieties and intensities of anxiety that help us and those that harm, and so on), and to simply let the chapters speak for themselves. If they speak clearly, they will tell a story about how anxiety and philosophy are tangled up with each other. About how anxiety itself is one of the great, perennial philosophical themes. About how anxious minds seem uniquely drawn to philosophical questions and how philosophers tend to be an unusually anxious bunch. About how anxiety is one of the major instigators of philosophical reflection, and how philosophical reflection in turn can sometimes serve as a powerful form of anti-anxiety self-help.

1
The Dizziness of Freedom

> [I]n the eyes of the world it is dangerous to venture. And why? Because one may lose. But not to venture is shrewd. And yet, by not venturing, it is so dreadfully easy to lose that which it would be difficult to lose in even the most venturesome venture, and in any case never so easily, so completely as if it were nothing... one's self. For if I have ventured amiss—very well, then life helps me by its punishment. But if I have not ventured at all—who then helps me? And, moreover, if by not venturing at all in the highest sense (and to venture in the highest sense is precisely to become conscious of oneself) I have gained all earthly advantages... and lose my self? What of that?
>
> —Søren Kierkegaard, *The Sickness Unto Death*

Søren Kierkegaard is an infuriatingly difficult philosopher. Even world-renowned scholars of his work have been known to concede the opaqueness and impenetrability of his books and other writings.[1] And still, despite the immense difficulty of his work, people are continually drawn to Kierkegaard. Anxious sufferers especially seem to find themselves responding viscerally to his ideas. As Daniel Smith notes, readers can tell right away that Kierkegaard was someone who "understood anxiety from the inside.... His descriptions of anxiety are some of the most vivid we have.... Even Kierkegaard's abstractions have the feel of lived truth" (Smith 2012, 88). It's safe to say that many of his readers can spot in Kierkegaard a little something of themselves, a "kindred soul to that household of millions who find themselves troubled by feelings that answer to the names 'anxiety' and 'despair.'" (Marino 1998, 309)[2]

Kierkegaard himself was a terribly anxious person. He regarded anxiety as a "congenital" affliction, and claimed to have felt it even while still in the womb (Alessandri 2023, 149). "All existence makes me anxious," he confessed in a journal entry from 1839, "from the smallest fly to the mysteries of the Incarnation. . . . My distress is enormous, boundless" (Kierkegaard 1980, 170). He came to believe that anxiety and distress were bequests from his father. In his journals he would reflect on "the anxiety with which my father filled my soul, his own frightful depression" and identified this as "the dark background" of his own life trajectory (Kierkegaard 1980, 171–172). As Clare Carlisle recounts in her captivating biography, "Whenever he traces the roots of . . . [his] unrest, reaching back to his dimmest memories, he encounters the large, looming figure of his father, whose gloomy presence seemed to fill the house" (Carlisle 2019, 67).

By outward appearances Kierkegaard lived a dull, uneventful life. Aside from a few visits to Germany and Sweden, he never left his beloved Copenhagen. Unmarried and childless, he spent his time contemplatively wandering the streets and writing fervently in his journals. Kierkegaard was fascinated with questions of literary genre and obsessed with his own voice as an author. As Jane Chamberlain and Jonathan Rée point out, "the main preoccupation of Kierkegaard's days and nights was the laborious cultivation of the arts of philosophical prose. In seclusion, he worked fanatically, composing draft after draft, reading his output aloud to himself to check it for rhythm and tone, and then recomposing over and over again" (Chamberlain and Rée 2001, 1). Kierkegaard was a ludicrously prolific writer. When he died in 1855 at the young age of forty-two (likely from tuberculosis), he left behind thirty-four published volumes and thousands of meticulously revised written pages.

Kierkegaard was an obsessive and passionate person. He felt a lot, and felt intensely, but also seemed constitutionally incapable of joy and happiness. "So great is my unhappiness," he wrote. "I am so lacklustre and joyless that not only have I nothing to fill my soul, I cannot even conceive of anything that could possibly satisfy it— alas, not even the bliss of heaven" (Kierkegaard 1996, 102; 133). By all rights Kierkegaard should have been happier than he was. He was, after all, a wealthy and brilliant young man, loved by an intelligent, beautiful woman (his sweetheart, Regine Olsen, with whom he abruptly ended his engagement to be married in 1841). And yet, as Carlisle points out, Kierkegaard "made life exceptionally difficult for himself. This deep and mysterious fact of Kierkegaard's psychology was inseparable from his philosophical stance towards the world" (Carlisle 2019, xv). Kierkegaard was not only unhappy in his life, he also dwelled philosophically in unhappiness.

Kierkegaard is noteworthy for developing what is probably the first account of *existential* anxiety (or *Angest* in his native Danish). On this account, anxiety, while certainly something felt or experienced, is not just one more emotion or mood, like sadness, anger, pride, or disgust. Rather than something ephemeral and merely unpleasant, like a headache, which can be cured by popping a pill or taking a nap, Kierkegaard maintains that anxiety is fundamentally connected with the self and with freedom—indeed, with our very nature as spiritual beings.

In the first half of this chapter, I give an overview of Kierkegaard's thinking about the nature and meaning of anxiety: about the kind of affect he takes anxiety to be; about why we are anxious and where anxiety comes from on his view; about what he means when he says that, "Whoever has learned to be anxious in the right way has learned the ultimate" (Kierkegaard 1980, 155). Kierkegaard was a passionately religious person, and his account of anxiety is, unsurprisingly, an unabashedly religious one. In *The Concept of Anxiety*, for instance, it's claimed that anxiety is at the root of "original" and "hereditary" sin. Our anxious apprehension of future possibility—the always alarming "possibility of *being able*"—is where sinful disobedience and our loss of innocence first enter the world (Kierkegaard 1980, 44). Anxiety, we are told, underpins The Fall of Man. These will strike many readers as baffling claims. Still, I think that a lot of what Kierkegaard has to say about anxiety and despair can be translated into a more secular idiom, and that many of his central insights can be appreciated by religious and non-religious ears alike. I take for granted in what follows that such translation is both possible and fruitful.[3] While Kierkegaard's famous argument that anxiety is like a discombobulating "dizziness" that we experience in the face of our freedom has much to be said in its favor, as we will see, the second half of the chapter considers how anxiety and freedom can be experienced as incompatible, even negatively correlated, states. That is, how anxiety has a tendency to supress the sense of a person's freedom, and conversely, how a gain in freedom implies a corresponding diminution of anxiety.

At the beginning of *The Sickness Unto Death*, writing under the pseudonym *Anti-Climacus*, Kierkegaard proclaims that human beings are *spiritual* creatures, as opposed to merely minds and bodies.[4] "Man is spirit" (Kierkegaard 2013, 11). Kierkegaard of course has something explicitly religious in mind here. According to the biblical story, we humans are the only creatures made in God's "own image" (Genesis 1:27). The only creatures that bear a "likeness" to God, that manifest the stamp of their creator. We are related to a higher power in a way that other creatures are not (and cannot be) and we occupy a special position in the cosmic order of things in virtue of this fact. On the biblical story, human beings are fundamentally different from the apple trees, the alligators, and the antelopes—higher than the rest of living nature on the *scala natura*. Unlike the other plants and animals, human beings have a spark of divinity in them. Given the Lutheran pietism to which he was obsessively devoted, it's safe to assume that, strictly speaking, Kierkegaard would have agreed with this biblical account. But Kierkegaard also thought that "true Christianity" required more than dispassionate belief in a set of doctrines. What matters centrally is how an individual's own commitment to these doctrines unfolds in the course of living a life. The task of "arranging the truths of Christianity in paragraphs" is of secondary importance (Kierkegaard 1992, 15). With this emphasis in mind, it's helpful to be reminded that "spirit" for Kierkegaard involves "the power of the will to self-consciously choose . . . the part of the self that chooses" (Beabout 2009, 60). We are spiritual creatures in virtue of our capacity to make choices (or, put the other way around, we have the capacity to make choices in virtue of the fact that we are spiritual creatures). Crucially for Kierkegaard, it is our status as spiritual beings with the capacity to choose that makes anxiety and despair possible for us.

In a journal entry from 1844, Kierkegaard writes that, "animals do not suffer anxiety, just because they are by nature not qualified as spirit. They fear the present, tremble, etc., but are not anxious. They no more have anxiety than they can be said to have presentiment" (Kierkegaard 1980, 185). Human beings can be anxious (not merely afraid like the other animals), because we are alive in a unique way to the choices by which we negotiate the future (Allen 2004, 124). As Emily Dickinson beautifully puts it, we humans "dwell in possibility" (Dickinson 1960, 327). Our capacity to envisage future possibilities, to have new information shape our sense of what is possible or likely, provide anxiety the distinctive arena within which it operates. The very same capacities that make us agents—that is, beings capable of ascribing meaning and significance, of imaging possibilities and predicting outcomes, of moving through the world according to a plan and with an identity to some extent of our own authoring—also creates the space for a special kind of anxious worry to get its foothold.[5] This is a central premise in the story Kierkegaard tells about the indissoluble link between freedom and anxiety. If we were not spiritual beings, we would not be free, at least not in the sense in which anxiety and despair inhere in our freedom. But what exactly does it mean to be a spiritual being? And what is the special kind of freedom that this status supposedly confers?

Consider dolphins. Dolphins are conscious and sentient creatures. There is something it is like to be a dolphin, something it's like to inhabit the unique subjectivity and embodiment characteristic of dolphin life. Dolphins are not merely objects in the world, like sticks and stones, but beings for whom different things appear as nourishing, predacious, innocuous, dangerous, and so on. Borrowing some terminology from Swedish philosopher Martin Hägglund, we might say that dolphins are *natural* beings. Natural beings are alive and embodied. They are subject to various biological and physical constraints: the need for nourishment, the facts of their environment, the aerodynamic limitations of their bodies, and so on. Natural beings are also capable of self-movement, and they are responsive to a practical distinction between *how things might at first appear* and *how they really turn out to be*. Any conscious creature—any creature that "relates to the environment through its own sentience and responds to what happens in light of its own ends"—is a natural being, and thereby enjoys natural freedom (Hägglund 2019, 173–175). There can be no doubt that dolphins are natural beings in this sense. (I'm less confident that the shrimp on which dolphins occasionally dine are natural beings, too, since I honestly don't know whether there is something unique it is like to be a shrimp, whether shrimp life is animated by the kind of agency and normativity that dolphin life features. But we can let these armchair conjectures pass.)

What makes us humans *spiritual* beings, in addition to natural beings, is not only our responsiveness to various norms and principles, but a second-order ability to ask whether the norms and principles to which we are currently beholden should be modified or jettisoned. This is how Hägglund explains it:

> as long as we have a self-relation—as long as we lead our lives in any way at all—the question of who we *ought* to be is alive for

us, since it is at work in all our activities. In engaging the question "what should I do?" we are also engaging the question "who should I be?" and there is no final answer to that question. This is our spiritual freedom. (Hägglund 2019, 176)

Part of what it means to be a *spiritual* being—and on this point Kierkegaard and Hägglund are fully in agreement, as far as I can tell—is that we have the capacity to change course, to transform ourselves, to give new shape and meaning to our lives. We have the ability to renounce old commitments and ideals and to adopt new ones in their place. Human beings are not merely bound by norms and principles. We also have the ability to call those very norms and principles into question, to interrogate their status, and ultimately to revise or discard them.

There is also an important difference between the kind of freedom enjoyed by merely natural beings (viz., *natural freedom*) and the kind of freedom enjoyed by spiritual beings like us (viz., *spiritual freedom*).

Natural freedom has a single *ought* structure, since the agent cannot question its guiding principles and ask itself what it should do. Spiritual freedom, by contrast, is characterized by a *double ought* structure. As a spiritually free being, I can ask myself what I should do, since I am answerable not only for my actions but also for the normative principles that guide my actions. There are not only demands concerning what I ought to do; there is also the question *if I ought to do what I supposedly ought to do*. (Hägglund 2019, 179)

Being the spiritual creatures that we are, and having the spiritual freedom that we do, is a double-edged sword, an ambiguous mixture of good and bad elements. On the good side, it allows us to dream up marvellous new things—to imagine a life, and a world, wonderfully different from the present one. On the bad side, it makes us susceptible to forms of pain and psychic suffering that would be unthinkable for creatures who could exercise only natural freedom.[6]

For Kierkegaard, it is our status as spiritual beings with spiritual freedom that makes what he calls "despair" (*fortvivlelse*, in the original Danish) virtually unavoidable. Despair is a "sickness of spirit" to which all spiritual beings are predisposed. It arises because the future is unknown and uncertain. As Hägglund explains, for Kierkegaard,

> there is a trembling of anxiety in every relation to the future, since we cannot know what will happen and may lose what we want to keep. The more we are devoted to something, the more powerful the anxiety, since our own being is at stake. Thus, if I am a father, the prospect of losing my son is anxiety producing, both because I care about him in his own right and because I would be devastated if I lost him. To live with such anxiety . . . is according to Kierkegaard to live "in despair." (Hägglund 2019, 137)[7]

In a view he shares with St. Augustine, Kierkegaard believes that only an authentic religious (Christian) faith can save a person from despair.[8] Such faith is a state in which despair is "completely eradicated" (Kierkegaard 2013, 13). Nothing finite and this-worldly—no "merely human love"—can ever fully cure this sickness.

> Deep within every person's soul . . . there is a secret anxiety that even the one in whom he has the most faith could also become unfaithful to him. . . . No merely human love can completely drive out this anxiety, which can very well remain hidden and undetected in the friendly security of a happy life-relationship, but which at times can inexplicably stir deep within and which, when the storms of life begin, is immediately at hand. (Kierkegaard 1997, 284)

Other people, even family and friends with whom we are closest, might let us down. Merely human loves sometimes crack. But God is unfailing. He "remains faithful, every day of your life," Kierkegaard says, "whatever happens to you; he remains faithful to you in death; he meets you again in the hereafter as a trustworthy friend" (Kierkegaard 1997, 284).

Kierkegaard's argument about the despair-cancelling power of Christian faith can be summarized like this: (i) *everyone who is a "true Christian" does not suffer with despair, however, (ii) everyone who is "outside of Christendom" does. Therefore, (iii) if a person suffers despair, it follows that they are not a true Christian after all* (Kierkegaard 2013, 21). Kierkegaard spent a lot of time obsessing about the adequacy of his and other people's Christian faith, and this line of thinking is a good example of the puritanical zeal that sometimes fills his pages. Even so, the argument is not so easily dismissed. If a person wholeheartedly believed that a benevolent and all-powerful God designed the world with them in mind, and has a great ending in store for them, it's difficult to see how anxiety and despair would be possible for such a person. Kierkegaard was not naïve about how immensely difficult it is to maintain this kind of unswerving religious faith. But for the individual who has pulled off this most difficult of feats (the one Kierkegaard calls the "knight of faith," whom he describes as the "only happy man"), anxiety and despair are non-existent (Kierkegaard 1983, 50).[9]

Everyone "who lives outside of Christendom" has some despair, even if they cannot name it or recognize it definitively for what it is.

> Just as the physician might say that there lives perhaps not one single man who is in perfect health, so one might say perhaps that there lives not one single man who ... is not to some extent in despair, in whose inmost parts there does not dwell a disquietude, a perturbation, a discord, an anxious dread of an unknown something, or of something he does not even dare to make acquaintance with, dread of a possibility of life, or dread of himself. . . .

[I]n the remote depths, in the most inward parts, in the hidden recesses of happiness, there dwells also the anxious dread which is despair. (Kierkegaard 2013, 21; 25)

And similarly, from an 1837 journal entry:

Deep within every human being there still lives the anxiety over the possibility of being alone in the world, forgotten by God, overlooked among the millions and millions in this enormous household. A person keeps this anxiety at a distance by looking at the many round about who are related to him as kin and friends, but the anxiety is still there. (Kierkegaard 1980, 171)

Again, the ultimate source of this "anxious dread of an unknown something" is the fact that we are spiritual creatures, endowed with spiritual freedom. Such freedom orients us toward an essentially uncertain future, and this orientation makes anxiety virtually inescapable. The future is unknown. Things may turn out badly. The people we love might get hurt, or worse. We may lose what we cherish. For those of us without the requisite Christian faith, despair is always there.

Anxiety and despair are the natural consequences of having things matter for us. To have no anxiety whatsoever would be, in a sense, to have nothing one cares about—no loves or attachments the loss of which would expose one to pain and suffering. It would be like having an attitude of indifference and unconcern toward the future. To feel as though one had nothing at stake, for better or for worse, in how things panned out. This doesn't mean that anxiety and despair must have specific objects. On the contrary, Kierkegaard was probably the first thinker to argue that anxiety differs from ordinary fear in having no fixed, determinate object. Anxiety, he says, "is altogether different from fear and similar concepts that refer to something definite" (Kierkegaard 1980, 42). Freud of course became well known for advancing the same idea decades later, when he distinguished between *realistic* anxiety, which is "fear of particular external situations of danger," and *neurotic* anxiety, which is "completely enigmatic" and by all appearances "pointless" (Freud 1989, 782; 774). Neurotic anxiety isn't about anything in particular (Freud 1952, 103). As Freud says, it's "anxiety in regard to a danger which we do not know" (Freud 1963, 113). Similarly, what Kierkegaard calls *Angest* is amorphous and free-floating, not bound up with any specific worry or outcome. There is nothing *in particular* onto which it fastens.[10] As Alastair Hannay notes, for Kierkegaard, *Angest* is a kind of "generalized apprehensiveness" or "global uneasiness."

> I can be anxious about my children's meeting with the youth culture, about the outcome of an interview, about a meeting with my psychiatrist. These are all forms of apprehensiveness, a fear of a possible and definite but as yet undecided outcome. Fear or even dread itself, as we use these terms, is even more focussed; we are afraid not just "in case" something will happen, but *that* it will happen. "*Angest*" in Kierkegaard's sense is a generalized apprehensiveness with no particular "in case" in view, one might call it a state of global uneasiness. (Hannay 2001, 213)

Anxiety on this view is about everything and nothing: about *everything* we might decide to do with our freedom and simultaneously about *nothing* in particular.

An obvious rejoinder to Kierkegaard here is to point out that, while anxiety is sometimes experienced as nebulous and unspecific, sometimes the object of anxiety is clear and well-defined. If I suffer panic attacks when driving a car on the highway, for example, or if I feel anxious about an upcoming test, it's not "an unknown dread" I am contending with. It's perfectly clear what my anxiety is about in these cases. Kierkegaard would have replied that what he calls *Angest* does not refer to everyday episodes of anxious worry per se, but to a more fundamental existential predicament. *Angest* denotes the "concept" (or *begreb* in the Danish) of anxiety, not its various materializations. *Angest* itself is vague and objectless, but the everyday episodes of anxiety that bubble up in its name can and frequently do have specific content. So, odd though it may sound, the panic attacks I have while driving on the highway have a clear object, but such episodes are merely expressions or realizations of a deeper "unknown dread" which is itself objectless.

Freedom, Possibility, and the Future

"Possibility" is the keynote of both freedom and the future. It's also the raw substance of anxiety. As Kierkegaard writes, in what is probably the most famous passage from his work:

> Anxiety may be compared with dizziness. He whose eye happens to look down into the yawning abyss becomes dizzy. But what is the reason for this? It is just as much in his own eye as in the abyss, for suppose he had not looked down. Hence anxiety is the dizziness of freedom, which emerges when . . . freedom looks down into its own possibility. . . . In anxiety there is the selfish infinity of possibility. (Kierkegaard 1980, 61)

The full scope of a person's freedom never sits in plain view. No one can actively consider that many possibilities at the same time. Yet when we happen to look into the "yawning abyss"—that is, when we are suddenly made aware of the overwhelming number of different things we can do and be, of all the different paths we might go down—this makes us feel frightened and dizzy. Freedom is always directed toward the future, in the direction of what's possible. But freedom is never possible as soon as it's actual (Kierkegaard 1980, 22). We ruminate on the endless number of things we can or might do, and we occasionally tremble with anxiety while staring into the abyss of possibility. But once actualized, our freedom dissolves from possibility into actuality. The same way that the future continually spills over into the past. Kierkegaard says that anxiety is what *mediates* the transition from possibility to actuality. "[P]ossibility is to *be able*," he writes. "In a logical system it is convenient to say that possibility passes over into actuality. However, in actuality it is not so convenient, and an intermediate term is required. The intermediate term is anxiety" (Kierkegaard 1980, 49). Anxiety, in short, is the nervous uncertainty inherent in the exercise of our freedom: it represents that momentary gap in between the endless possibilities of the future, on the one side, and the concrete actualities of the past and present, on the other.

Another important rejoinder to Kierkegaard here involves pointing out that anxiety can and does arise, not just as a consequence of the exercise of freedom (about what we do and refrain from doing). It also arises in the form of general worry about what the future holds in store, whether as a result of our actions or not. Jean-Paul Sartre helpfully distinguishes between "anguish" (*Angst, angoisse*) and ordinary fear by noting that the latter arises from external threats or possibilities whereas the former "is anguish before myself" (Sartre 1956, 65). In Sartre's anguish (like Kierkegaard's *Angest)* the locus of the worry is what we can or might do with our freedom. In his *War Diaries*, Sartre describes anguish as "freedom becoming conscious of itself" and "the existential apprehension of our freedom" (Sartre 1984, 133). After all, we really could jump down from the cliff we are now standing on. We really do have the power to steer the car into oncoming traffic. Sartre's explicit indebtedness to Kierkegaard here should be glaring. But the main point is that anxiety need not involve the exercise of our freedom. It's possible for a person to feel anxious about what might simply happen to them, independent of any exercise of agency (like getting struck down by lightning or receiving a grim medical diagnosis).

Kierkegaard's argument about anxiety as the dizziness of freedom is beautifully summed up by Clare Carlisle as follows:

> Anxiety... is a spiritual awareness unknown to animals, which are merely physical creatures. But human beings are not angels, either. We live in the world anchored by gravity, feet on the ground, rooted in actuality—our mortal bodies, our circumstances, the facts of our lives. And yet we breathe the air of possibility, and the force of gravity is seldom so strong that we cannot lift a foot into this air and take a step, one way or another. We all long to claim our freedom, and when actuality becomes a swamp we gasp desperately for air. Yet this same freedom, with its dizzying proliferation of possibilities, fills us with anxiety the moment we experience it. An open future is, like the nothingness of death, an unknown abyss. Glancing down, afraid of falling, we anxiously grasp and cling onto anything solid we can find—possessions, money, food, drink, other people—in an effort to steady ourselves. Thus we live, clutching at things in the world, whether or not it is for our good, or theirs. (Carlisle 2019, 174)

The picture presented here links anxiety with our essence as spiritual creatures. We are finite, mortal beings who find ourselves contending with the uncertainty inherent in the future and in our ability to choose, and this makes anxiety unavoidable for us (at least those of us residing "outside Christendom"). These are grand claims about the human condition. But I think that elements of Kierkegaard's account also ring true in more simple, everyday contexts. Consider that many people suffer spikes of anxiety when faced with chunks of open, unstructured time. A day without obligations or plans. One way to interpret this kind of affective state in Kierkegaardian terms is to say that such people are suffering with a profusion of choices, an excess of freedom. There is too much "possibility" to comfortably navigate, too many different ways one's time and energy might be spent. Such people are usually more comfortable with a tighter schedule of activities—an outing, some exercise, a list of errands or chores to get through. Anything to fill in the details of this wide-open time. Anything to avoid staring into the dizzying abyss of our freedom. Kierkegaard might have rejoined that (for the non-Christian at least) anxiety is never finally conquerable so long as more possibility lies ahead. There is always a further stretch of future time to worry about, additional *what ifs* to weigh and stew over. There never comes a point at which a person can say, *All that open possibility has given me so much anxiety, but thankfully it's over now*. Freedom is not a project that can be completed, just as an abyss has no bottom. In short, and despite whatever temporary relief we non-Christians may find for ourselves, as long as there is "possibility" in the future, as long as there is more freedom of which to make use, anxiety will be impending. As Kierkegaard puts it, in a stunning phrase, "What is anxiety? It is the next day" (Kierkegaard 1997, 78).

The structure of anxiety on Kierkegaard's view is our ambiguous relationship with the future (Beabout 2009, 77). Anxiety is a forward-looking affective state. It aims at figuring out what to do in the future, *going forward*, rather than correcting a wrong already done (Kurth 2018, 214–215). Kierkegaard thinks that anxiety necessarily affixes on the future—on what's *possible* rather than what's *actual*. He says that "accurate and correct linguistic usage ... associates anxiety and the future." It's basically a category mistake to say that a person might be anxious about the past, which is not to deny that anxious feelings are sometimes stirred by memories and thoughts about what has already transpired. Kierkegaard would have insisted that, even when anxiety is triggered by something in the past, it's still fundamentally directed toward the future. When an anxious mind hones in on a blunder or mishap from the past—when we are lying awake at night obsessing over some embarrassing thing we might have said or done—that is because we are worried about what may yet happen as a result. Even when we're confident that we will never again see the people who witnessed our embarrassing episode and we conclude that their opinion of us therefore has no obvious consequence, an anxious mind can still concoct scenarios about how this might hurt or humiliate us in the future (Wright 2017, 35–36). There is always the chance that we will become the unwitting protagonist in someone's hilarious story. Unbeknownst to us, strangers could be howling in laughter about that thing we said or did.[11] As Kierkegaard sums it all up: "When it is sometimes said that one is anxious about the past, this seems to be a contradiction.... If I am anxious about a past misfortune, then this is not because it is in the past but because it may be repeated, i.e. become future." If a misfortune is properly in the past, Kierkegaard writes, then a person "cannot be anxious but only repentant" in relation to it (Kierkegaard 1980, 91–92).

There is a useful distinction between two sorts of future-oriented emotions—*anticipated* emotions and *anticipatory* emotions—the drawing of which sheds light on Kierkegaard's view about the necessarily future-facing nature of anxiety.[12] Anticipated emotions are the emotions we predict we will have if something occurs (e.g., *I'm going to feel anxious if I'm asked to give a toast at this social event*). The latter are the emotions that we are currently experiencing because we are thinking about something in the future (e.g., *I'm scheduled to take a long flight next week and the thought of being trapped on an airplane, squirming uncomfortably in my seat for hours, is giving me anxiety now*). As the examples just given confirm, anxiety can be both an anticipated emotion and an anticipatory one. Indeed, anxiety might be unique among the emotions in its tendency to make virtually all *anticipated* instances of itself simultaneously *anticipatory* ones. It's an extremely common form of anxious worry that arises precisely because a person is thinking about how they are likely to feel anxious at some point in the future. *Predicting or anticipating that one will feel anxious in the future is a surefire way to become more anxious now*. As Montaigne unforgettably put the point all the way back in 1580, "Anyone who is afraid of suffering suffers already from being afraid" (Montaigne 2003, 1243).[13]

This helps explain why, on Kierkegaard's view, the *actual* predicament an anxious person finds themselves in, even if rather bad, is never quite as terrifying as the *possibilities* they conjure for themselves. He writes, "The hypochondriac is anxious about every insignificant thing, but when the significant appears he begins to breathe more easily. And why? Because the significant actuality is after all not so terrible as the possibility he had fashioned" (Kierkegaard 1980, 162). We can deal with almost anything when it is known, when we can see it clearly for what it is. "Possibility is the weightiest of all categories," Kierkegaard says. The "terrible things in life" are always "weak by comparison with those of possibility" (Kierkegaard 1980, 156–157). The suggestion here is that the *anticipation* of fear and pain is almost always more difficult than struggling in the present moment. Emily Dickinson puts it like this: "While we were fearing it, it came / But came with less of fear... Tis harder knowing it is due, than knowing it is here" (Dickinson 1960, 558). It helps to be reminded that things almost never turn out as badly as an anxious mind imagines they will, and that the anticipation of future suffering—"knowing it is due"—is frequently the worst part of the ordeal.

Despite the obvious pain and suffering it causes, Kierkegaard believed that anxiety can be a powerful resource for our spiritual education (Marino 1998, 309). There are profound, otherwise inaccessible truths that we can learn from being anxious—truths about our own lives and the human condition, about our finitude, about the nature of freedom, about sin and faith and God. Kierkegaard thinks that there is "educative" value in facing one's anxiety squarely, in being a "pupil of possibility." We benefit immensely, he thinks, from learning how to be anxious "in the right way" (Kierkegaard 1980, 159; 155). Once again, Clare Carlisle sums it all up perfectly.

> [Kierkegaard] tries to confront his anxieties with clear-sighted courage, to let them move through him and experience all their power and subtlety. He sees anxiety as a blessing as well as a curse, a privilege as well as an affliction, a mark of spiritual nobility;

after all, Jesus prayed anxiously in the garden at Gethsemane before he faced his death, and Socrates, condemned to die by drinking hemlock, raised his poison cup as if toasting his own anxiety. "The more profoundly a human being is in anxiety, the greater he is," for anxiety "consumes all finite ends and discovers their deceptiveness." When a human being "passes through the anxiety of the possible"—an indeterminate horror of existence that finds no worldly foothold , since it senses an infinite nothingness beneath every step—he will be "educated to have no anxiety, not because he can escape the terrible things of life but because these always become weak by comparison with those of possibility." Kierkegaard imagined such a man saying, as a patient might say to his surgeon when a painful operation is about to begin: Now I am ready. "Then anxiety enters into his soul and searches out everything and anxiously torments everything finite and petty out of him." (Carlisle 2019, 175)[14]

But Kierkegaard also believed that he lived in a "cowardly" age. He observed that most people construct diversionary preoccupations that help them supress or avoid their anxiety. "Anxiety can contrive a hundred evasions," he wrote. People will do everything they can to "keep away lonely thoughts by diversions," just as "in the American forests wild beasts are kept away by means of torches, shouting, and beating of cymbals" (Kierkegaard 1980, 154; 120). It's hard to disagree with the observation that people frequently search for ways to evade or supress uncomfortable thoughts and feelings.[15] But in calling this state of affairs "cowardly," Kierkegaard's point is not that people are wimpier or less resilient than they might otherwise be. It's that we humans are constitutionally restless, never fully at peace in the world. Such restlessness is a central feature of our human nature and is endemic to all human existence. Even Adam had these kinds of feelings in the Garden of Eden. What Kierkegaard ultimately finds "cowardly" about his age is that, in his estimation, so many people refuse to face up to this deep truth about themselves—"not daring in the deeper sense to think about such things." Instead of giving their attention to the "highest spiritual trials," people occupy themselves with "the pandering conflicts between men and between man and woman" (Kierkegaard 1980, 120).

In the end, Kierkegaard believes that the real truth about anxiety cannot be grasped "medically-therapeutically"—as if anxiety were something that could be overcome with "powders and with pills" (Kierkegaard 1980, 121). Anxiety is much more than an unpleasant affect. At its most fundamental level, *Angest* is bound up with a person's recognition of their freedom, with the always striking awareness that we are spiritual beings able to do and be otherwise.

Feeling Anxious and Feeling Free

So far, we've been considering Kierkegaard's thesis that anxiety and freedom are two sides of the same existential coin. Anxiety, we saw, is like a distressing "dizziness" that we experience alongside and as a consequence of our freedom. It arises when a person becomes cognizant of what's possible for them, of the incalculably many options among which they can and must choose. Anxiety bubbles up with our recognition of the vast ocean of possibilities that we invariably navigate in living a life, with our awareness of the spectacular variety of different things we might do and be. In short, we are anxious because we become mindful of our freedom. And every occasion of freedom—every possibility we imagine, every choice we consider, every prospect we entertain—has a corresponding dose of uncertainty and anxiety written into it.

Yet experience also tells us that anxiety and freedom are sometimes negatively correlated, such that an expansion of the one goes hand in hand with a contraction of the other. The more anxious a person feels, the more diminished the feeling of their own freedom, and conversely. The experience of anxiety has a tendency to metaphorically shrink its sufferer's world. To the extent that it diminishes the range of possibilities a sufferer sees for themselves, to the extent that it speaks in the language of constraint or limitation, of avenues that are closed, anxiety itself constitutes a form of unfreedom.[16]

In his famous 1962 essay, "Freedom and Resentment," P.F. Strawson argued that our everyday moral practices of praising and blaming (what he called our moral "reactive attitudes") would be unaffected if it turned out that determinism was in fact true (Strawson 2008). So, too, I suggest, for freedom and anxiety. Even if the universe is wholly determined—even if, as Nietzsche unforgettably put it, "the acting man is caught in his illusion of volition"—the connections between freedom and anxiety that I want to explore in what follows would remain intact.[17] Those connections are phenomenological, not metaphysical. They would neither receive extra validation if determinism turned out to be false, nor would they be undermined if determinism turned out to be true.

What is the experience of freedom like? What does it mean for a person to feel free? The simplest and most intuitive answer is that a person feels free when they have that indelible and normally unreflective sense that they are agents with the ability to makes choices. To go one way or another. Philosopher Galen Strawson (eldest son of the P.F. Strawson I cited a moment ago) describes this instinctual, everyday feeling of freedom in his customarily colorful style.

> Suppose tomorrow is a holiday and you're wondering what to do. You can climb a mountain or read Lao Tzu. You can restring your ukulele, or go to the zoo. Right now you're reading about free will. You're free to go on reading, or stop now. You've started on this sentence, but you don't have to.........finish it. Right now, as so often in life, you have a number of options. Nothing forces your hand. Surely you're entirely free to choose what to do, and responsible for what you do do? ... This is what being a free agent *is*. This is it. (Strawson 2018, 93)

No one denies that this is how things *feel* for us. Barring anything unusual that might impinge on a person's sense of their own volition (an extreme psychological disorder, being under the influence of drugs, being an infant, etc.), everyone knows what it feels like to be a free agent.[18]

It's also possible for a person to enjoy the experience of freedom in a more visceral and emotionally charged way. Consider philosopher Jonathan Gingerich's gloss on an ideal he calls *spontaneous freedom*:

> Sometimes I have a feeling that the future of my life is open, rather than closed, that the possible paths into the future that stretch out before me are uncountable, and that I could do or become anything. I feel free. This experience of freedom is part of a family of cognate experiences, feelings, moods, and attitudes, which encompasses the sense that my life is open before me, the attitude that I hold when I regard an activity as "free time" or "leisure" rather than work, a feeling of refuge that I might find in privacy, a feeling of relief at not having to do things that I want to avoid, the sense of a beginning when I set out on an adventure, the excitement of discovery, a mood of spontaneity, and the attitude that I have toward my art when I creatively make aesthetic objects. At the center of this family of feelings and related cognitive states is the experience of freedom that one can have about the future of one's own life not being fixed or determined. (Gingerich 2018, 834–835)

The experience of spontaneous freedom does not refer to a solitary affective state but a cluster or "family" of different feelings, moods, thoughts, emotions, inklings, notions, and attitudes. As a result, it's probably not possible to locate precisely where the experience of spontaneous freedom ends and other nearby kinds of experiences begin. The range of human feeling is broad here. Experience is rich. Borders are fuzzy. And there is room for reasonable people to disagree about borderline or controversial cases.[19]

The experience of spontaneous freedom incorporates but goes beyond the mundane feeling that we are free agents with the capacity to make choices. At the heart of this kind of experience is the ideal of the "free spirit" (Geuss 2005, 74). Spontaneous freedom involves a powerful sense of unscriptedness about our lives. A rich sense of possibility. A feeling that one's future is wide open, that there are uncountably many options among which to choose, innumerably many different paths to go down. The experience of spontaneous freedom is bound up with the feeling that our life story is as yet unwritten and that we ourselves are the lead authors of that story. We are alive in a special and vivid way to the marvellous variety of different things that we could be or do. We feel light and "free as a bird."

Some of the most powerful examples of spontaneous freedom come to us from literature. Richard Yates's 1961 novel, *Revolutionary Road*, offers a striking case. At the center of the novel is a married couple, April and Frank Wheeler, who are contemplating an escape from their bland 1950s suburban American life by moving to Paris. Frank initially expresses some reluctance about the couple's newly hatched plan. He wonders what exactly he is supposed to be doing in Paris, to which April responds, avidly,

> Don't you see? Don't you see that's the whole idea? You'll be doing what you should've been allowed to do seven years ago. You'll be finding yourself. You'll be reading and studying and taking long walks and thinking. You'll have *time*. For the first time in your life you'll have time to find out what it is you want to do, and when you find it you'll have the time and the freedom to start doing it. (Yates 2000, 109)

Later on, Frank is having a martini-laced lunch with his colleague and best friend at Knox Business Machines—a happy-go-lucky alcoholic named Jack Ordway. He tells Ordway about the plan to move to Paris. Ordway is mildly skeptical but ultimately unmoved. On their way back to work, tipsy from the martinis, Frank experiences an unusual and "splendid" sense of freedom.

> The sun was pleasingly warm. In another few days it would be hot, but it was perfect now. In the cool marble depths of the bank, whose Muzak system was playing "Holiday for Strings," he entertained himself by pretending it was the last time he would ever stand in line here, the last time he would ever shift his feet and finger his paycheck as he and Ordway waited their turns at one of the ten tellers' windows that were reserved at lunchtime, twice a month, for Knox employees.
>
> He pretended it was the last time . . . he would ever join this slow promenade of office people in the sunshine, the last time the approach of his own polished shoes would ever cause these wobbling pigeons to take fright and skitter away across the spit and peanut shells of the sidewalk, to flap and climb until they were wheeling high over the towers with alternatively black and silver wings.
>
> And Goodbye, goodbye, he could say in his heart to everyone they passed—a chattering knot of stenographers clutching packages from the dimestore, a cynical, heavy-smoking group of young clerks who leaned against a building front in their shirtsleeves—goodbye to the whole sweet, sad bunch of you. I'm leaving. It was a splendid sense of freedom. (Yates 2000, 170–172)

Another powerful example of spontaneous freedom can be found in Virginia Woolf's 1925 masterpiece, *Mrs. Dalloway*. Peter Walsh, who had been living in India, returns to England to arrange a divorce for Daisy Simmons, his lover whom he intends to marry. Shortly after arriving in London, Peter is casually strolling through the city. As he stands in Trafalgar Square, he catches himself having a remarkable and moving experience.

And just because nobody yet knew he was in London, except Clarissa, and the earth, after the voyage, still seemed an island to him, the strangeness of standing alone, alive, unknown, at half-past eleven in Trafalgar Square overcame him. What is it? Where am I? And why, after all, does one do it? he thought, the divorce seeming all moonshine. And down his mind went flat as a marsh, and three great emotions bowled over him; understanding; a vast philanthropy; and finally, as if the result of the others, an irrepressible, exquisite delight; as if inside his brain by another hand strings were pulled, shutters moved, and he, having nothing to do with it, yet stood at the opening of endless avenues, down which if he chose he might wander. He had not felt so young for years.

He had escaped! was utterly free—as happens in the downfall of habit when the mind, like an unguarded flame, bows and bends and seems about to blow from its holding. I haven't felt so young for years! thought Peter, escaping (only of course for an hour or so) from being precisely what he was, and feeling like a child who runs out of doors, and sees, as he runs, his old nurse waving at the wrong window. (Woolf 2005, 51, cited in Gingerich 2022, 41–42)

Spontaneous freedom is obviously a desirable kind of experience. All else being equal, it's the sort of thing a person would want more of rather than less. I'm not claiming it cannot be overdone. It probably can—in theory certainly if not also in real life. Too much free spiritedness could put a person in the position Sartre (1956) called "meta-stable," never really standing anywhere because always metaphorically on the move. Always accentuating the freedom to choose but never quite choosing anything as a result. But surely the much more common and serious problem involving spontaneous freedom has to do not with an excess but with a deficiency. It's that so many people enjoy too little spontaneous freedom in their lives.

There are a thousand ways for a person to feel—and to be—spontaneously unfree. Feeling trapped in a bad relationship.

Drowning in bills and debt. Working at the sort of mind-numbing job that leaves a person feeling exhausted and spiritually empty. Suffering with a mental disorder.[20] Physical sickness or injury.[21] There are certain moods and emotional states that also contribute to a person's feeling as though they are hemmed in and unfree. Depression seems especially potent in this regard. In a moving autobiographical tidbit, Virginia Woolf describes her depression (the "dumb horror" that so gravely afflicted her) in terms that explicitly suggest a loss of freedom. "Again I had that hopeless sadness," she writes, "that collapse I have described before; as if I were passive under some sledge-hammer blow; exposed to a whole avalanche of meaning that had heaped itself up and discharged itself upon me, unprotected, with nothing to ward it off" (Woolf 1985, 78). Depression has a tendency to immobilize its victim, pinning them under a metaphorical avalanche or sledge-hammer blow. Depression can also inhibit a person's sense of freedom by altering the terms by which they measure success and failure. It makes setbacks look more formidable than they might have looked otherwise. Disappointments appear heavier. Small missteps can feel catastrophic. A depressed person is also more likely to draw negatively fatalistic conclusions about the everyday obstacles they encounter. As philosopher Iain Law eloquently explains:

> When I'm depressed, every job seems bigger and harder. Every setback strikes me not as something easy to work around or get over but as a huge obstacle. Events appear more chaotic and beyond my control: if I fail to achieve some goal, it will seem that achieving it is forever beyond my abilities, which I perceive to be far more meagre that I did when I was not depressed. (Law 2009, 355)[22]

Depression may be the more ruthless killer of spontaneous freedom, but I think it's obvious that anxiety belongs in this category as well. An anxious person sees frightening obstacles more quickly than exciting possibilities. Anxiety makes us tight and constricted rather than loose and freewheeling. If spontaneous freedom conveys a sense of openness and opportunity, of all the exciting possibilities that lie before us, anxiety shrinks our comfort zone by telling us that potential disaster lurks around every corner. Matthew Ratcliffe puts the point crisply: "a world where dread is all-pervasive is a world where things cannot entice one to act in a confident, habitual, effortless way" (Ratcliffe 2015, 168). Experientially speaking, anxiety is on the other side of spontaneous freedom.

Anxiety is also a species of unfreedom in virtue of the exhausting vigilance it demands. Years ago, I had a panic attack while delivering a lecture to my students on some topic in the philosophy of law. It's impossible to explain to someone who has never experienced one what the horror of a full-blown panic attack is like, but I remember becoming overwhelmed with the terrifying thought that I must flee, must somehow escape this room. (*But how? A quick, panicked glance at the clock told me that the lecture was barely fifteen minutes old.*) My knees wobbled as I snatched desperate, shallow breaths. My vision became blurry. I remember that the sound of my own voice seemed strange and foreign. I gripped the lectern tightly with both hands. Some time passed. Instinctually, I lobbed a question to my students, something to deflect attention away from me. Something to buy a minute or two while I tried to pull myself together. One student mercifully raised his hand and babbled out some words, then another student after him. A few moments later the panic abated (as it always does, as it must) and somehow, nerves frayed and body still trembling, I navigated my way to the end of the class period.

Even now, all these years later, on days when I am scheduled to teach, a special anxiety-instigated itinerary is scrupulously adhered to. There are numerous little rules and rituals that need to be followed to keep the anxiety at bay. A second cup of coffee is not permitted on teaching days (too much caffeine makes me jumpy).

Some pre-lecture exercise is also required, to dampen the roiling anxiety. I arrive at campus early, leaving plenty of time to review my lecture slides one more time, to make a few handwritten notes, and to purchase a camomile or peppermint tea from the café near my office (herbal tea apparently has anxiety-calming properties). I need to arrive at the lecture hall early, too, leaving enough time to set things up in just the right way. Lights at the correct dimness. Lectern positioned thus and so. Stool placed nearby, in case I need to unexpectedly sit down for a moment, in case my wobbly agoraphobic legs get a little too wobbly. Water bottle here. Freshly purchased herbal tea over there. Other belongings organized in a neat stack. And on and on. Feeling yoked to my little itinerary is unpleasant, but it's not the end of the world. I manage. Yet there is obviously a kind of unfreedom in all of the care and planning anxiety demands of me, and in the "forethought of grief" (Wendell Berry's beautiful phrase) that yokes me to my little itinerary in the first place. I sometimes fantasize about what it might be like to throw the itinerary away: to wander into the lecture hall, loose and relaxed, without a care in the world, excited to share my love of philosophy with students. What a wonderful gift of freedom that would be. The conclusion is not only that that anxiety robs its sufferer of equanimity (that much is probably true by definition), but also that equanimity is an important variety of freedom in its own right.

Another connection between freedom and anxiety involves the idea of control. Anxiety frequently has the quality of being driven by some process over which we have no power. "Part of what is most horrendous about ... anxiety and panic," writes Andrew Solomon, "is that it does not involve volition: feelings happen to you for absolutely no reason at all" (Solomon 2001, 225). Unwelcome thoughts intrude uninvited. Physical symptoms show up unannounced, without our consent or foreknowledge. Those flashes of panic strike without warning, indifferent to what David Hume famously called our "willings and desires" (Hume 2009, 98). Solomon likens the physical experience of severe anxiety to the feeling that attends tripping and falling. It's a mixture of vertigo, adrenaline-filled helplessness, and terrible urgency.

> There is a moment, if you trip or slip, before your hand shoots out to break your fall, when you feel the earth rushing up at you and you cannot help yourself, a passing, fraction-of-a-second terror. I felt this way hour after hour after hour. Being anxious at this extreme level is bizarre. You feel all the time that you want to do something, that there is some affect that is unavailable to you, that there's a physical need of impossible urgency and discomfort for which there is no relief, as though you were constantly vomiting from your stomach but had no mouth. (Solomon 2001, 50)

It's not only that anxiety arrives on the scene against our will, like an involuntary spasm of the muscles. It's also that, at its worst, the experience of anxiety can call into question a person's sense of their own volition, raising doubts about who or what is really in control.[23]

The close relationship between anxiety and control has been taken up extensively by psychiatric professionals, who note that feeling out of control is one of the hallmark features of the experience of anxiety (Craske and Barlow 2007, 51). Psychologist David Barlow writes that, at the core of anxiety, "is an abiding sense of unpredictability and *uncontrollability* concerning future events." He argues further that the "process of worry seems to be associated with (failed) attempts to predict potential future negative outcomes, and *with the belief that this prediction allows for increased control over these outcomes*" (Barlow 2004, 498; emphasis added). On this view, the reason we anxious sufferers spend so much time worrying about catastrophic outcomes—about every little thing that might go wrong—is that this somehow delivers a feeling of being in control. Or *more* in control than one might have felt otherwise. The sequence of thought seems to go something like this: *The more we worry, the more vigilant and punctilious we are, the more accurate predictors of outcomes we believe we will be. And if we are more accurate predictors of outcomes, we will thereby have more control over a fundamentally uncertain situation.* Someone who has prepared for all contingencies is more in control than someone who hasn't. Someone who "sees it coming" (so to speak) is to that extent more in control than someone who is blindsided.

Many people respond to the essential uncontrollability of anxiety by searching for something else in their lives over which to exert control. A new diet or fitness regimen. Another imperative or prohibition about their finances or health or something else. Anxious people will often impose new rules on themselves. They will say things like: *"I won't spend any money at restaurants this month"* or *"I'm only allowed to check my work email at such and such times"* or *"From now on I will walk at least ten thousand steps per day"* or *"No more looking at my phone in bed."* And so on. Solomon speculates that this kind of response, this longing for something over which to have control, also helps explain the high incidence of substance abuse, which is well documented, among sufferers of anxiety and other mental disorders. It's not only that drugs and alcohol can "take the edge off," as the old expression has it. They also replace "uncontrollable suffering which the user does not understand" with a "drug-induced dysphoria which the user does understand." In Nepal, apparently, "when an elephant has a splinter or spike in his foot, his drivers put chili in one of his eyes, and the elephant becomes so preoccupied with the pain of the chili that he stops paying attention to the pain in his foot, and people can remove the spike without being trampled to death (and in a fairly short time, the chili washes out of his eye)." For many people with anxiety and other mental health illnesses, drugs and alcohol are the equivalent to the chili. No one is suggesting that this is ideal. But sometimes, turning to something over which one has at least some control (even if potentially harmful) can serve as a distraction from the "uncontrollable suffering" of anxiety, and can provide respite as a result (Solomon 2001, 225).[24]

It goes without saying that the relationship between freedom and anxiety is a complicated and contested one. We saw earlier in the context of Kierkegaard that anxiety is the fundamental mark of human freedom. And yet, we also considered how freedom and anxiety sometimes pull in different directions—how they appear as incompatible, even antagonistic ideas. The Kierkegaardian response to this apparent paradox involves pointing out, once again, that the concept of *Angest* is not identical to all those anxious feelings that routinely bubble up in our lives (the intrusive thoughts, the irrational worry, the panic attacks, the phobias, and all the rest). *Angest* is not just one more mood or a feeling, on a par with all the others. Rather, on the story Kierkegaard tells, anxiety is essential to human existence. It is the mark of our nature as spiritual beings.

2
When Something Bitter Rises Up

> In the healthiest and most prosperous existence, how many links of illness, danger, and disaster are always interposed? . . . Take the happiest man, the one most envied by the world, and in nine cases out of ten his inmost consciousness is one of failure. Either his ideals in the line of his achievements are pitched far higher than the achievements themselves, or else he has secret ideals of which the world knows nothing, and in regard to which he inwardly knows himself to be found wanting.
> —William James, *The Varieties of Religious Experience*

It's hard to imagine any philosopher more richly attuned to the vicissitudes of mental health and sickness than William James. James's writings—beautiful stylistic specimens—reveal a preoccupation with the nature of mental hardship and also with the conditions under which we might (with effort and luck) cultivate healthier habits of living and coping.

A lot of professional philosophy focuses on the minutiae of arcane intellectual puzzles. Not so for James. Deep, humanly momentous questions—about freedom of the will, the existence of God, the nature of the emotions and conscious experience, about the "vital difference" between significant and insignificant lives—were seemingly always at the center of his philosophizing. John Kaag puts it well when he says that, for James, "Philosophy was never a detached intellectual exercise or a matter of wordplay. It wasn't a game, or if it was, it was the world's most serious. It was about being thoughtful and living vibrantly" (Kaag 2020, 3–4). James was sanguine about human potential but darkly realistic about human nature. He believed that we humans are essentially damaged creatures, inescapably prone to all sorts of sickness and fear, and yet, at the same time, he maintained that it was possible (though of course there are never any guarantees) to fashion healthy and rewarding lives for ourselves.

In this chapter, I want to consider James's diagnosis of our human condition—a fascinating blend of existentialist anguish and Pragmatist hope—and also to give a sketch of some of the strategies by which he thought we could become better and healthier than we presently are, more vital and energetic, more hopeful and less susceptible to psychic suffering. Despite the pain and sickness which is a constitutive feature of our nature as human beings, James reminds us that we are not merely passive recipients of suffering, lacking any say in the matter. He reminds us that we are agents with the capacity to take action, to heroically push back. In short, James saw that suffering is a deep and unavoidable fact of human existence, as the first Noble Truth of the Buddha teaches. But he also insisted that hope for improvement springs eternal.[1]

It's not an embellishment to say that, from the late 1880s until his death in 1910, William James was the most famous philosopher in the United States. Along with his brilliant and cantankerous friend Charles Sanders Peirce, James was a co-founder of the quintessentially American school of philosophy: Pragmatism. He was also closely associated with the founding of functional psychology in the late 19th century, although his relationship to "functionalism" was a complicated one. As a world-famous Harvard professor, James would cross paths with a number of notable people. He met with Sigmund Freud in 1909, during Freud's only visit to the United States, at a conference for psychologists at Clark University in Worcester, Massachusetts. He was a mentor to the great sociologist W.E.B. Du Bois, the first African American to receive a PhD from Harvard, who referred to James in his *Autobiography* as "my friend and guide to clear thinking"

(Du Bois 1968, 143). One of James's extremely average undergraduate students at Harvard was a brash teenager from New York City named Theodore Roosevelt. Roosevelt and James would turn out to disagree sharply about many things—most consequential of which, the U.S. imperialist foreign policy in Cuba and the Philippines that Roosevelt championed and James loathed. As James wrote in a Boston newspaper in 1899 about the U.S. intervention in the Philippines: "It is horrible, simply horrible. Surely there cannot be many born and bred Americans who, when they look at the bare fact of what we are doing . . . do not blush with burning shame" (James 2010, 206).

James came from a wealthy and absurdly talented family. His paternal grandfather—an Irish immigrant who settled in Albany, New York, who came to be known as "old Billy James"—was one of the first millionaires in the United States. His father, Henry James Sr., was a well-known Swedenborgian theologian. His little brother by a year—Henry James Jr.—is regarded by many as one of the finest novelists ever to write in the English language. Their younger sister, Alice, was a famous diarist who, despite her tragically short life, wrote many insightful, witty things about English life and manners. The great Ralph Waldo Emerson was James's godfather.

Life Is a Tragic Situation

James suffered mightily with depression and anxiety (that "most evil of all maladies," as he once referred to it), especially as a teenager and during early adulthood (James 2010, 13). He was also diagnosed with what in those days was called "neurasthenia" (a general weakness of the nerves or nervous exhaustion), a condition to which it was thought hardworking, stressed-out Americans were unusually susceptible.[2] The young William James would also battle an assortment of other ailments and illnesses: poor eyesight, insomnia, headaches, a weak stomach, constipation, and chronic back pain. As he would casually remark in 1891, "I was entirely broken down before I was thirty" (Feinstein 1984, 206).

In *The Varieties of Religious Experience,* James cited a detailed personal account of anxiety from a mysterious, unnamed "French correspondent" (the account is almost certainly James's own) who described it as "a horrible dread at the pit of my stomach . . . a sense of the insecurity of life . . . it was as if something hitherto solid within my breast gave way entirely, and I became a mass of quivering fear. . . . It gradually faded, but for months I was unable to go out into the dark alone" (James 1982, 160). *A sense of the insecurity of life* is an excellent way to describe what the experience of anxiety is like at its core. Anxiety arises because life is essentially insecure. We are vulnerable creatures who inhabit a world replete with danger and uncertainty. At bottom, nothing can really keep us safe. All the money in the world won't keep the cancer away. No precaution can render our children impervious to illness or accident. Nothing protects against bad luck. In the end, and despite our best efforts, the possibility of injury and loss is always there.

We saw earlier that for Kierkegaard (who died when James was thirteen years old), anxiety is bound up with uncertainty about the future. James would have agreed that such uncertainty is one of anxiety's central elements. (It's worth remembering that how to cope intelligently in a fundamentally uncertain world is basically the hallmark of the Pragmatist philosophy that James helped found shortly after the American Civil War.) But more than simply not knowing in detail how things will turn out, James also believed that, in one way, things will always turn out badly. Human life is a "tragic situation," he wrote. Even when things go smoothly and well—as smoothly and well as can reasonably be hoped—some good things will be sacrificed for the sake of others. Even in the best of all possible worlds, there will be suffering and loss. We will miss out on something of value no matter what we do. "All demands conjointly cannot be satisfied in this poor world," he says. "Some part of the ideal must be butchered" (James 2000, 255–256).

Having to make agonizing choices and dealing with the attendant loss, James has it, is a deep and unavoidable fact about the human condition. As he explains, "there is always a *pinch* between the ideal and the actual which can only be got through by leaving part of the ideal behind." And he goes on:

> There is hardly a good which we can imagine except as competing for the possession of the same bit of space and time with some other imagined good. Every end of desire that presents itself appears exclusive of some other end of desire. . . . Doesn't the fact of "no" stand at the very core of life? Doesn't the very "seriousness" that we attribute to life mean that ineluctable noes and losses form a part of it, that there are genuine sacrifices somewhere, and that something permanently drastic and bitter always remains at the bottom of its cup? (James 2000, 254; 129)

We can and do feel this sense of loss, of having missed out on something valuable, even when we are pleased with the choices we have made. Even when things have worked out favorably by our own lights. Human lives are finite, and with our finitude comes the necessity of making choices. (It's spacio-temporally impossible to pursue all good things.) And with the necessity of making choices comes the inescapability of loss. In saying "yes" to some good (a career, a spouse, an adventure), we are thereby saying "no" to something else (a different career, another spouse, an alternative adventure). In opting one way rather than another, we necessarily suffer the loss of something valuable. Isaiah Berlin puts the conclusion crisply: "We are doomed to choose, and every choice may entail an irreparable loss" (Berlin 1990, 13).[3]

And yet, despite the "tragic" nature of human affairs, decisions do, after all, get made. James's view is that we more or less fumble ahead, without method or compass, ever mindful of the fact that things may turn out badly. It occasionally happens that people find themselves frozen in a state of indecision, immobilized like Buridan's Ass. But James would have emphasized that doing nothing is a certain kind of choice, too. He would have further insisted that there is no ethical algorithm to consult in these kinds of cases. No fundamental principle or theory or decision-procedure will supply the right answer for us.

Often enough, we have no choice but to turn these kinds of decisions over to our emotions, what James calls our "passional nature" (James 2000, 205). When the intellectual reasons run out, we will be compelled to lean on our existential commitments—our vague, usually inchoate, "more or less dumb sense of what life honestly and deeply means" (James 2000, 7). Such commitments are not themselves undergirded by something else. While not "foundational" in the specifically philosophical sense of that term, these commitments are where our evaluative thinking comes to the end of the line. It is where we reach "bedrock" and our "spade is turned" (Wittgenstein 1998, 85). As Hilary Putnam explains on James's behalf,

> Someone who only acts when the "estimated utilities" are favorable does not live a meaningful human life. Even if I choose to devote my life to a calling whose ethical and social value is certain, say, to comforting the dying, helping the mentally ill, curing the sick, or relieving poverty, I still have to decide, not whether it is good that someone should do that thing, but whether it is good that I, Hilary Putnam, do that thing. The answer to that question cannot be a matter of well-established scientific fact, no matter how generously "scientific" is defined. (Putnam 2017, 260)

James ends his most famous essay, "The Will to Believe," with this bracing quotation from James Fitzjames Stephen. It sums up perfectly James's diagnosis of the "tragic" situation we invariably find ourselves in, and the attitude he thinks it's best to adopt in the face of uncertainty and agonizing choices.

What do you think of yourself? What do you think of the world? ... These are questions with which all must deal as it seems good to them. They are riddles of the Sphinx, and in some way or other we must deal with them.... In all important transactions of life we have to take a leap in the dark.... If we decide to leave the riddles unanswered, that is a choice. If we waver in our answer, that too is a choice; but whatever choice we make, we make it at our peril.... Each must act as he thinks best, and if he is wrong so much the worse for him. We stand on a mountain pass in the midst of whirling snow and blinding mist, through which we get glimpses now and then of paths which may be deceptive. If we stand still, we shall be frozen to death. If we take the wrong road, we shall be dashed to pieces. We do not certainly know whether there is any right one. What must we do? "Be strong and of a good courage." Act for the best, hope for the best, and take what comes. ... If death ends all, we cannot meet death better. (Stephen 1874, 353, quoted at James 2000, 218)

This is the moral and spiritual equivalent of working without a net. The future is unknown. Uncertainty lurks in every corner. We will suffer loss no matter what we do. And yet, "taking a leap in the dark" is our best and only recourse. We may wish for something more objective and solid to grab hold of here, but it's at the very heart of Jamesean Pragmatism to insist that, ultimately, it is not to be had. "Objective evidence and certitude are doubtless very fine ideals to play with," he wrote in 1896, "but where on this moonlit and dream-visited planet are they found?" (James 2000, 207). Men and women will forever be agonizing over difficult choices, taking risks, making sacrifices, incurring losses, compromising some good things for the sake of others. We may wish it were otherwise, but navigating uncertainty and enduring loss is our fate.

I think that some of James's reflections about uncertainty and loss—about life as "a tragic situation"—help explain why anxiety is so pervasive. We anxious sufferers are constantly worried about taking the wrong path, obsessed with not incurring any more loss than is absolutely necessary. But we also know, deep down, that a modicum of pain and loss is unavoidable no matter how we proceed, no matter how things turn out. In sum, Kierkegaard was right to maintain that uncertainty about the future is the fundamental breeding ground of anxiety, the soil in which it naturally grows. But James was correct to add an additional dark caveat to that formulation. Though we can never know in detail how things will transpire in the future, we can be certain that the future will inevitably bring about pain and loss, even when things unfold comparatively well. This is ultimately what "The pit of insecurity beneath the surface of life" comes to (James 1982, 160). Anxiety is unavoidable, in short, because life is a tragic situation, because uncertainty and loss are inescapable facts of human existence.

Earlier, I described James's attitude about our human condition as a blend of existential despair and Pragmatist hope. So far, I have been emphasizing the darker, existential side of James's thinking. This is the James who says things like: "Our civilization is founded on the shambles, and every individual existence goes out in a lonely spasm of helpless agony. If you protest, my friend, wait till you arrive there yourself!" (James 1982, 163). Or, equally darkly, "Mankind is in a position similar to that of a set of people living on a frozen lake, surrounded by cliffs over which there is no escape, yet knowing that little by little the ice is melting, and the inevitable day drawing near when the last film of it will disappear, and to be drowned ignominiously will be the human creature's portion" (James 1982, 139). But there is a hopeful and fortifying side of James's work, too. This is the James who assures us that, through "sweat and effort," we can make better, happier lives for ourselves. This is the James who believes that we can become more energetic, more cheerful and vital, by intentionally cultivating healthier habits of living (James 1962, 133).

Which of these two Jameses is correct about the situation we find ourselves in? Is facing up to the uncertainty of the future ultimately an occasion for anxious despair, or for hope? James himself would have insisted that this is not the kind of question that can be settled intellectually. There is no fact of the matter about which emotional stance—anxiety or hope—is the more apt or predictively sound one. Just as anxiety has a tendency to produce *false positives* (we feel anxious about things that are not genuinely worrisome) and *false negatives* (we don't feel anxious about things that are genuinely worrisome), so too do we frequently feel hopeful in genuinely hopeless situations and hopeless about situations for which a modicum of hope is realistic and warranted (Kurth 2022, 123). In the end, for James, the choice between anxiety and hope is best explained in terms of a distinction between two fundamental human dispositions or temperaments—between a temperament "organically weighted on the side of cheer" on one side, and a temperament that lingers "over the darker aspect of the universe" on the other (James 1982, 83).

Sick Souls

James spends several lectures in *The Varieties of Religious Experience* distinguishing between those people who live out a "religion of healthy mindedness" from those who are afflicted with what he calls a "sick soul." The phrase "sick soul" refers to those people (James himself certainly counted among them) who cannot, as a matter of temperament, "swiftly throw off the burden of the consciousness of evil, but are congenitally fated to suffer from its presence" (James 1982, 132–133). The sick-souled are those for whom "something bitter rises up: a touch of nausea, a falling dead of the delight, a whiff of melancholy. . . . The buzz of life ceases at their touch as a piano-string stops sounding when the damper falls upon it" (James 1982, 136).

Sick souls obviously come in different shapes and sizes. No two are exactly the same. Nor does a particular sick soul correspond with a single diagnosis or condition. Most are "mixed cases," James says. Incidentally, James was always adamant that we should take various psychiatric diagnoses with the healthy grain of salt he thought they deserved—"we should not treat our classifications with too much respect" (James 1982, 148). It's obviously anachronistic to insert James into contemporary debates about the soundness of psychiatric diagnoses, but his view would have almost certainly been that there is no fact of the matter about when anxiety crosses a threshold from the normal to the pathological. There is no "natural dividing line" we can appeal to (Horwitz 2013, 15). More generally, there is no decisive place at which something new and different called "disorder" or "illness" emerges on the scene. Similarly, there is no unique piece of information that tells us when or if some episode of pain is too much for a person to bear. Everything is on a continuum. Human experience is endlessly rich. No two minds are perfectly alike. Variation abounds. Some of this variation we find it convenient to classify as "normal," some of it "pathological." But this is not because someone has discovered, out there in the nature of things, a distinction between "normal" and "pathological." It's not because we have finally succeeded at carving nature at the joints. For James, nature has no joints which our various descriptions might or might not succeed at carving. "Every way of classifying a thing is but a way of handling it for a particular purpose," he writes in impeccably Pragmatist fashion (James 1956, 70). Every psychiatric diagnosis has a dose of built-in arbitrariness (*Why should the line be here rather than there? Why are those the specific diagnostic criteria, anyway? Why not others instead? Why not more criteria, or fewer? And why must a person exhibit x-number out of y-number diagnostic features in order to qualify for formal diagnosis? What would be so fundamentally mistaken about different values for x and y?*, and so on). A psychiatric diagnosis is a practical exercise, "abbreviated trade talk between professionals to indicate a course of treatment" (Feinstein 1984, 23). It no more zeroes in on the deep metaphysical truth about anxiety and other mental disorders than do a million other ways of drawing lines or establishing borders. Or so I am confident James would have insisted.[4]

James would have also insisted that every psychiatric diagnosis is rough and partial. No diagnosis can perfectly capture the full richness of a person's emotional experience. Something will always be left out. Consider novelist Paul Auster's description of his anxious mother:

> At the other end, the extreme end of who she was, there was the frightened and debilitated neurotic, the helpless creature prey to blistering assaults of anxiety, the phobic whose incapacities grew as the years advanced—from an early fear of heights to a metastatic flowering of multiple forms of paralysis: afraid of escalators, afraid of airplanes, afraid of elevators, afraid to drive a car, afraid of going near windows on upper floors of buildings, afraid to be alone, afraid of open spaces, afraid to walk anywhere (she felt she would lose her balance or pass out), and an ever-present hypochondria that gradually reached the most exalted summits of dread. In other words: afraid to die, which in the end is probably no different than saying afraid to live. (Auster 2012, 141)

Several familiar psychiatric diagnostic categories seem in point here (Generalized Anxiety Disorder or GAD; panic disorder with agoraphobia or PDA; Hypochondriasis, phobias of various sorts). But there also seems to be something more nebulous—a general manner of character or temperament; an overall anxious disposition—that eludes formal diagnostic categories (Horwitz 2013, 6–7). James would have regarded such elusion as unavoidable. No formal diagnosis can do justice to the fullness of what things feel like for us on the inside. There will always be something that escapes the diagnostic net. As if the richness and complexity of a person's emotional experience was wholly translatable into the categories of the most recent edition of the *Diagnostic and Statistical Manual* (*DSM*).

James defines sick souls broadly, as vague and generalized predispositions to psychic suffering, a "sensitiveness and susceptibility to mental pain" (James 1982, 145). This can obviously manifest in different ways and to different degrees. "Sometimes," James says, it is "mere passive joylessness and dreariness, discouragement, dejection, lack of taste and zest and spring." At other times, it's a "positive and active anguish" which can assume a variety of different qualities and characteristics: "loathing; irritation and exasperation; self-mistrust and self-despair; suspicion, anxiety, trepidation, fear" (James 1982, 145; 147).

As we have already seen, having a sick soul is not an all-or-nothing affair. Sick souls do not come with necessary and sufficient conditions, and there is no diagnostic checklist that determines whether a particular soul is "sick" in James's sense, and, if so, to what extent. Most people experience some of these feelings and inclinations from time to time. Even people who are generally cool and calm can find themselves unexpectedly tight with panic. Habitually happy and optimistic people can sometimes find themselves in moods of darkness and resignation. James cites the example of Goethe—that "conquering optimist"—who nevertheless proclaimed in 1824 that his existence had been "nothing but pain and burden, and I [Goethe] can affirm that during the whole of my 75 years, I have not had four weeks of genuine well-being. It is but the perpetual rolling of a rock that must be raised up again forever" (Goethe, in James 1982, 137). James himself was prone to these moods (if that is the right word for them), in which everything seems gloomy and pointless. In such moods, he says, the world can look "remote, strange, sinister, uncanny. Its color is gone, its breath is cold, there is no speculation in the eyes it glares with" (James 1982, 141; 151).

James sometimes wrote as if sick souls were written into the nature of things, as if to suggest that our prehistoric ancestors suffered with these same kinds of feelings, more or less as we do. "There are morbid minds in every human collection," he says (James 2000,

127). There's at least a little bit of sick soul in all of us. We are all cut from the same human cloth. A fundamental similarity unites us all. Every human existence has pain and darkness in it. "In the deepest heart of all of us there is a corner in which the ultimate mystery of things works sadly" (James 2000, 219). "The normal process of life," James writes, "contains moments as bad as any of those which insane melancholy is filled with, moments in which radical evil gets its innings and takes its solid turn. The lunatic's visions of horror are all drawn from the material of daily fact" (James 1982, 163).

No one really knows where sick souls come from. And different factors impact different people in different ways, and to different degrees. In the case of anxiety in particular, it's widely acknowledged that parents and upbringing often have a significant role to play. In his influential self-help workbook, *The Anxiety and Phobia Workbook*, Edmund J. Bourne lists the following "childhood circumstances" as major causes of anxiety disorders:

- Your Parents Communicate an Overly Cautious View of the World
- Your Parents are Overly Critical and Set Excessively High Standards
- Emotional Insecurity and Dependence
- Your Parents Suppress Your Expression of Feelings and Self-Assertiveness. (Bourne 2010, 35)

The first item on Bourne's list—an instance of what psychologists sometimes call "parental modelling"—is almost certainly what most impacted me as a child. My memories of childhood, happy on the whole though they are, are colored by a vague sense of a world replete with hazard and a corresponding imperative to be on the lookout for danger—to be alert, cautious, vigilant about safety. There are no distinct episodes I single out, just a standing, ever-present directive to *be careful*. It was subtle. But looking back now with adult eyes, it was also pervasive and unmistakable. Nowadays, a parent myself, I fear that I'm infecting my children with the same bitter poison—little drop by little drop—every time I tell them to be careful, to stay away from the road, not to play too close to the ledge, and so on. In his 2012 memoir of anxiety, *Monkey Mind*, Daniel Smith writes movingly about anxiety and parental influence.

> But a child is a sensitive instrument. You can hide the factual truth from a child, but you can't blanket influence. Your agitation will out, and over time it will mold your child's temperament as surely as water wears rock. It was not until I was nearly twenty, deep into my own way with anxiety, that my mother spoke to me explicitly about her anxiety and the grief it caused her. But by that time she was essentially talking to herself. I'd become her. It wasn't merely genetics. It was the million little signals ... the jolting movements, the curious fears, the subtle avoidances, the panic behind the eyes, the terror behind the hugs, the tremor in the caresses. ... A child registers who's raising him. (Smith 2012, 29)

Wherever they come from exactly, and despite the obvious pain and suffering they are responsible for, James believes that sick souls are philosophically significant. There is much to learn about life and death, about our very humanity, from "the secrets of their prison-house." "Let us see," James proposes, "whether pity, pain, and fear, and the sentiment of human helplessness may not open a profounder view and put into our hands a more complicated key to the meaning of the situation" (James 1982, 135–136). In short, James is prepared to look sick souls in the face, to listen to their point of view, to accept darkness and fear as essential (and sometimes instructive) elements of our human condition.[5] A worldview that fails "to accord to sorrow, pain, and death any positive and active attention" is less comprehensive than one that does, James thinks. This is why he concludes, at the very end of the lecture on sick souls, that "the completest religions" (and he names Buddhism and Christianity as exemplars) would be the ones "in which the pessimistic elements are best developed." Both Buddhism and Christianity—not only them, but perhaps them preeminently—believe that suffering can lead to growth and enhancement. Both religions affirm in their different ways the possibility of overcoming, of liberation through pain and hardship. Both give us an account about how "man must die to an unreal life before he can be born into the real life" and are for that reason, James concludes, "essentially religions of deliverance" (James 1982, 165).

Taking seriously the possibility of deliverance is an abiding theme in James's philosophy and in the American Pragmatist tradition more generally. James and his fellow Pragmatists sometimes use the word "meliorism" to describe this possibility. Meliorism does not purport to predict how, in fact, things will unfold. It merely accentuates the possibility—the chance and the corresponding hope—that things will be better in the future. This is how James glosses it:

> There are unhappy men who think the salvation of the world impossible. Theirs is the doctrine known as pessimism. Optimism in turn would be the doctrine that thinks the world's salvation inevitable. Midway between the two there stands what may be called the doctrine of meliorism. . . . Meliorism treats salvation as neither necessary nor impossible. It treats it as a possibility, which becomes more and more of a probability the more numerous and actual conditions of salvation become. (James 2000, 124–125)

James's friend and fellow Pragmatist philosopher, John Dewey, describes meliorism as the belief "that the specific conditions which exist at one moment, be they comparatively bad or comparatively good, in any event may be bettered" (Dewey 1957, 178). It's hard to take issue with that. A meliorist perspective accentuates the possibility that we might feel a little bit better tomorrow. No matter how hopeless or scared or gloomy we feel in the present moment, the possibility of improvement, even if only slight, is always there. Deliverance is never guaranteed, but neither is it ever ruled out. A meliorist perspective reminds us that improvement is possible, and more, that human effort has a role to play in bringing it about. It reminds us that we needn't sit back and passively accept the current situation as our fate. The dice is never loaded. We are agents with the capacity to courageously fight back, to take action against pain and suffering.

But how, exactly? What are we supposed to do? James's answer is deceptively simple. We can endeavor to feel better through a combination of sheer willpower and the meticulous cultivation of the right habits.

Habit, Will, and Emotion

Habit is a pivotal theme in James's philosophy. All living creatures are "bundles of habits," he thinks. Yet, unlike wild animals, whose behavior seems "implanted at birth," James maintains that human habits are largely "the result of education" (James 2007a, 104). Unlike other animals, we are schooled into and out of our habits.[6]

Habit and will are closely related concepts in James's philosophy. Both enjoy great causal power: almost everything a person does and refrains from doing is regulated to some degree by habit and the will. Habit and will also mirror each other. Genuinely habitual action is in a sense involuntary and unwilled. It happens unreflectively, almost mechanically. A genuinely willed action by contrast seeks to overcome inhibition and disrupt previously established habit. James believed that every idea that represents an action shall—necessarily, as a matter of course—translate itself into an action unless something stands in its way, unless it is blocked by another inhibitory idea. Sometimes, the overcoming of inhibition occurs without effort, by way of "a fortunate lapse of consciousness." In other cases, the overcoming of inhibition is more difficult and requires attentive, repeated effort. In these kinds of cases, new habits are formed through the deliberate training of the will. But this is James's crucial insight: once a habit is properly formed, once it has sufficiently taken root, it develops a momentum of its own and no longer requires the will to sustain it. Part of the challenge, then, involves cultivating the right habits so that acting and feeling in certain ways occurs naturally, unthinkingly. The picture this evokes is someone who glides effortlessly through life—who acts in certain ways as a matter of unthinking habit—rather than someone for whom strained, laborious willing is continuously required. As James writes in his masterwork, *The Principles of Psychology*, "There is no more miserable human being than one in whom nothing is habitual but indecision, and for whom the lighting of every cigar, the drinking of every cup, the time of rising and going to bed every day, and the beginning of every bit of work, are subjects of express volitional deliberation" (James 2007a, 122).

There is an extremely important link for James between the establishment of new habits and improved mental health. This is because, contrary to what common sense might tell us, causation between action and thought—between bodily symptoms and inwardly felt emotional states—flows in both directions. The commonsense view that James sets himself against says: "we lose our fortune, are sorry and weep; we meet a bear, are frightened and run; we are insulted by a rival, are angry and strike" (James 2007b, 449–450). James maintains that the order of this sequence (roughly: a stimulus causes an emotion and an emotion then causes an action) is incorrect, or at least incomplete. What's missing from the sequence is an account of the unique bodily state that accompanies each instance of an emotion. Emotions do not just occur in the head. On the contrary, they are physical and bodily through and through. They are "constituted by, and made up of, those bodily changes which we ordinarily call their expression or consequence." An "emotion dissociated from all bodily feeling,"

James writes, "is inconceivable." "A purely disembodied human emotion is a nonentity" (James 2007b, 452).

To make his case for the fundamentally physical and bodily character of the emotions, James invites his readers to participate in a thought experiment. Can you imagine being in an emotional state of rage, he asks, without any of the physical symptoms characteristic of rage—no "ebullition in the chest, no flushing of the face, no dilation of the nostrils, no clenching of the teeth, no impulse to vigorous action, but in their stead limp muscles, calm breathing, and a placid face?" Surely not. James thinks what you would be imagining in this case is not the emotion we know and refer to as rage but rather "some cold-blooded and dispassionate judicial sentence, confined entirely to the intellectual realm" (James 2007b, 452). There is simply no emotion of rage without its sensory and bodily corollaries. And so too for all the other emotions in their turn. If we try to think of an emotion in abstraction from "all the feelings of its bodily symptoms," we will find, James argues, that there is "nothing left behind" (James 1961, 246).[7]

Anxiety is invariably physical and bodily—one of the most physical and bodily of all the emotions (Ratcliffe 2017, 73). The bodily nature of anxiety is even suggested by the etymology of the word "anxiety" itself. Consider that,

> The English word "anxiety" and its European equivalents (e.g., *angloisse* in French, *angoscia* in Italian, *angustia* in Spanish, *Angst* in German, and *angst* in Danish) come from the Latin *anxietas*, which, in turn, has roots in the ancient Greek *angh*. Although *angh* was sometimes used by the Greeks to mean burdened or troubled (i.e., *angu*ished), it was primarily employed in reference to physical sensations, such as tightness, constriction, or discomfort. For instance, the word "angina," a medical condition in which chest pains occur in relation to heart disease, comes from *angh*. (LeDoux 2016, 2)

When we are anxious, our bodies are reacting as if a threat to our safety or well-being is impending. We begin to sweat. Our stomachs nervously churn. Muscles tighten. Heart palpitations and difficulty breathing may also occur. Some of us suffer with sensations of "depersonalization" (the highly disturbing feeling that our experience is not properly tracking reality, that we are watching our own lives unfold as if from the outside). There is nothing to be afraid of—deep down we probably know this—but the brute physical and physiological response to perceived danger, honed evolutionarily over the course of thousands of generations, is still there.[8]

No one really doubts that emotions have the physical and bodily aspect James insists they do. But James is often taken to have argued for a much stronger and more controversially reductive kind of claim: that the physical and bodily symptoms associated with an emotion *just are* the emotion itself. James was admittedly unclear and inconsistent on this point. But it's important to see that when James identifies emotions with feelings of bodily change, he is not thereby attempting to divorce emotions from cognition and from our more general experience of the world. As Matthew Ratcliffe nicely explains,

> For James, feelings or affects are not *mere* accompaniments to distinct cognitive states and processes but inextricable from them. . . . Rather than taking a conception of intentionality for granted and identifying emotions with bodily feelings that are distinct from intentional states, James reconceptualizes intentionality so as to include bodily feeling in its structure. Emotions are thus essential to the structure of world-experience. In this role, they also shape our decision-making and behaviour. (Ratcliffe 2008, 222)

In other words, rather an assuming a sharp distinction between private mental events, on the one hand, and bodily sensations, on the other, and then reducing the former to the latter, James's actual view is that thought and feeling come together in a rich conception of what he calls "pure experience." Thought and feeling arise for us as an "indistinguishable combination" (James 1982, 151). We can talk about them separately, if and when the context calls for it, but our actual experience of the world arises as a seamless mixture—James calls it a "mosaic"—of cognitive and bodily elements (James 1996, 42). Here is Ratcliffe again:

> A phenomenology without emotional feeling is a phenomenology that guts the world of all its significance. The experienced world is ordinarily enriched by the feelings that are sewn into it, that imbue it with value and light it up as an arena of cognitive and behavioral possibilities. So cognition without feeling is not, according to James, in any sense complete. It is an extreme phenomenological privation that strips the world of all meaning, akin to extreme depression or "melancholia." (Ratcliffe 2008, 227–228)

In short and to sum up, James does not emphasize the importance of bodily feelings *at the expense* or *to the exclusion* of thought and cognition. Rather, the picture of the emotions he defends encourages us to recognize "how much our mental life is knit up with our corporeal frame"—how thought and bodily feeling come together, virtually imperceptibly, in the rich flow of our experience (James 2010, 14). In the age-old philosophical struggle "between the spirit and the flesh," James concludes, "neither party will definitively drive the other off the field" (James 2010, 16).

James is sometimes interpreted as saying that every emotion has its own distinct fingerprint in the body, but that too is not quite right, as Lisa Feldman Barrett has perceptively shown. "James actually wrote that each *instance* of emotion, not each category of emotion, comes from a unique bodily state ... [which] means you can tremble in fear, jump in fear, freeze in fear, scream in fear, gasp in fear, hide in fear, attack in fear, and even laugh in the face of fear" (Barrett 2017, 160–161). Every instance of emotion might involve a unique bodily state, but there is no essential bodily state from which every category of emotion (anger, sadness, fear, anxiety, and all the rest) must derive.

One important implication of James's theory of emotion is that we can sometimes change the way we feel by changing what we do. We tend to think that action follows from feeling, but James insists that "action and feeling go together." If we can regulate our action, therefore, "which is under the more direct control of the will, we can indirectly regulate feeling, which is not" (James 1962, 99–100). Here is how James explains it:

> The sovereign voluntary path to cheerfulness, if our spontaneous cheerfulness be lost, is to sit up cheerfully, to look round cheerfully, and to act and speak as if cheerfulness were already there.... To wrestle with a bad feeling only pins our attention on it, and keeps it still fastened in the mind: whereas, if we act as if from some better feeling, the old bad feeling soon folds its tent like an Arab, and silently steals away. (James 1962, 100)

And similarly, from *The Principles of Psychology*:

> There is no more valuable precept in moral education than this, as all who have experience know: if we wish to conquer undesirable emotional tendencies in ourselves, we must assiduously and in the first instance cold-bloodedly go through the *outward movements* of those contrary dispositions we prefer to cultivate. ... Soothe the brow, brighten the eye ... pass the genial compliment, and your heart must be frigid indeed if it does not gradually thaw! (James 2007b, 463)

If we can will ourselves to *act* in a happier and more healthy-minded manner—"as if from some better feeling"—this might well help us *feel* happier and healthier, too. The action itself can help bring about the more desirable affective state. The simplest and most obvious example is probably the one that James himself gives, in his 1884 essay called "What Is an Emotion?" James there writes of a friend who suffers from panic attacks and "morbid fear." According to the anonymous friend (though, again, one wonders whether this is really James's own testimony), "the whole drama seems to centre about the region of the heart and the respiratory apparatus, that his main effort during the attacks is to get control of his inspirations and to slow his heart, and that the moment he attains to breathing deeply and to holding himself erect, the dread, *ipso facto*, seems to depart" (James 2010, 13).

James is certainly not arguing that deep breathing is some magical cure for anxiety and panic attacks. But if the intentional regulation of breathing sometimes helps to diminish feelings of anxiety and panic (as many of us know firsthand that it does), that fact alone seems to be enough to vindicate the central Jamesean thesis. To be sure, the suggestion is not that we can change all of our emotions completely at will. Some emotional states will be stubbornly resistant in the face of these efforts. As Robert C. Roberts sensibly puts it, and as James would have agreed completely, there is a "mixture of voluntariness and involuntariness in our emotions" (Roberts 2003, 81).[9] But even after conceding that some of our emotions will be impervious in the face of attempts to change them, James's claim about the two-way causal relationship between feeling and action emerges unscathed.

It's easy to see why habit was so central in James's thought. If we can cultivate the habits of better mental health, the thought seems to be, better mental health may come as the result. The formation of new habits is a serious, difficult business. James was not delusional about that. He knew all too well that many attempts along these lines fail. Even so, he offered his readers plenty of practical advice and bracing encouragement to help maximize the chances of success. Following the Scottish philosopher Alexander Bain, he sets forth three maxims for the successful formation of new habits. First, in acquiring a new habit or in retiring an old one,

> we must take care to launch ourselves with as strong and decided an initiative as possible. Accumulate all the possible circumstances which shall re-enforce the right motives; put yourself assiduously in conditions that encourage the new way; make engagements incompatible with the old; take a public pledge, if the case allows; in short, envelop your resolution with every aid you know. This will give your new beginning such a momentum that the temptation to break down will not occur as soon as it otherwise might; and every day during which a breakdown is postponed adds to the chances of its not occurring at all. (James 2007a, 123)

Favorable circumstances play an important role in the successful acquisition of new habit. If someone wants to quit smoking, for example, they should avail themselves of "every aid" they can, organizing their environment so as to make the achievement of their goal more likely. They should ensure there are no cigarettes nearby; they should disrupt old patterns and triggers; avoid the places and people who will tempt one to smoke; "take a public pledge" to encourage support and accountability; etc. It doesn't cheapen the power of the human will to insist that "favorable circumstances" will improve our chances of success.

James's second maxim emphasizes the importance of momentum and inertia. When a new habit is not yet well rooted, even one small lapse can weaken or derail it. James urges us to "never suffer an exception to occur" until the new habit is rooted securely in our lives.

> Each lapse is like the letting fall of a ball of string which one is carefully winding up; a single slip undoes more than a great many turns will wind again. Continuity of training is the great

means of making the nervous system act infallibly right. . . . It is surprising how soon a desire will die of inanition if it be never fed. (James 2007a, 123)

And finally, third, James implores us not to wait on the implementation of our plan. The acquisition of new habits requires resolution and decisiveness. Delays, deferrals, and rationalized procrastination only weaken the chances of success. The advice here is to commit and to act right away, not to vacillate. "Seize the very first possible opportunity to act on every resolution you make," James writes, "and on every emotional prompting you may experience in the direction of the habits you aspire to gain" (James 2007a, 124).

Once again, James was the first to admit that all of this is more easily said than done. Developing new habits requires sustained effort. And even then success is never guaranteed. When it comes to the acquisition of new habits, James seems to recommend a kind of monkish training of the will. He urges that we inure ourselves "to habits of concentrated attention, energetic volition, and self-denial in unnecessary things."

Keep the faculty of effort alive in you by a little gratuitous exercise every day. That is, be systematically ascetic or heroic in little unnecessary points, do every day or two something for no other reason than that you would rather not do it, so that when the hour of dire need draws nigh, it may find you not unnerved and untrained to stand the test. (James 2007a, 126)

In short, and now to sum up, James's maxims emphasize the possibility and hope that we can cultivate better habits of living (a schedule of regular exercise, for example, not too much caffeine or alcohol, a practice of meditation, and many others things). Because action and feeling "go together," moreover, the cultivation of healthy habits can sometimes and to some degree make us feel a bit happier and less anxious as a result. Matt Haig is right to note that there are no "foolproof" cures for anxiety, no "magic thunderbolts." Even so, it feels good to "build up, over the years, things that you know do—on occasion—work. Weapons for the war that subsides but that can always ignite again" (Haig 2015, 154). This is exactly the right way to think of James's maxims. The cultivation of better habits will not magically eradicate feelings of worry and anxiety from our lives. It will not cure our sick souls. Nothing can do that. But it might give us more of a fighting chance in our war against unwanted anxiety.

3
Anxiety Reveals the Nothing

> He who pretends to look on death without fear lies. All men are afraid of dying, this is the great law of sentient beings, without which the entire human species would soon be destroyed.
> —Jean-Jacques Rousseau, *Julie, or the New Eloise*

It's tempting to think that contemplation of death lies at the root of anxious suffering. Many people think of death as the worst outcome, the greatest loss. And the fear of death as the "most basic, most universal and inescapable" of fears (Tillich 2014, 40).[1] As Arthur Schopenhauer put it: "The greatest of evils, the worst thing that can threaten anywhere, is death; the greatest anxiety is the anxiety of death" (Schopenhauer 1966a, 465).

Reflection on the connection between anxiety and death can be found in immense swaths of writing, from the Hebrew Bible to Sigmund Freud, from the Stoics to Michel de Montaigne and Blaise Pascal, from Hindu and Buddhist sources to the Romantic poets, from Epicurus and Lucretius to contemporary analytic philosophy. But it's probably in the European existentialist tradition—in figures like Kierkegaard, Heidegger, Karl Jaspers, Sartre, Paul Tillich, and others—where the intimate association between death and anxiety has been most comprehensively theorized.

This chapter explores existential anxiety through the philosophy of death. Martin Heidegger will be serving as our primary guide in what follows, and we will consider a handful of prominent Heideggerian theses about the close, mutually constitutive relationship between anxiety and death. In particular:

(1) that contemplation of death is a (or *the*) preeminent source of anxiety
(2) that the "mood" of anxiety is always, at bottom, about the nothingness (or *Nichtigkeit*) of death
(3) that anxiety has much to teach us about the attitude it is best to adopt in the face of the fact that, one day, we will be dead.

One important locus of philosophical debate in this area concerns whether it is rational or even possible to fear "nonexistence" or "nothingness" as such, or whether this is better understood as the fear of some more concrete loss, of all the experiences and pleasures that sentient life affords. Richard Rorty has argued that, "There is no such thing as fear of inexistence as such, but only fear of some concrete loss. 'Death' and 'nothingness' are equally resounding, equally empty terms," he writes. "To say one fears either is as clumsy as Epicurus's attempt to say why one should not fear them" (Rorty 1989, 23). Robert C. Solomon puts the same point more harshly. Like Rorty, Solomon sees the need to render the fear of death more tangible, to fill in the details, to specify precisely what will be lost when death arrives. When we do that, however, we see that it is not death or nonexistence *as such* that is the object of our anxiety. The truth, Solomon has it, is much less flattering.

> We worry about the pain of dying, or the pain that precedes dying. We vainly worry about the disposition of our bodies after death. We worry about the people we care for, but then we also worry that they will be fine without our care.... The idea that death is nothing, too, may not be so much a matter of metaphysics as an awkward sense of absence. Put in the least flattering way, we might say that my death is a bad thing because it deprives the universe of me.... I watch someone date and marry my wife, raise my children, refute my books. Death may be nothing, but it is a nothing that *hurts*. All of this is not grand metaphysics ... but

petty selfishness... morbid solipsism, an image of death solely in terms of the self. (Solomon 1998, 174–175)

Rorty and Solomon agree that what really bothers us is not death itself —that is, the condition of being dead— but all the losses that lie in death's wake. The prospect of such losses obviously can and does make us afraid. And yet, while it's extremely difficult to spell out clearly, Heidegger's view is that nothingness or "nullity" (to use a term that appears frequently in his pages) is itself a genuine and distinct object of anxiety, which is to say that anxiety about death cannot be reduced to or subsumed by our other death-related fears (fears about physical pain and loss, cognitive or mental decline, thwarted goals, unrealized hopes, harm to loved ones, and so on).[2] I hope to make all of this much clearer in what follows. But let's begin with a few biographical snippets.

Martin Heidegger was born in 1889, in Messkirch, a town of a few thousand inhabitants near the edge of the Black Forest in the German state of Baden-Württemberg. The Heidegger family was traditional, rural, and working class to the core. Heidegger's father earned a living as a barrel-maker and a sexton at the village church. His mother was a housewife. The Heideggers were proudly, devoutly Catholic. As a young man, Heidegger enrolled at a Jesuit seminary with the goal of becoming a priest. That plan was short-lived, however, as he was dismissed a mere two weeks into his time there after a health exam revealed what was thought to be a psychosomatic heart condition.

One of the most notorious aspects of Heidegger's biography has to do with his support for the rise of Hitler and Nazism. Given Heidegger's provincial background and his grouchy, reactionary, cultural sensibilities, it's not particularly surprising that he would have been enthusiastic about Hitler in 1933. (Heidegger joined the Nazi Party officially on May 1, 1933, ten days after becoming the rector of the University of Freiburg.) Richard Rorty has suggested that what is most unforgiveable about Heidegger is not necessarily his early enthusiasm for Hitler, but his "postwar silence" and "hysterical denial" about Nazism and the Holocaust (Rorty 1999, 192–196).[3] Heidegger lived a long time after the war (more than three decades), and he had ample opportunity to take responsibility for his actions. In 1966, he gave an interview to the German magazine *Der Spiegel*, in which he rationalized his involvement with Nazism. He insisted there that his main goal, as rector, had been to insulate his university from politicization and this required some pragmatic compromise with the Nazis. He also claimed that he had in fact changed his mind about Nazism in 1934, a claim for which sufficient historical evidence is widely agreed to be lacking. (Heidegger had been adamant that the *Der Spiegel* interview be released posthumously. It was published five days after his death, in 1976).

Heidegger was thirty-five years old, married with two sons, when he began a four-year-long affair with one of his students at the University of Marburg, an eighteen-year-old Jewish woman named Hannah Arendt. As Daniel and Birgit Maier-Katkin write about the famous Heidegger-Arendt affair:

> Theirs was a hidden, adulterous love, conducted in strict secrecy. Elfride, Heidegger's wife, was not to know, and in a small university town this meant that no one must know. Often the lovers met in Arendt's attic apartment; sometimes Heidegger sent cryptic notes in code specifying the place and the time of their next rendezvous with a system of signals of lights to be switched on and off to show if he was in his study. (Maier-Katkin 2007, 35)

When Hitler became chancellor in January 1933, and especially after the burning of the Reichstag the following month, Arendt became convinced (correctly) that it was no longer safe for her to remain in Germany. Reports of Heidegger's anti-Semitic behavior at Freiburg, and rumors that he had been giving speeches at Nazi meetings, were acute sources of anger and betrayal for her. Rüdiger Safranski recounts that:

At the beginning of 1933, shortly before her emigration, Hannah Arendt wrote to Heidegger. Certain reports had come to her ears. Was it true "that he excluded Jews from his seminars, didn't greet his Jewish colleagues on the campus, rejected his Jewish doctoral students, and behaved like an antisemite?" . . . [According to a paraphrased account of his reply:] He answered in a furious tone, in what was his last letter to Arendt until 1950: "One by one he listed the favors he accorded to Jews—his accessibility to Jewish students, to whom he generously gave of his time, disruptive though it was to his own work, getting them stipends and discussing their dissertations with them. Who comes to him in an emergency? A Jew. Who insists on urgently discussing his doctoral degree? A Jew. Who sends him voluminous work for urgent critique? A Jew. Who asks him for help in obtaining grants? Jews." (Safranski 1998, 255)

Despite Heidegger's reprehensible behavior before and during the war, and despite the cowardly postwar silence, Arendt seems to have forgiven him in the end.

Although she did not trust him or hold his character in high regard, there was for Arendt both the memory of love and continuing admiration for Heidegger's genius. For Arendt, neither Heidegger's disgraceful behavior in the critical year 1933–34, nor the weakness of character that made duplicity rather than candor his principal defensive strategy in the postwar years, were of such a magnitude as to place him outside of the human community within which, she believed, reconciliation is always a possibility. (Maier-Katkin 2007, 44)

There is no denying Heidegger's philosophical brilliance and originality, nor the gigantic influence of his work on twentieth-century European philosophy. There is also no denying that he is remembered for the most part as a largely unpleasant man. Stanley

Cavell gets it exactly right about Heidegger in my opinion when he notes his "arrogance and intellectual vulgarity . . . his routine disparagement of the assumed (underdescribed) superficiality of others, his repeated claims to profundity, his sometimes facile spirituality" (Cavell 2010, 501). Heidegger was massively self-aggrandizing. He displayed an overweening pride in his philosophical ability, and harbored few doubts about the awesome, world-historical power of his work. He simply took it for granted that he was operating at a level of philosophical sophistication and spiritual depth that no one else could even get close to. Heidegger eventually came to believe that, "the only 'philosophers' of importance were Heraclitus, Anaximander, Parmenides, and himself" (Rockmore 1996, 121).

Heidegger was an avid lover of the outdoors. Mountain hikes and skiing (at which he was apparently quite skilled) were favorite activities. He also had reclusive predilections and seemed to find contentment in seclusion. In 1922, he moved into a tiny cabin (approximately six meters by seven) that was built for him near the village of Todtnauberg, high in his beloved Black Forest mountains. He called his little dwelling *die Hütte* ("the hut"), and some of his most important writings, including his 1927 masterwork, *Being and Time*, were extensively labored on there.

Making sense of Heidegger's philosophy on its own terms is a daunting, time-consuming undertaking that requires the mastery of a whole new language—what is sometimes now referred to (usually not in the spirit of a compliment) as "Heideggerese."[4] Inculcating oneself into this Heideggarian dialect (and slogging through the laborious sentences that fill Heidegger's pages) is a perfectly legitimate intellectual undertaking. But it's not the undertaking that interests me here. The aim in what follows is not to provide a comprehensive exposition of Heidegger's thought *ad pedem litterae*. More modestly, I want to reflect on the *spirit* of Heidegger's thinking about anxiety and death with an eye to better understanding what he means when he says that anxiety is our fundamental "mood," how the mood of anxiety supposedly "reveals the nothing," and what all of this suggests about the stance we should try to adopt in the face of these unsettling revelations.[5]

Considering Death from Within and Without

There are many points of view from which to contemplate one's own death and the death of other people. And different points of view tend to stimulate different valences. Thinking about a person's death from a cosmic perspective, as one among billions of other deaths occurring over vast stretches of time (trillions if we include non-humans in the tabulations), can make it look like a trivial speck. But there is nothing trivial about that same death considered from the point of view of surviving family and friends, people for whom it will be a solemn and momentous event. And the prospect of our own death looks dramatically different when considered *externally* (as just another event in the world) as opposed to *internally* (as the permanent end of subjective consciousness, the termination of one's world).

Human beings have existed for about 200,000 years. And there have been by some estimates about 107 billion of us, approximately 7 billion of whom are alive today. This means, as Richard Holloway muses, "that the skeletons of 100 billion of us have faded into the earth. Occasionally we come across one that has been buried for thousands of years, and we wonder about the life it had, its joys, its sorrows and what it made of the world it found itself in" (Holloway 2018, 7). It's arresting to contemplate one's own skeleton as a thing in the world. But it's also hard to avoid the thought that, from the point of view of approximately 100 billion *Homo sapien* deaths, our own single death is no big deal.

The French essayist and critic Charles du Bos coined the wonderful phrase, *Le réveil mortel* (roughly, "the waking-up to mortality") to describe the first awakening or realization a person has about the fact that he or she must die. Here is novelist Julian Barnes, wondering how du Bos's phrase is best translated:

> "The wake-up call to mortality" sounds a bit like a hotel service. "Death-knowledge," "death awakening"?—rather too Germanic. "The awareness of death"?—but that suggests a state rather than a particular cosmic strike. In some ways, the (first) bad translation of du Bos's phrase is the good one: it *is* like being in an unfamiliar hotel room, where the alarm clock has been left on the previous occupant's setting, and at some ungodly hour you are suddenly pitched from sleep into darkness, panic, and a vicious awareness that this is a rented world. (Barnes 2008, 24)

The *réveil mortel* marks a person's graduation into a new form of anxious fear. Innocence is lost. Things will never really be the same now. A new kind of anxiety and dread, previously impossible, now becomes a genuine prospect. Now we really grasp the painful truth that we inhabit a world in which suffering, fear, and ultimately death, are unavoidable. Yet there is a certain ambiguity about what exactly the *réveil mortel* is meant to denote. Does it consist in the commonplace knowledge that death is a brute, inescapable fact in the order of living things? Or is it the more personal realization that *I* one day will be dead, that *this* consciousness will be extinguished for good?

I'm not exactly sure when I first learned about the fact of death. (I believe it occurred after encountering a dead bird as a young boy, and the ensuing, clumsy conversation with my parents about what it means for a once living thing to be "dead." But this is a murky memory.) I'm visited by the second sort of *réveil mortel*—the panicked realization that *this* life will be gone forever—much more frequently than I'd prefer. The realization is always sudden, always terrifying. It's like (or *is*) a panic attack, and usually comes for me, when it does, late at night or very early in the morning. Unluckily for me, these attacks have been occurring more regularly the older I get, as death gets factually closer.[6]

These episodes are extremely distressing. But I take a tiny bit of comfort in knowing that I'm not all by myself in suffering with them. Philosopher James Baillie vividly describes an experience very much like the sort I have in mind:

> Last night I entered into a state of mind unlike anything I had experienced before. I realized that I will die. It may be tomorrow, it may be in fifty years time, but one way or another it is inevitable and utterly non-negotiable. *I no longer just knew this theoretically, but knew it in my bones. The knowledge of my death was real to me, as if for the first time (in a way that it no longer is as I write these words).* It was as if I had been given a glimpse of an aspect of reality that had previously been closed to me. It was as if the blinders had been removed, and I was the only person to have woken up from a collective dream to grasp the terror of the situation. It was to be defenseless against this fact, and without the possibility of defense. This new awareness was completely out of my control. I have no idea how it came about. All attempts to turn my attention to other matters failed completely. I could only wait, traumatized, in the hope that it would pass. I was in this state for the longest ten minutes of my life. (Baillie 2013, 189; emphasis added)

Julian Barnes similarly describes one of his sudden and horrifying "awakenings," which he concedes are difficult to describe accurately. These flashes of terror, much like extreme physical pain, have a tendency to "drive out language."

> Only a couple of nights ago there came again that alarmed and alarming moment, of being pitchforked back into consciousness, awake, alone, utterly alone, beating pillow with fist and shouting "Oh no Oh No OH NO" in an endless wail, the horror of the

moment—the minutes—overwhelming what might, to an objective witness, appear a shocking display of exhibitionist self-pity. An inarticulate one, too: for what sometimes shames me is the extraordinary lack of descriptive, or responsive, words that come out of my mouth.... We know that extreme physical pain drives out language; it is dispiriting to learn that mental pain does the same. (Barnes 2008, 124–125)

The distinction underlain by these two interpretations of the *réveil mortel*—between grasping death as an abstract fact and grasping it personally and viscerally—is central in Heidegger's discussion of death and anxiety.[7] Everyone knows that they will die, but this abstract knowledge is rarely in front of our minds. A full, intimate recognition of our finitude usually gets pushed aside, or hides in the quotidian business of daily life. It requires a certain pause and reflection to really get hold of. We keep knowledge that we must die at a certain distance, as it were, and this is part of what's so unsettling about those panicked episodes when that knowledge comes charging back into unobstructed view.

Because they reveal what normally lies hidden, these panicked episodes of death anxiety closely resemble a kind of affective state that Heidegger calls "uncanny" (*unheimlich*, in the original German). Our default mood or state is something like an unthinking familiarity with the world we are inhabiting. We are cruising along on auto-pilot, living our lives, performing various tasks and activities, more or less oblivious. When something happens to interrupt or "unsettle" that default state, the world can suddenly appear "uncanny." We are "thrown into uncanniness," Heidegger says (Heidegger 1962, 394). All of a sudden we lose our sense of connectedness with things. The world appears strange and foreign. For Heidegger, as Matthew Ratcliffe points out, "Anxiety is the most extreme form of the uncanny" (Ratcliffe 2008, 179). Anxiety makes us feel "inhibited" and "bewildered"—like strangers inhabiting a strange world. "Everyday familiarity collapses"

(Heidegger 1962, 395; 233). The entire matrix of relations that constitutes my normal dealings with things and people suddenly seems incomprehensible and groundless.[8] The world "sinks into insignificance" (Heidegger 1962, 393).

Richard Polt gives an eloquent account of the "uncanniness" of anxiety in Heidegger's thought and is worth quoting at length:

> I am weeding in my garden when my activity suddenly seems pointless. "What is the meaning of all this?" "Who am I?" I ask. I am alienated from myself as a gardener and from the garden as part of my world. In fact, I am uncomfortable with *every* role I can play in the world, and indifferent to everything around me: all this seems meaningless. What is left over? Simply the naked truth that I find myself in a situation where I am forced to make something of myself. But this is precisely what I realize when I face up to mortality.... When I feel that this could be the last moment of my life, I necessarily ask myself what my life adds up to and who I am. Do I really want to live and die as a gardener (a sculptor, a politician, a priest)? In anxiety, I face up to mortality because I feel the fragility of my life and the necessity of deciding what it all means. (Polt 1999, 88)

These moments of uncanniness and anxiety (like the panic attacks about death that resemble them) need not be triggered by anything in particular. They just arrive, unannounced and usually uninvited. Anxiety "can awaken in existence at any moment," Heidegger writes. "It needs no unusual event to rouse it." Even when we are engrossed in our daily activities, feeling basically happy and calm, anxiety is "only sleeping" and "always ready" (Heidegger 1993, 106).

For Heidegger, anxiety (*Angst*) is essentially a mood (*Stimmung*). A mood in this sense suggests the idea of being "attuned" in a certain way. The full quality and range of experience is permeated, as if through a photographic lens or filter. We *are* a certain joy or sadness or anxiety. And the world itself now appears differently than it would have otherwise. As Heidegger says, a mood makes "manifest 'how one is, and how one is faring.'" We are always in one mood or another, or perhaps some combination of different moods. It's not possible on Heidegger's view for a person to be without any mood at all—to be mood-free, so to speak. Even though that "pallid, evenly balanced" affective state in which we pass a lot of our time does not necessarily feel as though it attaches to any particular mood, Heidegger insists that this kind of state is "far from nothing at all." In short, "Dasein always has some mood" (Heidegger 1962, 173). Anxiety occupies a special—"fundamental"—place in the catalog of human moods. Anxiety is not merely a *Stimmung*, it is the *Grundstimmung*—"the shadowy queen among moods" (Safranski 1998, 152). Because anxiety is our fundamental mood, Heidegger believes that human beings are always anxious in some way, to some degree—"anxious in the very depths of [our] Being" (Heidegger 1962, 234).

Much like Kierkegaard before him, Heidegger takes pains to distinguish between fear and anxiety, while nevertheless conceding that the two are "kindred phenomena" (Heidegger 1962, 230). Fear is always directed toward something definite, whereas anxiety is vague and objectless. This maps onto a distinction between anxiety as "the fundamental mood" on the one hand, and the everyday "common anxiousness, ultimately reducible to fearfulness, which all too readily comes over us," on the other. The latter sort of anxiety—the "common anxiousness"—always has a determinate object and usually manifests as a discrete emotional episode. We are anxious "in the face of this or that . . . in this or that particular respect." But the "fundamental" mood of anxiety represents a deeper existential predicament, a state in which the contingency and groundlessness of existence is revealed to us. Such anxiety does not manifest as an object-directed episode, but more like a fog that envelopes the full range of experience (Aho 2020, 260).

The mood of anxiety reminds us that all our projects are shaky and insecure, and our lives finite and fragile. We human beings are essentially purposive, project-having creatures. The projects needn't be consequential or elaborate necessarily, but we are always doing or trying to do or thinking about doing something. A human life without projects of any kind is not a human life in any recognizable sense. As Raymond Geuss puts the point on Heidegger's behalf, "Even on my deathbed I shall presumably be trying one final time to look around the room or listen to the whispers of the prospective chief mourners assembled around my bed. To have *no* outstanding projects is to have no future, that is, to be dead" (Geuss 2017, 239). And yet, in having projects we are always ahead of ourselves, making plans, projecting ourselves forward into a contingent, indeterminate future. Some of our plans are hatched for more or less immediate execution (*I need to climb the stairs now to answer the ringing telephone*). Others lie a little further in the future (*I need to make an appointment next week with a lawyer to finalize my will*), and still others come with only a vague timeline of execution (*I would love to visit India one day*). Many of our plans are elaborately interwoven with one another, such that the execution of one depends on the prior execution of others (*I should respond to my friend's email, to decline the invitation to the concert, because I need to save money, in order to buy a ticket for a flight, in order to get to India*, etc.).

The mood of anxiety is bound up with the realization that, (1) when death arrives it will abruptly smash *all* of my plans—big and small, simple and elaborate, proximate and far off, alike, and (2) death can quite literally arrive at any moment. To the extent that death will cut short all of my projects and plans, it will render them unfinished and a failure. This is not a possibility we're normally inclined to keep in clear view. On the contrary, we naturally recoil from it. To conceive of one's life in this way—a fragile chain of tasks and projects, abruptly snuffed out by death, all grounded upon nothing and ultimately leading nowhere—is liable to make one squirm. The mood of anxiety communicates to us (or, as Heidegger would say, "discloses") the uncomfortable truth that all of our projects are inherently unstable, which means that all of our living is unstable (Geuss 2017, 239). It discloses the contingency and groundlessness of who and what we are. All of our practices, plans, and projects are grounded in nothing more than additional practices, plans, and projects. All the way down. Resting ultimately on nothing firmer than the contingent truth that, somehow, we're here now. As one commentator on Heidegger sums it all up: "The mood of anxiety is so disturbing because it reveals that 'at bottom' we are nothingness, that our existence is ultimately groundless, and that we are essentially finite and mortal. In the face of such disclosures, little wonder that most people flee from the mood of anxiety" (Zimmerman 1993, 245).

Our propensity to flee from the mood of anxiety is a central theme in Heidegger's thought, as it was also in Kierkegaard's. The "nothingness" that anxiety reveals is extremely unsettling, and so we typically do our best to keep it at bay. We push these kinds of thoughts aside, diverting our attention to more trivial matters like whether it might rain tomorrow, or whether we should purchase those shoes we've had our eye on, or how the local football team has been playing recently.[9] This strategy of diversion is what Heidegger calls "idle talk" (*Gerede*). Idle talk serves as a distraction from having to face the prospect of our death squarely and authentically. In "idle talk" we are going through the conversational motions, engaging in what Matthew Ratcliffe nicely calls "habitual banter" (Ratcliffe 2008, 262). Idle talk consists in "gossip," "hearsay," and "passing the word along." It's a way of "keeping things moving" (Heidegger 1962, 218). Virtually everyone learns how to participate in this kind of low-stakes chitchat. Knowledge about the rules by which idle talk operates, Heidegger says, "spreads in wider circles and takes on an authoritative character" (Heidegger 1962, 212).

The inclination to flee from the mood of anxiety is not only or always something that individuals do all by themselves. Raymond

Geuss explains on behalf of Heidegger that Western philosophy itself is one of the forms such fleeing can take. All of Western philosophy is, in a sense, "a reaction to anxiety in the face of death, although it is a reaction that tries to cover up the phenomenon."[10] What I really am, Geuss writes, is "a continual spiralling of possibilities, possible ways of being in the world, oriented toward my death. But how reassuring it would be if I were not that, but just one more thing with fixed and immutable properties, like the things I encounter in the world."

> The repression of the anxiety which is a constituent of human life is not ever fully successful, but what Greek philosophy did was to initiate a long and gradual process . . . in which the more philosophy develops, the more complex conceptual schemes it elaborates, and the more elaborate the schemes, the further away they take us from and occlude Being (and also my death). (Geuss 2017, 240–242)

I'm not sure I know how to properly assess the plausibility of this story. But it remains an excellent question why Western philosophy has been so preoccupied, famously since Thales and continuously down through the ages, with questions about the fundamental substance out of which this or that thing is composed. Heidegger's answer, roughly, is that this way of conceiving of things diverts us from the anxiety of death. It's not easy to confront the nothingness that anxiety discloses, to face directly "the sheer brutal contingency of the world, which at any moment can cease to exist (with my death)." It's much less anxiety inducing to think about our existence in the terms proliferated by Greek philosophy, terms like "substance," "matter," "subject," "object," "essence," "cause," "property," and the like (Geuss 2017, 242).

It's clear that anxiety and the contemplation of death are intimately connected on Heidegger's view. Yet it's important for his analysis that we not think of our death merely as an event in the world. What we're trying to envision is an *internal possibility*, one that will instantly and permanently cut off all other possibilities. The word "possibility" is important here because a person's death can only ever be possible—never actual—for the person whose death it is (Heidegger 1962, 297). From an internal point of view, our future death is something we can anticipate and plan for. But it's also something that will never quite arrive, since its arrival will obliterate the very internal point of view from which we are trying to grasp it. If death deprives its subject of the ability to experience anything at all, it follows that no one gets to undergo or experience their own death (Heidegger 1962, 73). Remember Freud's claim according to which no one can really imagine their own death, since "whenever we try to do so we find that we survive ourselves as spectators" (Freud 2018, 18). If all the things we might do, and all the things that might happen, constitute the "horizon" against which our lives unfold, then our death is not really on the horizon but is just on the other side of it. This is exactly the point that the young Wittgenstein had in mind when he wrote that, "Death is not an event of life. Death is not lived through. . . . Our life is endless in the way that our visual field is without limit" (Wittgenstein 1999, 106).

And here again, the distinction between the two interpretations of the *réveil mortel* comes into the foreground. It's one thing to know that everyone "owes nature a death" (as Freud beautifully put it) and to know that everyone, oneself included, must eventually make good on this debt. Everyone dies. I am someone. So, someday, I will die. Even young children can master this syllogism. But such syllogistic knowledge is the upshot of viewing death externally, from the outside. To grasp death internally—to grasp it as "ownmost" (*eigenst*) in Heidegger's jargon—is to regard it as a genuine possibility *for me*.[11] This helps untangle the meaning behind Heidegger's claim from *Being and Time* that death is the "possibility of the impossibility of comporting oneself towards anything, of every way of existing" (Heidegger 1962, 307). Viewed internally in this way, my death is not just one more thing that will happen, one more incident in a world packed with incidents. It's the end of my world. The abrupt, final termination of subjective time and experience.[12]

Trying to think about one's death from the outside (as an event in the world) is easier, conceptually speaking, than contemplating the end of one's world, which is not to say that imagining one's death from an "external" perspective isn't unsettling and disorienting, too. Picturing the world carrying on after our death, indifferent to the fact that we're no longer in it, is not some happy thought exercise. People all over the world will wake up and go to their jobs. Stores and businesses will open. Conversations will take place. Meals will be consumed. Children will go to school. There will be traffic. It will be a day just like any other. The day after his son died, W.E.B. Du Bois observed movingly that the sun continued to shine, the birds still sang. "The day changed not," he wrote. "The same tall trees peeped in at the windows, the same green grass glinted in the setting sun" (Du Bois 1994, 129).[13] The world will carry on unperturbed after we die. We can be confident about this because the world always carries on unperturbed, despite the fact that roughly 150,000 people die each day. How could it possibly be any different when our turn comes? In sum, it hurts to think that the drama will continue on without us, and probably none the worse for that (Rorty 1983, 177). It's also disconcerting (Solomon would say it's "vain") to meditate on the prospect of one's corpse in the world. Trying to visualize one's own lifeless body being handled, moved, touched, and looked at is apt to make one extremely uncomfortable.

To make sense of our death from an internal point of view, to grasp it from within, Heidegger thinks we must adopt an "anticipatory understanding." It can be highly unsettling, but what Heidegger calls "anticipatory resoluteness" requires that we look forward to our death, to see it as a future prospect (Heidegger 1962, 310–311; 434). One of the first insights about our death that appears from this "anticipatory" point of view is that it is *not to be outstripped* (*unüberholbar*). This insight comes into focus in the light of two additional facts: (1) death is *certain*, but also, (2) death is *indefinite*, which is to say that, barring unusual circumstances, no one knows precisely when their death will come. As Havi Carel explains, for Heidegger:

> Because it is certain, the threat of death hangs over us constantly. Because it is indefinite, that is, we do not know when we shall die, we are constantly anxious about its time of arrival. As a result, we cannot outstrip or overtake death, we are not able to hold it fixed as we can with other events, such as a friend's visit. We can wait for a visit that is meant to take place next week. Eventually the visit takes place and once it has ended we can view it as a past event, as an event that has already taken place and that has been temporally surpassed. Death cannot be similarly overtaken or surpassed. As long as Dasein exists, it is always in front of it and always indefinite. (Carel 2006, 73)

In short and to sum up, while we are always "running towards" (*Vorlaufen*) our death, death never quite arrives. From an internal point of view, death is necessarily ahead of us, never actual, always impending (Heidegger 1962, 306).

Is it Irrational to Fear Our Death?

The Epicurean doctrine, elaborated by Lucretius, that death is and should be "nothing to us, and matters not at all," is a famous rejoinder to the kind of death anxiety we've been considering. Whereas Heidegger maintains that anxiety "reveals the nothing" of death, Epicurus and Lucretius rejoin that nothingness is nothing to be anxious about (Heidegger 1993, 101). After all, non-existence is not a state of affairs to be endured. It's nothing, an experiential blank. Since death is tantamount to the end of *me*, it makes no sense to fear death since *I* won't be there to suffer it. "If I am, then death is not," Epicurus wrote in his famous letter to Menoeceus. "If Death is, then I am not. Why should I fear that which can only exist when I do not?" (Epicurus 1940). Good question. It might be answered by noting that the Epicurean counsel that says, roughly, "It's irrational to fear nothingness because you won't be there to suffer it" won't help if "not being there" is precisely the source of the fear we are seeking to exorcise. Not being here, not being anywhere. What if *that* is what we're afraid of?

But why, Epicurus and Lucretius might ask in reply, should anyone be afraid of *that*? Another line of Epicurean argument in this neighborhood appeals to the apparent "symmetry" between prenatal and posthumous non-existence. Since there is nothing to fear or regret about the infinite stretches of empty time that elapsed before our birth, so, too, is our inevitable death nothing much to worry about. Being dead will be exactly like the time before we were born—which is to say, it will be nothing. Here is how Lucretius puts it:

> Look back again to see how the past ages of everlasting time, before we were born, were nothing to us. These, then, nature holds up to us as a mirror of the time that is to come, when we are dead and gone. Is there anything that looks terrible in this, anything that appears gloomy? Is it not more tranquil rest than any sleep? (Lucretius 1965)

Seneca offers a virtually identical argument (albeit in a less gentle tone than Lucretius). "Doesn't the person who wept because he had not been alive a thousand years ago seem to you an utter fool?" he asks. "Equally foolish is he who weeps because he will not be alive in a thousand years' time. These two are the same..." (Warren 2004, 70)

It's an interesting question why many people tend to regard prenatal non-existence as something innocuous, but the prospect of posthumous non-existence so unsettling. Aren't the two states—these two "eternities of darkness," as Vladimir Nabokov called them—"identical twins"? (Nabokov 1989, 19). I don't think they are. Prenatal non-existence was going to end with our miraculous arrival on the scene, with what Philip Larkin beautifully calls "the million-petalled flower of being here."[14] The prenatal abyss had an expiry date. Even more important, unlike the prior abyss of prenatal non-existence, this time there will be something for us to lose. This time we will be deprived of something that, had death not come when it did, we would not have been deprived of (Nagel 1979, 5).

Epicurus and Lucretius are clearly aiming to provide comfort. They're trying to neutralize the panic, to help take the sting out of the anxiety so many of us feel about death. That's a morally decent thing to try to do, and it would be nice if some people found their arguments therapeutically soothing in this way. I'm not one of those people. It seems to me that the kind of fear Epicurus and Lucretius are addressing is not fundamentally an intellectual or philosophical problem, an issue on which one might be swayed by reason and argument. This kind of fear is not something that anyone can be *convinced* into having or not having. "All attempts to argue it away are futile," Paul Tillich says about the fear of death (Tillich 2014, 40). All attempts to expose its irrationality leave us unmoved. So, for instance, it's possible to agree with Jay Rosenberg's Epicurean-*ish* claim that attitudes like fear and dread are "logically appropriate only to what could in principle be experienced, be lived through" while also observing that one's own fear is completely undented by any such argument (Rosenberg 1983, 199). We can agree with Ronald de Sousa when he says that, "there is no target of the fear of death; no experience about which we can ask whether it has a motivating aspect fitting the formal object of fear" (de Sousa 1987, 328). And yet the fear of death is still there, "always in the background of our existence," bubbling up periodically, reminding us of our vulnerability and finitude (Ben Ze'ev 2000, 16). Kieran Setiya gets it exactly right: "When I lie sleepless," he writes, "thinking of the final moments of my life, the final look, the final touch, the final taste, stunned by panic, I am not making a logical error. There is no refuting this despair, no conceptual distinction that will make it vanish" (Setiya 2017, 124). *Timor mortis conturbat me*, goes the old litany. The fear of death disturbs me. Even if death is the end, even if we are confident that there is nothing bad or painful on the other side of it, the very thought horrifies.

Having the Right Attitude toward Death

What attitude should we adopt in the face of our death? Is it better to be resigned or defiant? Shaking with fear or standing tall and valiant? Is it appropriate to feel sad that we will not have more time, or instead to cultivate a sense of gratitude for the time we were gifted (whether comparatively long or short)? Should we "rage" against death, as Dylan Thomas unforgettably urged, or is it better to cultivate a stiff upper lip, an attitude of Stoic acceptance?

Kai Nielsen recounts a story about the Oxford philosopher J.L. Austin, terminally ill with cancer, attending a lecture on death given by the French existentialist philosopher Gabriel Marcel. After the lecture, Austin reportedly said: "Professor Marcel, we all know we have to die, but why do we have to sing songs about it?" Among other things, the story sheds light on the contrast between regarding death as something deeply unsettling, something about which it is appropriate to have intense anxiety, on the one hand, and seeing it as a cold, hard fact that we grudgingly accept and more or less move on from, on the other (Scarre 2007, 65–66). Nielsen is clearly in favor of the latter kind of attitude. He thinks we should try to face up to the fact that we must die and, as he puts it, "get on with the living of our lives" (Nielsen 2000, 154–155). This is not an attempt to minimize death's seriousness, to be flippant or dismissive. What Nielsen is urging is the cultivation of rational acceptance. The recommendation is that we take a deep breath and try to make peace with a fact that, try though we might, we are utterly powerless to change. What's the alternative? Are we supposed to thrash around, kicking and screaming? Will it help to "engage in theatrics" or to "create myths for ourselves"? Could "singing songs" about our death possibly change anything? (Nielsen 1990, 186).

All of this bears directly on the question of how best to respond to the death anxiety that we've been considering in this chapter. Some philosophers advise attending to the prospect of our death more frequently and intensely than we might normally be inclined to do. Michel de Montaigne is a major source for this kind of view. Following a piece of Socratic wisdom according to which "to philosophize is to learn how to die," Montaigne's advice involves "having nothing on our minds as often as death." Since we cannot elude death, the best counterattack is to have death constantly in mind, to "await it everywhere." "I want Death to find me planting my cabbages," Montaigne famously wrote, "neither worrying about it nor the unfinished gardening" (Montaigne 2003, 99). This is like exposure therapy for death anxiety. If contemplating our death is the intellectual equivalent of staring at the sun, Montaigne is saying that we need to continually stare so as to become accustomed to the brightness. Diverting our gaze only makes the fear worse.

> Let us rid death of its strangeness, come to know it, get used to it. Let us have nothing on our minds as often as death. At every moment let us picture it in our imagination in all its aspects. . . . It is uncertain where death awaits us; let us await it everywhere. Premeditation of death is premeditation of freedom. . . . He who has learned how to die has unlearned how to be a slave. Knowing how to die frees us from all subjection and constraint. (Montaigne 2003, 96)

A strikingly similar line of argument is also found in Heidegger himself. Keeping the possibility of our death in clear view, reflecting on it frequently and intensely, makes one vividly aware of their freedom. Adopting this stance—what Heidegger calls authentic "Being-toward-death" (*Sein-zum-Tode*)—allows a person to escape the pettiness and mindless humdrum of everyday life, and ultimately to see their life as authentically their own, as through the particularity of their own experience. This is not intended to be some morbid exercise. On the contrary, Heidegger regards it as affirmative and emancipatory. In a passage that is widely but falsely attributed to Heidegger himself, Thelma Lavine sums up the core idea poignantly: "If I take death into my life, acknowledge it, and face it squarely, I will free myself from the anxiety of death and the pettiness of life—and only then will I be free to become myself" (Lavine 1984, 332).[15]

If Montaigne and Heidegger are suggesting in their different ways that genuine freedom is to be found in an attitude of confrontation, of going toward thoughts of death, a nearly perfect inversion of the same argument is famously found in Baruch Spinoza. "A free person," Spinoza writes, ". . . thinks about death less than anything, and his wisdom is a meditation not on death but on life" (Spinoza 2018, 209). It's not that the "free person" is delusional about their fate. They know as well as anyone else that their days really are numbered. It's that they are too busy appreciating all the wonderful things that life has to offer for thoughts of death to creep in all that much. If and when such thoughts do arise, they are more or less brushed aside, shrugged off. Contemplation of death doesn't trigger any anxiety or panic. "The free person's eyes are on the prize," writes Steven Nadler on Spinoza's behalf, "and the prize is right there with him: his own freedom and virtue. Instead of the irrational fear of death, he knows the rational joy of living" (Nadler 2020, 177).

So, a continuum emerges, with obsessive attention to death on one end and avoidance or indifference on the other. Where on this continuum is it optimal to be? It's difficult to say. On the one hand, what Montaigne or Heidegger is recommending strikes me as an extremely unpleasant way to live. (Candidly, as someone who already thinks about death quite a lot, I find the advice to think about it *even more* patently unhelpful.) On the other hand, it's much easier to intentionally bring a certain kind of thought before one's mind than it is to intentionally keep one out. Maybe we could train ourselves to "think of death less than anything" as Spinoza urges, to keep these disquieting thoughts out of mind and far away. But if your experience is anything like mine, unexpected, involuntary mental pivots to death are still likely to occur. The real trick, Spinoza might have rejoined, is not to block these morbid thoughts from entry altogether, but rather to learn how to be unaffected by them (or at least not too badly disturbed) when they do arrive. Cultivate the right habits of mind, Spinoza might have said, and the fear of death will take care of itself.[16]

Amélie Rorty has brilliantly argued that it is simultaneously appropriate and inappropriate to fear one's death, and I think her argument sheds useful light on some of the issues we've been considering. On Rorty's view, it is proper "to have irresolvably conflicting attitudes towards one's own death: it is inappropriate to fear death and yet it is also inappropriate not to fear it, or to attempt to cease fearing it." "Sometimes," she continues,

> when there are reasons for a course, and reasons against it, it is possible to weigh the strengths of the reasons on both sides, and to form a judgment about what is best, or most reasonable, all things considered. But in this case, the reasons for fearing death are not commensurable with those for not fearing it: no summary weighted judgment is possible. Both views are categorically valid, requiring full assent. (Rorty 1983, 175–176)

Fearing death is irrational for all the reasons Epicurus and Lucretius give. "Death as such is not to be feared; nothing in that state can bring us harm" (Rorty 1983, 188). And yet, it is also rational (or "appropriate"), because fear of death, even when it arises irrationally, is a "functional" psychological attitude that we'd be loath to do without. Much like certain varieties and intensities of pain, fear of death performs a valuable service for us on the whole. Such fear is "functional" insofar as it keeps us safe, making us alert and motivationally responsive to a wide range of dangerous situations. Rorty argues that a person:

> would choose to be capable of those fears that, among other things, issue in the fear of death. When fearing is the beginning of appropriate safeguarding motion from danger, and when it is the most rapid and efficient motivational assurance of safeguarding behaviour in certain sorts of circumstances, then the capacity for fearful reaction is desirable. Though it is not desirable to experience fear, it is desirable to be capable of experiencing it, and to tend to feel it when doing so is the most efficient trigger for moving us out of harm's way. (Rorty 1983, 180)

So, we can grant that the fear of death is irrational at the same time as we accept that, all things considered, it is a good thing that creatures like us have the capacity to be frightened in this way.

But what "function" does the sudden welling up of death anxiety serve? (Slote 1975, 20). What does the metaphysical fear of death we have been considering in this chapter—"*angst* at one's nonbeing"—have to do with those functional fears that keep us safe in the face of danger? After all, Rorty writes,

> A metaphysical fear of death is the sort that a person might have when there is no clear and present danger, a fear she might have sitting in her study and looking out of the window and brooding on the nature of things . . . anxious metaphysical fear ["the metaphysical terror of non-being"] is quite different from . . . functional fear . . . and it is this fear that might be thought irrational. It is this sort of gratuitous metaphysical fear, surely, that was the subject of Epicurean attack. (Rorty 1983, 185)

Rorty claims—and perhaps this is an issue that ultimately needs to be settled empirically—that these metaphysical fears "are by-products of functional fears." And so, just as a mind capable of certain kinds of causal reasoning cannot restrict the use of such reasoning, so, too, can we never guarantee that fear borne on good functional foundations won't float away into more irrational, non-functional waters (Rorty 1983, 186). The overall conclusion is that, "the two sides of the argument are not commensurable; they cannot be weighed and summarized in such a way as to allow us to determine what is, all things considered, the rational attitude towards death" (Rorty 1983, 188).

If it's appropriate to have irresolvably conflicting attitudes about our death, it seems to follow that philosophers should moralize less about this sort of thing and simply accept that the various attitudes people adopt toward their death is a highly personal, idiosyncratic business. Such attitudes probably answer less to the soundness of the arguments a person has in their arsenal and more to nebulous facts about their temperament. I acknowledge that I'm more frightened in this way than most people. But I think it's a consequence of Amélie Rorty's argument that there is no single, objectively correct attitude—the one true stance toward death; the one correct intensity of fear—that everyone should or must adopt. There is a range of reasonable feelings and attitudes here, and within that range it's not possible to say when or if someone has made a mistake. (What would it even be like to discover that one has been excessively frightened about death all this time, or perhaps not frightened enough?) If this is correct, the upshot is a liberal imperative of tolerance, a greater willingness to accede to the legitimacy of a wider range of attitudes and degrees of fear in regards to death.

Heidegger was not any kind of liberal, and we can be confident that he would have impatiently dismissed any call for more tolerance. For him, "anxiety in the face of death" is not some "random moment of weakness" that some people might succumb to and others not (Heidegger 1962, 295). Anxiety about death is not idiosyncratic, like a taste or preference that differs from one person to the next. For Heidegger, anxiety is a basic human state of mind that grips all of us whenever we thoroughly grasp the possibility of our death.

4
A New Lap in the Race

> No attained object of desire can give lasting satisfaction, but merely a fleeting gratification; it is like alms thrown to the beggar, keeping him alive today so that his misery may be prolonged till the morrow. Therefore, as long as our consciousness is filled by our will, as long as we are given up to the urgent prompting of desires with their constant hopes and fears, as long as we are the subject of willing, we can never have lasting happiness or peace.
> —Arthur Schopenhauer, *The World as Will and Idea*

Nietzsche once said that Arthur Schopenhauer was the nineteenth century's only "serious" moralist. Unlike his lesser contemporaries, Schopenhauer was prepared "to torment himself" with the deepest and most fundamental questions, to look suffering squarely in the face, and to ask whether life is worth it in the end. What Nietzsche apparently admires most about Schopenhauer, what makes him singularly "serious," was his willingness to "descend into the depths of existence with a string of curious questions on his lips: why do I live? what lesson have I to learn from life? how have I become what I am and why do I suffer from being what I am?" (Nietzsche 1997, 154). Schopenhauer's answers to these questions reveal his unrivaled gloominess. He believed that suffering is both overwhelming and inescapable. The world bankrupt and irredeemable. Genuine happiness is a mirage, always just beyond our reach. The future is bleak. Life, even if it contains moments of joy and fulfillment, is probably not worth it in the end.[1]

Despite this gloominess, or more likely because of it, Schopenhauer's work is a treasure trove of insight into the human condition. Schopenhauer did not have a great deal to say about anxiety as such.[2] He was interested in "suffering" more nebulously defined. Even so, there is much to be learned about the nature and meaning of anxiety from Schopenhauer's pessimistic philosophy. Or so I shall suggest in what follows.

Arthur Schopenhauer was born in 1788, in Danzig (what is now Gdánsk, on the Baltic coast of Northern Poland). His father was a wealthy merchant and shipowner. His mother was a well-known writer of essays, novels, and biographies. The Schopenhauer family was affluent and cosmopolitan. They were knowledgeable about world affairs, traveled extensively, and moved for the most part in highbrow, cultured circles. Politically speaking, they were avidly republican, both in their support for the French Revolution and in their opposition to Prussian imperialism. When Danzig was annexed by the Kingdom of Prussia in 1793, the Schopenhauers fled to the free city of Hamburg.

Schopenhauer's father, Heinrich Floris Schopenhauer, struggled tremendously with his mental health. He was prone to "loud outbursts" and erratic behavior, and could frequently be found pacing his room at night, mumbling incoherently to himself. He also became increasingly paranoid as his sickness deepened. He was constantly mistrustful of his employees, and would repeatedly hurl accusations of infidelity at his wife, Johanna, despite the groundlessness of his suspicions. The consensus seems to be that Heinrich's death in 1803 was a suicide, but details remain hazy and biographers concede that it might have been accidental.

> When he was found floating in the icy waters of the canal behind the family compound on 20 April 1803, both Johanna and Arthur viewed his death as a suicide, although it was possible that instead of jumping out of the warehouse loft, he may have fallen.... Schopenhauer was devasted by his father's death....

He ... claimed that as a result of his bereavement, "the darkening of my spirit so greatly intensified that it was close to becoming an actual melancholy." ... [Schopenhauer] would recognize his own depression, anxiety, and melancholy as descending from his father: "Inherited from my father is the anxiety which I myself curse ... and combat with all the force of my will." (Cartwright 2010, 88; 4)

After her husband's death, Johanna moved to the town of Weimar (Schopenhauer stayed behind in Hamburg), where she achieved renown as a writer and *salonnièrre*. Her salon parties were attended by many eminent literary figures, most notably the great Johann Wolfgang von Goethe, with whom she cultivated a friendship.

If their hostile correspondence is any indication, Schopenhauer and his mother didn't care much for each other. In Johanna's estimation, Schopenhauer was "irritating," "unbearable," and difficult to live with. As she wrote to him in a contemptuous 1807 letter:

All of your good qualities become obscured by your super-cleverness and are made useless to the world merely because of your rage at wanting to know everything better than others; of wanting to improve and master what you cannot command. With this you embitter the people around you, since no one wants to be improved or enlightened in such a forceful way, least of all by such an insignificant individual as you still are; no one can tolerate being reproved by you, who also still show so many weaknesses yourself, least of all in your adverse manner, which in oracular tones, proclaims this is so and so, without ever supposing an objection. If you were less like you, you would only be ridiculous, but thus as you are, you are highly annoying. (Cartwright 2010, 129–130)

It puts the point mildly to say that Schopenhauer was an odd and difficult person. By all accounts he was gruff, eccentric, rude, and bombastic. Human relationships were a perpetual struggle. He sometimes seemed to prefer the company of animals, especially his beloved poodles.[3] As Nietzsche corroborates, Schopenhauer "failed in his many attempts to establish firm and sympathetic friendships and was repeatedly obliged to return with a downcast eye to his faithful dog. He was a total solitary; he had not a single companion truly of his own kind to console him" (Nietzsche 1997, 139). Like his father before him, he trusted almost no one. As one well-known anecdote tells it, Schopenhauer was so paranoid that he refused to let his barber shave his neck. He would also sleep with a loaded pistol (and a sword!) by his bed. He also detested noise, once shoving a woman down a flight of stairs because she was apparently being too loud.

Schopenhauer was a unique and brilliant philosopher (perhaps the only one of his time and place to take Hindu and Buddhist thought seriously, for example), but given his complete ineptitude in the arena of human relations, it's not surprising that he could never secure a paid university post. Schopenhauer was critical (often rudely so) about many of the prominent philosophers of his day. His various tirades about Immanuel Kant, Johann Gottlieb Fichte, Friedrich Schelling, and especially G.W.F. Hegel, are both amusing and pathetic (Jacquette 2005, 7). He derided Kant's moral philosophy as "absurd moral pedantry," an "outrage to genuine moral feeling," and a "nursery-school morality" (Schopenhauer 1995, 66; 198). He also had an extremely low opinion of Fichte, whose famous lectures on the *Wissenschaftslehre* he had attended in Berlin, in 1811 and 1812. But it was clearly Hegel who received the harshest treatment. Schopenhauer judged Hegel a "sham" and his work "a lasting monument of German stupidity" (Schopenhauer 1966b, 437; 429).

> But the greatest effrontery in serving up sheer nonsense, in scrabbling together senseless and maddening webs of words, such as had previously been heard only in madhouses, finally

appeared in Hegel. It became the instrument of the most ponderous and general mystification that has ever existed, with a result that will seem incredible to posterity. (Schopenhauer 1966b, 429)

Schopenhauer's contempt for Hegel was off the charts. Working as an unpaid lecturer at the University of Berlin in the early 1820s, Schopenhauer went out of his way to schedule his lectures at the same time as Hegel's. Schopenhauer apparently thought he could debase his more famous colleague by stealing his students, but the plan was a spectacular flop. None of Hegel's students defected to Schopenhauer's concurrent lectures. Bitter and humiliated, Schopenhauer canceled his course and his brief teaching stint at the University of Berlin came to an end.

We know that Schopenhauer enjoyed the company of women and had a voracious sex drive. Like his other human dealings, however, sexual relations were consistently a source of frustration and disappointment. As Julian Young explains, "The women he was disposed to love would not sleep with him, and the women who would sleep with him—whores and actresses—he did not love. The one exception is the actress-singer Caroline Médon, with whom he had an on-off affair throughout the 1820s" (Young 2005, 2–3). Schopenhauer had baffling, Neanderthal views about women. The 1851 essay "On Women" is an unhinged, misogynistic rant. There is no good reason, he says there, "why a man whose wife suffers from chronic illness, or has remained unfruitful, or has gradually grown too old for him, should not take a second." He also notes in that essay that women are well suited to work as nurses and teachers "precisely because they themselves are childish, silly and short-sighted" (Schopenhauer 1970, 88; 81).

One of Schopenhauer's virtues, clearly, was his honesty. "Virtually all of the discreditable character traits and episodes in his life (his neurotic anxiety, his incapacity for friendship, his throwing of a noisy seamstress down a flight of stairs) we know from his own pen" (Young 2005, 15). He was also candid about the anxiety he suffered with. "Even when there is no particular provocation, I always have an anxious concern that causes me to see and look for dangers where none exist; for me it magnifies to infinity the tiniest vexation and makes association with people most difficult" (Schopenhauer 1988, 507). Most of all, Schopenhauer was honest—brutally so—in reflecting on the human condition and the suffering inherent in life. I think it's possible to read Schopenhauer's whole philosophy as a diagnosis of and a response to this suffering. As we'll see, both the diagnosis and the response speak volumes about anxiety. About why it might arise and what it feels like when we are in its grip. About how suffering with anxiety can transform us, over time, into more gentle and compassionate people.

Will, Toil, and Suffering

At the heart of Schopenhauer's pessimistic worldview is a dilemma about the will. Schopenhauer tells us that life is "an endless striving." Every person has goals and desires, and everything a person does and refrains from doing can be explained in terms of striving toward their fulfillment. If we were to have asked Schopenhauer why these goals and desires exist in the first place—why we are endowed with a will at all—the question would have been dismissed as "absurd." The existence of the will is "self-evident." Nothing more about its primal origins can be known (Schopenhauer 1998, 84).

A modicum of suffering is inherent in our relentless striving. This is because all of our striving "springs from deprivation—from discontent with one's condition" (Schopenhauer 1998, 195). We strive because we are unsatisfied with how things presently are, because we wish our circumstances were different. Without deprivation and discontent, we wouldn't be inclined to *want* or *do* anything. Suffering is like the gasoline that keeps our metaphorical engine running, propelling us forward. As Schopenhauer writes,

"One can even say that we *require* at all times a certain quantity of care or sorrow or want, as a ship requires ballast, in order to keep on a straight course." We obviously feel unhappy when things don't work out as we hope or expect. Unsatisfied desire provokes frustration. But there is an important respect in which these sorrows and wants are needed. Without them we would be rudderless and lost. A life without striving would be a "deadening languor," Schopenhauer says, characterized by a "dreadful" and "stultifying" boredom (Schopenhauer 1995, 85). If the "pressure of want, toil, calamity and frustration" were removed from life, where would we find motivation? What would spur us on? To what end and in the name of what would we strive? (Schopenhauer 1970, 43).

Schopenhauer's dilemma comes into focus when we realize that it is virtually impossible to obviate the suffering produced by the will. Here is an important passage from the 1850 essay "On the Suffering of the World."

> Work, worry, toil and trouble are indeed the lot of almost all men their whole life long. And yet if every desire were satisfied as soon as it arose how would men occupy their lives, how would they pass the time? Imagine this race transported to a Utopia where everything grows of its own accord and turkeys fly around ready-roasted, where lovers find one another without any delay and keep one another without any difficulty: in such a place some men would die of boredom or hang themselves, some would fight and kill one another, and thus they would create for themselves more suffering than nature inflicts on them as it is. (Schopenhauer 1970, 43)

If we are unsuccessful in our strivings, we will obviously be frustrated and unhappy. But if we are successful—and this is Schopenhauer's crucial insight—we will immediately need new wants and desires to replace the freshly satisfied ones. "Every satisfied wish at once makes room for a new one," he writes. Our attempt to forestall suffering by successfully fulfilling desires and goals is a fool's errand, an interminable project. The joy of satisfaction never lasts. "Every goal attained is the starting point of a new lap in the race, and so on *ad infinitum*" (Schopenhauer 1998, 119; 85). Successfully achieving goals is always merely the beginning of a new striving. The unfortunate conclusion is that suffering is "essential to life" and "cannot be thrown off" (Schopenhauer 1998, 200). "Want and boredom are . . . the twin poles of human life" (Schopenhauer 1970, 45). If we have no desires or goals, we will languish in boredom. If we do have desires and goals we will either fail to achieve them (which is painful and frustrating), or we will succeed in achieving them, in which case we shall then require something new toward which to strive, lest we fall back into the abyss of boredom.

It should be clear that Schopenhauer's thinking here is importantly indebted to Buddhist philosophy. His dilemma about the relentless striving of the will overlaps neatly with the first two Noble Truths of the Buddha, which famously proclaim that (i) all existence is suffering (*dukkha*), and (ii) the cause of suffering is craving (*taṇhā*). Schopenhauer is claiming that we're stuck on a treadmill: there is desire or craving, then a bit of momentary satisfaction if and when desire is satiated, then boredom, which invariably leads back again to desire. And so on, for the rest of our days. Unless we can find a way to get beyond desire itself, unless we can achieve the cessation of craving (*nirodha*) that Buddha's third Noble Truth expounds, suffering of one kind or another will always be there.[4]

The Emotional Meaning of Schopenhauer's Dilemma

Schopenhauer's dilemma conveys something sad and tragic about life. It accentuates feelings of repetition, futility, the emptiness of satisfied desire, of life's overwhelming effortfulness. It seems to ask: *What's the point of all this striving? What does this exhausting sequence of tasks and projects come to in the end?* I think that the gloomy contours of Schopenhauer's dilemma can be glimpsed, between the lines, in Andrew Solomon's vivid recounting of his experience living with depression.

> The opposite of depression is not happiness, but vitality, and it was vitality that seemed to seep out of me. I didn't feel very excited or enthusiastic about any of the things that had previously filled me with joy and pleasure. I remember particularly that, coming home and listening to the messages on my answering machine, I would feel tired instead of being pleased to hear from my friends, and I'd think, That's an awful lot of people to have to call back. I was publishing my first novel at the time, and it came out to rather nice reviews. I simply didn't care. All my life I had dreamed of publishing a novel, and now here it was, but all I felt was nullity. That went on for quite a while. Then the sense of life's being effortful kicked in. Everything began to seem like such an enormous, overwhelming effort. I would think to myself, Oh, I should have some lunch. And then I would think, But I have to get the food out. And put it on a plate. And cut it up. And chew it. And swallow it. And it all began to seem like the stations of the cross. (Solomon 2013, 510–511)[5]

As I hear it, Schopenhauer's dilemma sings in this sad, resigned key. Yet, as philosopher Kieran Setiya has shown in his wonderful book *Midlife: A Philosophical Guide*, it also speaks to the powerful sense of disquiet and restlessness many people experience at midlife. Setiya explicitly connects Schopenhauer's dilemma with these feelings. He begins by telling us that life at the age of forty is rich and rewarding. It's filled with valuable pursuits and accomplishments. With travel and excitement. Fulfilling work, family, and friends. On paper everything seems great, but when Setiya considers his life as a whole, something seems inexplicably, disconcertingly, off.

I turn forty, a tenured professor with a wife and a child, two books, and twenty-odd articles in print. I love the profession of philosophy but not with the fire I had ten years ago. The novelty of accomplishment is gone: first publication, first lecture, first day of class. I will finish the paper I am writing; it will eventually be published; and I will write another. I will teach these students; they will graduate and move on; I will teach more. The future is a tunnel of glass: the rest of life goes by, in its variety, elsewhere. My son will grow, my wife and I grow older. My body creaks and sags; back pain is a trusted companion, not a sometime visitor; I use a standing desk. My parents are getting on, their health increasingly precarious. I feel the finitude of life: the years are numbered; time is moving fast. (Setiya 2017, 22)

He goes on:

I knew I was lucky to be doing what I loved. And yet there was something hollow in the prospect of doing more of it, in the projected sequence of accomplishments stretching through the future to retirement, decline, and death. When I paused to contemplate the life I had worked so hard to build, I felt a disconcerting mixture of nostalgia, regret, claustrophobia, emptiness, and fear. (Setiya 2017, 2)

The view expressed here is not nihilism. Goals and accomplishments have value. But at the same time, Setiya says (in impeccably Schopenhauerian fashion) that the numerous accomplishments which give his life meaning and direction are "bittersweet." They are "longed for, pursued, and ultimately, disappointingly complete. That's over with. What now?" (Setiya 2017, 128). Setiya's midlife crisis seems to involve a mixture of different thoughts and feelings: nostalgia for the open possibilities of youth, restlessness, regret, perhaps a twinge of envy about the things that other people are doing and have done, a whiff of melancholy, a sense of loss over the different possible lives one might have lived instead, an anxious recognition of one's finitude, a feeling of urgency as the years steadily tick by, fear of death.

Setiya has some ingenious therapeutic advice to offer people trapped in Schopenhauer's dilemma, which I will describe and comment on in a moment. Setiya's advice is designed with a different kind of pain and trouble in mind, but I argue that it is tailor-made for the anxious sufferer as well. This gives us reason to think that, while depression may be the emotional keynote of Schopenhauer's dilemma, anxiety is an important part of the story here, too.

One interesting connection between Schopenhauer's dilemma and anxiety involves the observation that when we are trapped in Schopenhauer's vicious pendulum between desire and boredom, we are necessarily ahead of ourselves, always "getting ready to live" (Berman 1995, xxxi). Our happiness is always being planned for, anticipated, projected forward into the future. Our attention is locked in on the various things we want to do, on what we hope we will accomplish. We're thinking about whether we will be successful in achieving our goals, and about the pain and disappointment we'll have to cope with if things end up not working out as we want. But notice that we are now securely on anxiety's home turf: ruminating about the future, imagining possibilities, inventing scenarios, mind churning, nervously expecting the worst.

Another connection centers on the feeling of interminability. It's not only feelings of emptiness and futility that are the result of continuously meeting goals and completing projects. This is also an apt description of the ebb and flow of anxious fear over time. Just like the relentless striving of Schopenhauer's will, anxiety is forever in search of a new project. An anxious mind is always on the hunt for something else to obsess about, some new object onto which the anxiety can be projected. There is always a new emergency in what feels like a never-ending chain of emergencies. "Anxiety," Samantha Harvey poignantly notes, "often has no object and transmutes itself into worry by finding objects to attach to, in order to justify its existence" (Harvey 2020, 100).

This aspect of the experience of anxiety has been aptly described in the metaphor of *Bees in a Tree*. The specific object to which one's anxiety is attached can be removed. You can cut down the tree, so to speak. But the bees simply relocate and find a new tree to buzz around. And the bees always seem to find a new tree. I will feel anxious about some event or obligation to come (a class to teach, a party to attend, a deadline to meet). Time goes by. The dreaded event passes without the catastrophe that I'd imagined. *Disaster averted. Everything's okay. A moment of peace.* But I know that my anxious mind is already scanning for something else about which to roil and obsess and prognosticate. D.H. Lawrence makes the point beautifully in a short poem from the 1916 collection *Amores*:

> He has passed us by; but is it
> Relief that starts in my breast?
> Or a deeper bruise of knowing that still
> She has no rest. (Lawrence 1993, 100)

Anxiety keeps us on guard by presenting new thoughts and symptoms, by using our own care and vigilance against us. The introduction of fresh doubt is anxiety's most efficient weapon. *I know that that tightness in my chest is anxiety. I've felt it before. Tightness in the chest is an extremely common physical symptom of anxiety. Besides, it's on the right side and I know that cardiac pain is supposed to present on the left side of the chest, where the heart is. This is just tight muscles. Just stress and tension. Take a deep breath. Everything is okay, you're alright. But wait, here's a new one. This time in my right calf. I've never felt that before. Isn't pain in the calf the hallmark of a blood clot? Didn't I read somewhere that calf pain is one of the telltale signs of a pulmonary embolism? What's the mortality rate for pulmonary embolisms? Is my life insurance policy in order? It's been a while since I checked. My children are too young to be without their father.* In my heart of hearts, I know that this is an outlandish sequence of thoughts. I know that it's unreasonable to travel stepwise from a random twitch in the calf to an image of my fatherless children. And yet, if you suffer with anxiety like I do, you can probably relate.[6]

Just like Schopenhauer's dilemma, anxiety communicates to its sufferer a sense of interminability, a sense that there is always "another one" waiting in the wings. Like the relentless striving of Schopenhauer's will, anxiety conveys the sense that life is like a treadmill. No closure. No lasting relief. Fresh doubt always on the horizon. A novel profile of symptoms, a new scenario to concoct, more fear, always just around the corner. *Every frightening episode overcome the starting point of a new lap in the race.* Part of what's so painful and exhausting about living with anxiety is the sense of its endlessness. To live with anxiety is to inhabit a world where fear is always lurking nearby. Even on our best, happiest days we anxious sufferers are ever alert to the possibility that anxiety will make an unwanted appearance. Even more perversely, anxiety will use those happy days as a premise in an argument whose conclusion leads right back to itself. *I'm feeling fine now, but I know that anxious thoughts and feelings are coming back soon. I'm due. Feeling good never lasts forever.* And of course, the unsettling prospect of its coming back indicates that anxiety is really already there. To be expecting anxiety's return is really already to be suffering with it. Once again, Samantha Harvey sums it all up perfectly:

> You will need to stand guard in case, in case. Forever in case. Standing guard will make the perceived threat seem more real, which necessitates a more vigilant standing guard. Fear ends when the threat is gone, while anxiety, operating in a hall of mirrors, self-perpetuates. As a friend once said to me: there is no grace for the imagination. You cannot be saved from an assailant that doesn't exist. (Harvey 2020, 90)

It's not necessarily anxiety in the present moment (frightening and painful as that can certainly be) that is normally the worst part of the ordeal. It's the "deeper bruise" of knowing that we are trapped in an exhausting and interminable cycle.

Telic and Atelic Activities

Schopenhauer thinks that we can escape his perpetual seesaw of pain and boredom by strangling the will, thereby achieving what the Buddhists call Nirvana. As Moira Nicholls notes, despite a few minor differences, "both Nirvana and [Schopenhauer's] denial of the will signify the end of craving or willing and the cessation of suffering" (Nicholls 1999, 193). There's an obvious paradox in the view that the will might somehow deny itself. Wouldn't any such denial *just be* another manifestation of the very same will? How can a person consistently will not to will? (Welchman 2017, 437). But paradox aside, is it really so bad to have projects and goals? Is satisfying desires and then needing to replace them really the unbridled misery that Schopenhauer makes it out to be? Is our only hope really the full renunciation of the will, a smothering of all desire—a feat, incidentally, that only a tiny number of people will actually be able to pull off?

Setiya thinks that a more promising "path of spiritual progress" (which also draws inspiration from Buddhist thought, albeit in a different way than Schopenhauer) begins with the appreciation of an ancient distinction between two kinds of activities: *telic* and *atelic*.[7] Consider the various activities that make up your life: driving home from work, eating sushi, shoveling snow, listening to music, washing the dishes, and so on. Some of these activities are "telic." They "aim at terminal states, at which they are finished and thus exhausted. . . . Driving home is telic: it is done when you get home. . . . Other activities are 'atelic': they do not aim at a point of termination or exhaustion, a final state in which they have been achieved." Playing with your children, doing yoga, or listening to music are all examples of atelic activities. You can and will stop doing these things, obviously. (No one can do yoga forever!) But the activities themselves cannot be completed. "They have no limit, no outcome whose achievement exhausts them and therefore brings them to an end" (Setiya 2017, 133; 134).

Setiya thinks that a propensity for the telic is the jet fuel that powers his midlife crisis. He has grown accustomed to successfully achieving goals, to getting things done. But a certain feeling of futility and emptiness is the result. *Is this all there is? Just more goals? Further items on a constantly replenishing checklist?* "I have spent four decades acquiring a taste and aptitude for the telic," he writes, "for achievement and the next big thing, for personal and professional success—only to feel the void within. Fulfillment lies always in the future or the past. That is no way to live" (Setiya 2017, 135). Setiya's advice is not to renounce the will completely, as Schopenhauer and the Buddha would recommend, but rather to afford atelic activities a more prominent place in one's life. There is more to life than getting things done. "There is pleasure in going for a walk, just wandering or hiking, not to get anywhere, but for the sake of walking itself. Walking is atelic: unlike walking home, it does not aim at its own completion, a point at which there is no more to do" (Setiya 2017, 140).

Spending more time on activities that cannot be completed, that have no inherent terminus, will help us feel less like hamsters running on a wheel. It will soothe the sense of interminability and futility that accompanies Schopenhauer's dilemma. A healthy human life should have within it space for activities that are not accomplishments, which is not to say that accomplishments don't matter. They obviously can and do. But the point is that we human beings are not merely machines for the completion of projects, and our lives should be lived in a way that reflects this important truth. Spending more time on atelic activities can also help reduce anxiety insofar as such activities naturally provide an escape from anxiety's home turf: the future-looking point of view from which we ruminate about how things may turn out, obsess about our plans, worry about achievements and goals. That future-looking point of view belongs decisively to the telic mindset and it's where anxiety lives and thrives.

A telic activity cannot technically be transformed into an atelic one (an activity is either exhaustible or it isn't), but a telic activity can be performed in an atelic way, with an atelic spirit. There is a difference between the *kinds* of activities one can perform and the *attitude* or *ethos* with which an activity is performed. These can and frequently do come apart. A person can perform an atelic activity in a telic spirit, and conversely, it's possible to perform a telic activity in an atelic spirit. Meditation is a quintessentially atelic activity. It has no built-in terminus, no natural point of termination or exhaustion. And yet, you could easily imagine someone who judiciously keeps track of how much they are meditating, who carefully logs each session. You could even imagine them getting competitive about it, fixated on the goal of logging the most meditation hours, of becoming the "best" or most consistent meditator in their group of fellow meditators.[8] This is a strange way to approach the activity of meditating (to treat it as yet another project rather than a momentary hiatus from one's projects), but it's far from impossible. I have an app on my phone that encourages users to "set goals" for their meditation practice. The app keeps track of the number of meditation sessions a user has completed, their "streak" of consecutive days meditating; total minutes meditated per day, per week, and so on.

Conversely, one can also perform a telic activity in an atelic spirit. This possibility is expressed beautifully by Zen master Thich Nhat Hanh, who describes how a person can conceive of washing the dishes—a telic activity to the core—in a more atelic spirit.

> While washing the dishes one should only be washing the dishes, which means that while washing the dishes one should be

completely aware of the fact that one is washing the dishes. The fact that I am standing there and washing these bowls is a wondrous reality. I'm being completely myself, following my breath, conscious of my presence, and conscious of my thoughts and actions.

He tells his friend, an American named Jim, that:

"There are two ways to wash the dishes. The first is to wash the dishes in order to have clean dishes and the second is to wash the dishes in order to wash the dishes." ... If while we wash the dishes, we think only of the cup of tea that awaits us, thus hurrying to get the dishes out of the way as if they were a nuisance, then we are not "washing the dishes to wash the dishes." What's more, we are not alive during the time we are washing the dishes. In fact we are completely incapable of realizing the miracle of life while standing at the sink. If we can't wash the dishes, the chances are we won't be able to drink our tea either. While drinking the cup of tea, we will only be thinking of other things, barely aware of the cup in our hands. Thus we are sucked away into the future—and we are incapable of actually living one minute of life. (Hanh 1975, 4–5)

Washing the dishes is paradigmatically telic: we wash dishes in order to complete the task, to have clean dishes, and the task is exhausted and brought to its natural conclusion when the dishes have been cleaned. And yet the suggestion here is that we try to adopt an atelic attitude toward the performance of this task. Hanh is urging his readers to be conscious and mindful, to focus not on the completion of the activity they are performing but on the "wondrous reality" of the present moment.

Another way to think about this involves the idea that every telic activity has an atelic "counterpart." So that, as Setiya writes, "When you cook dinner for your kids, help them finish their homework, and put them to bed—telic activities through and through—you engage in the atelic activity of parenting" (Setiya 2017, 141). This is not some clever linguistic trick, a novel way to re-describe the various activities that fill our days. At its core, it's a powerful shift of perspective, a new way of relating to the world and of recognizing value in what one is doing.

In short and to sum up, the wisdom here is not only that we should make more room in our lives for atelic activities. It's also that we should try to adopt a more atelic attitude to *all* of our various tasks and activities. Not necessarily all the time and no matter what, but more frequently and habitually than many of us are accustomed to do. If we focus more on atelic activities and try to bring a more atelic mindset to all of our daily doings, we are likely to enjoy more peace and happiness in our lives. If Thich Nhat Hanh is right to claim that "Anxiety, the illness of our time, comes primarily from our inability to dwell in the present moment," it seems to follow that a greater focus on atelic activities will help reduce the anxiety so many of us struggle with (Hanh 1999, 78). Striving always to be accomplishing something is exhausting, dispiriting, and anxiety-producing. That's no way to live.

Schopenhauer on Suffering and Compassion

Schopenhauer was one of the first European philosophers to emphasize the moral significance of compassion. Here again his indebtedness to Indian philosophy is unmistakable. In Hindu and Mahayana Buddhist traditions, compassion (*Karuna*, in the Sanskrit) is one of the most important characteristics of ethical life. Schopenhauer clearly agrees. Just as it is a lack of compassion "that stamps a deed with the deepest moral depravity and atrocity," he writes, so, too, is compassion the only "real moral incentive" (Schopenhauer 1995, 170).

I think Schopenhauer's arguments about compassion also shed light on an interesting moral dimension of anxious suffering. Like the Hindu and Buddhist thinkers from whom he draws inspiration, Schopenhauer thinks that compassion is both borne *of* suffering and our most properly human response *to* suffering. At the heart of this view is the ancient truth that suffering is our best moral teacher, that our own suffering can make us more attuned and responsive to the suffering of others. Anxiety is obviously only one variety of suffering among innumerably many, and the ancient truth that Schopenhauer extols applies to all suffering, not just the anxious variety. Still, as we'll see, Schopenhauer's moral vision shows us how suffering with anxiety can transform us over time into more forgiving, gentle, and compassionate people.

Schopenhauer argues that compassion (*mitleid*) is the only genuine basis for morality. But what is compassion exactly, and what makes it so special from a moral point of view? Here it's helpful to contrast compassion with its purported opposite—namely, cruelty. Schopenhauer would have agreed with Montaigne, who said in his famous essay on the subject that cruelty is "the extreme of all vices"—the "ultimate vice of them all" (Montaigne 2003, 480–481). This is because what makes an action cruel (as opposed to merely bad or unpleasant or harmful) is that it is undertaken with the specific aim of causing pain and suffering. Causing pain and suffering is the *point* of cruelty, its raison d'être. Most of us are accustomed to some bad, unethical behavior in ourselves and others. We encounter lying, cheating, dishonesty, selfishness, and greed frequently enough. Cruelty, however, is of a different order. Other actions cause pain and suffering accidentally, or even as a foreseen by-product, but cruelty is "malicious joy put into practice," and this makes it almost incomprehensible to us (Schopenhauer 1995, 136).

> Nothing shocks our moral feelings so deeply as cruelty does. We can forgive every other crime, but not cruelty.... When we obtain information of a very cruel deed, as for example, the case ... of a

mother who murdered her five-year old son by pouring boiling oil down his throat and her younger child by burying it alive ... we are seized with horror and exclaim: "How is it possible to do such a thing?" (Schopenhauer 1995, 169)

What makes cruelty the only crime we cannot forgive is that "it is the very opposite of compassion." When we wonder how a person could do such a thing we are in effect wondering, as Schopenhauer asks, "How is it possible to be so utterly bereft of compassion?" (Schopenhauer 1995, 169–170). How can a person be so heartless, so indifferent to someone else's suffering?

Notice that compassion on this view is something like our natural state, our default setting. Compassion is an "everyday phenomenon," and it can be spotted everywhere we look (Schopenhauer 1995, 144).

[It] happens every day; everyone has experienced it within himself; even to the most hard-hearted and selfish it is not unknown. Every day it comes before our eyes, in single acts on a small scale, wherever, on the spur of the moment, and without much reflection, one man helps another, hastens to the assistance of one whom he has seen for the first time, and in fact sometimes exposes even his own life to the most obvious danger for the sake of that man, without thinking of anything except that he sees the other's great distress and danger. It appears on a large scale when, after long deliberation and difficult debates, the magnanimous British nation gave twenty million pounds to purchase the freedom of the Negro slaves in its colonies; this it did with the joy and approbation of the whole world. (Schopenhauer 1995, 166)

Compassion is obviously not an all-or-nothing affair. It comes in degrees. A person can be more or less compassionate, but everyone has or should have *some* compassion. Schopenhauer regards compassion as an "inborn" trait, a primal human instinct, even if its origins are ultimately "mysterious" (Schopenhauer 1995, 170). What needs accounting for is not that one person would be moved by the suffering of another. That's the normal manner of things. What needs accounting for is that someone could be so *unmoved* by another's suffering. What's shocking and baffling is the absence of compassion, not its presence. Cruelty, not compassion, is the incomprehensible phenomenon.

Schopenhauer argues that compassion is the ultimate foundation of morality. "This wholly direct and even instinctive participation in another's sufferings—compassion—is the sole source of such actions when they are said to *have moral worth*" (Schopenhauer 1995, 163).

> Boundless compassion for all living beings is the firmest and surest guarantee of pure moral conduct, and needs no casuistry. Whoever is inspired with it will assuredly injure no one, will wrong no one, will encroach on no one's rights; on the contrary, he will be lenient and patient with everyone, will forgive everyone, will help everyone as much as he can, and all his actions will bear the stamp of justice, philanthropy, and loving-kindness. (Schopenhauer 1995, 172–173)[9]

Compassion is the only "pure" moral motivation. When we act from a sense of compassion, we are not seeking instrumental advantage or personal gain. To be motivated by compassion is simply to be moved by another's suffering, to "participate" in it viscerally and instinctually.[10] Schopenhauer thinks that compassion is never directly stirred in us by someone else's well-being or happiness, which tends to leave us for the most part "unmoved." On the contrary, "only another's suffering, want, danger, and helplessness awaken our sympathy directly and as such." This doesn't mean that we cannot share in someone else's joy and happiness. We can and sometimes do. But Schopenhauer regards this as "secondary" because, as he puts it, "pain is something... that automatically makes itself known," whereas "satisfaction and pleasures are something *negative*, the mere elimination of the former" (Schopenhauer 1995, 146).

I have doubts that pleasure and satisfaction are really nothing more than the absence of pain and suffering, but let that pass. The more important idea is that the suffering of others resonates with us because in it we can dimly recognize our own suffering. Compassion is stirred in us when we "identify" with another's suffering, when we "participate" and see ourselves in it. "As soon as compassion is aroused," Schopenhauer says, "the weal and woe of another are nearest to my heart in exactly the same way... as otherwise only my own are. Hence the difference between him and me is now no longer absolute" (Schopenhauer 1995, 144). Only through compassion does another person's "need, distress, and suffering directly become my own.... I share the suffering *in him*, in spite of the fact that his skin does not enclose my nerves" (Schopenhauer 1995, 166). This sort of thing happens all the time, Schopenhauer thinks, even if we cannot really identify how or why.

From the perspective of compassion, every bit of suffering deserves its due. It's wrong to let the suffering of each concrete individual dissolve, metaphorically speaking, into a vast ocean of aggregated suffering. Individual suffering should never get lost in the math. It's a mistake to ignore individuals, each one unique and important, by trying to weigh vast sums of suffering and utility across millions (or billions) of creatures. All suffering matters, on its own terms and for its own sake. Whether some quantity of suffering is comparatively more or less than some other quantity is not the decisive moral question. A compassionate perspective requires forgoing comparisons and trying to see all suffering in its own light. If someone is in pain, it's not a decent or compassionate reply to say, "Oh well, other people are in even greater pain," or to say, "Fine, but people from disadvantaged groups suffer much more." From the point of view of compassion, every last bit of suffering counts, be it comparatively small or comparatively large. A properly compassionate moral perspective will accentuate the suffering and hardship of the discrete individual, suffering creatures one by one. "For that thousands had lived in happiness and joy would never do away with the anguish and death-agony of one individual" (Schopenhauer 1966a, 576). Questions about the totality of suffering in the universe or about how some quantity of suffering compares in size or intensity to another quantity are less important.[11]

Someone might plausibly complain that all of this raises more questions than it answers. How can we make ethical decisions without weighing and comparing? What does it mean—concretely, in the real world—to give all suffering its due? And what about counterarguments to the effect that, because they are prone to potentially harmful biases, compassion (and similar virtues like sympathy and empathy) are unsound bases for ethics?[12] These are difficult questions. But it's important to appreciate that Schopenhauer is not using compassion to develop a comprehensive moral theory. The virtue of compassion will not determine how competing interests or claims are correctly weighed, or how dilemmas of this or that sort are rightly navigated. No ethical algorithm or decision procedure follows from the virtue of compassion (or from any other virtue for that matter). Nor does compassion tell us much about the *content* of morality, which Schopenhauer sums up in the pithy slogan: "Harm no one; rather, help everyone as much as you can" (Schopenhauer 2009, 140).[13]

Instead, Schopenhauer tells us that his ambitions in ethics follow a "modest path" which involves "the task of clarifying and explaining ways of acting among human beings that are extremely morally diverse, and tracing them back to their ultimate ground" (Schopenhauer 2009, 189). He is interested primarily in differentiating between those actions that have moral worth (actions which are good or praiseworthy) and those actions that lack moral worth, and to ask how and in virtue of what they have these respective qualities (Puryear 2022, 14). On the assumption that there is genuine morality out there—on the assumption that actions with moral worth are a "given phenomenon" that we are trying to give an account of (Schopenhauer 2009, 189)—Schopenhauer maintains that, "Only insofar as an action has sprung from compassion does it have any moral value" (Schopenhauer 1995, 144).

While the virtue of compassion discourages the making of comparisons between one instance of suffering and another, it's also true, in another way, that measuring our own suffering against the suffering of others is necessary for the cultivation of compassion. In a poem that I'm confident Schopenhauer would have appreciated, Emily Dickinson writes:

> I measure every grief I meet
> With analytic eyes;
> I wonder if it weighs like mine,
> Or has an easier size.
>
> I wonder if they bore it long,
> Or did it just begin?
> I could not tell the date of mine,
> It feels so old a pain

Dickinson notes that it somehow gives solace to "measure" other griefs against her own. To wonder how they compare. "A piercing comfort it affords," she says:

> To note the fashions of the cross,
> Of those that stand alone,
> Still fascinated to presume
> That some are like my own. (Dickinson 1982, 32–33)

The suggestion here is not that other people's suffering exists to be medicinal for us. That's a perverse, egomaniacal idea. It's that suffering alone is much worse than suffering with others, and that "measuring" other griefs is part of the attempt we make to suffer together rather than alone. Schopenhauer is inclined to agree. "The most effective consolation in every misfortune and every affliction," he says, "is to observe others who are more unfortunate than we" (Schopenhauer 1970, 42). *Solamen miseris socios habuisse doloris.* It is a comfort to the wretched to have companions in misery.[14]

Like Schopenhauer, Dickinson recognizes that suffering is particular to each individual. Suffering "individualizes." Everyone struggles in their own unique way. Each person fights their own private battle. But there is a larger truth that these private bouts of suffering converge upon. It's that suffering is the fundamental similarity that unites us all, the distinctive stamp of the human. The details are always specific, but the fact of suffering universal. Our private battles confirm that we all share the same essential core. We are all members of one large human family, alone in our individual holes, so to speak, but simultaneously together as companions in suffering. As Schopenhauer writes, "The appropriate form of address between man and man ought to be, not *monsieur, sir,* but *fellow sufferer, compagnon de misères.*" (Schopenhauer 1970, 50)

An appreciation for the universality of suffering engenders compassion. It encourages us to think about the vast army of fellow sufferers—men, women, and children from literally every country on earth—struggling in some way like us. It's possible to feel a vague solidarity with this enormous group of strangers. To be moved by the thought that we are all cut from the same human cloth. Brothers and sisters in suffering.[15] Recognition of this fact also makes us more mindful and responsive to the private battles other people are fighting. We're reminded that a lot of suffering is concealed, intentionally kept hidden, and we are inclined to be gentler and more forgiving with people as a result. The point is expressed powerfully by a woman named Laura Anderson, who explains how her own brutal suffering with depression has enlarged her sense of compassion and forgiveness.

> Depression has given me kindness and forgiveness where other people don't know enough to extend it. I'm drawn toward people who might put off others with a wrong move or a misplaced barb. I had an argument about the death penalty tonight with someone, and I was trying to explain, without being too self-referential, that one can understand horrifying actions, understand the terrible links between mood and job and relationships and the rest of everything. I would never want depression to be a public or political excuse, but I think once you have gone through it, you get a greater and more immediate understanding of the temporary absence of judgment that makes people behave so badly. You learn even, perhaps, how to tolerate the evil in the world. (Solomon 2013, 529)

I think I understand *exactly* what she means. As a result of my own suffering with anxiety, the world now looks a little bit different to me, too.

The world is awash with anxiety, but a lot of it is hidden from view. We anxious sufferers are typically quite skilled at keeping our anxiety concealed. To the outside observer, everything seems fine, but deep inside, as the composer Hugo Wolf wrote, "the heart bleeds from a thousand wounds" (Wolf, in Jamison 1995, 39). People with anxiety are "adept at the art of subterfuge," writes Daniel Smith. "For the sake of propriety, ambition, desire, or privacy . . . [anxious sufferers] learn to seal their anxiety off from public view. They learn to cork their anxiety within themselves like acid in a vial" (Smith 2012, 28). So they do.[16] Yet part of the compassion I now feel for others is bound up with my ability to discern anxiety in places I would not have been able to notice it before. A friend unexpectedly cancels on a plan to meet; a conversation partner tightly grips the arms of his chair for support; that person's fingernails are gnawed; this person keeps nervously looking at their phone. Anxiety's little clues are everywhere: sweaty palms, fidgety movements, restless legs, shallow breathing, excessive blinking, all sorts of ticks and idiosyncrasies, that nervous flicker in the eye. Thanks to my own suffering with anxiety, I've become an expert at spotting them. And a new compassion and softness now extends to the strange and sometimes off-putting behavior I observe in others. I can live with odd slights and misplaced barbs now. Quirky or even rude behavior that previously might have offended or angered me, I'm now mostly able to view with forgiveness and compassion.

Compassion makes us more inclined to see things from the point of view of suffering. We can tell ourselves that suffering is ubiquitous, that everyone is struggling in their own way, trying their best to cope. We're now better able to empathically reverse perspectives with others. And we now have a deeper appreciation for the fact that pain and suffering make people behave in ways they might not have otherwise behaved, makes them do things they might not have otherwise done. We're more inclined to think: *What if I had suffered as they suffered? What if I had walked the path they walked and went through what they went through? Maybe in that case the rude or badly behaved person would have been me, not them. There but for the grace of God go I.* From this perspective, almost anything can be forgiven.

But isn't it also true that pain and hardship sometimes make us stronger and more resilient? Like Kierkegaard before him, Nietzsche is famous for arguing that suffering is productive and valuable. Pain and struggle are conducive to growth, discovery, and occasionally even greatness. This is how he puts it in *The Will to Power*:

> To those human beings who are of any concern to me I wish suffering, desolation, sickness, ill treatment, indignities—I wish that they should not remain unfamiliar with profound self-contempt, the torture of self-mistrust, the wretchedness of the vanquished: I have no pity for them, because I wish them the only thing that can prove today whether one is worth anything or not—that one endures. (Nietzsche 1967, 481)[17]

Suffering is obviously unpleasant, but on Nietzsche's view it's ultimately good for the soul. Suffering is responsible for "all the elevations of humanity," he says. "Examine the lives of the best and most fruitful people and peoples," he writes in the *Gay Science*, "and ask yourselves . . . whether misfortune and external resistance, whether any kinds of hatred, jealousy, stubbornness, mistrust, hardness, greed, and violence do not belong to the *favourable* conditions without which any great growth even of virtue is scarcely possible?" (Nietzsche 2001, 43). From this perspective, it's a mistake to regard compassion as any kind of virtue at all. On the contrary, compassion is a character defect, a form of weakness. One more residue in our moral thinking of a slavish, wimpy, Christian morality.

I agree that there can sometimes be value in suffering, that we can sometimes grow and benefit from it. I also grant that suffering can sometimes help make a person deeper and more thoughtful. It can give them, as Freud beautifully put it, "a keener eye for the truth" (Freud 2005, 206). It's also possible to develop over time a sense of gratitude for the suffering one has had to endure. A person can come to recognize how their suffering has shaped them, for better or worse, into who and what they are. I accept the value in these sorts of discoveries.[18] But notice that such discoveries can only ever be made retrospectively, with the benefit of hindsight, once the storm has passed, so to speak. No one can presume to know in advance that some bout of suffering—our own or someone else's—will be safely navigated. If suffering is sometimes conducive to growth and greatness, it's also true that sometimes we are not better off for having endured it. Anne Rice puts the point movingly in her novel *The Queen of the Damned*: "It's an awful truth that suffering can deepen us, give a greater lustre to our colours, a richer resonance to our words. That is, if it doesn't destroy us, if it doesn't burn away the optimism and the spirit, the capacity for visions, and the respect for simple yet indispensable things" (Rice 1988, 3).

In short and to sum up, we can agree with Nietzsche that suffering has the capacity to be productive and redemptive. We can agree with him, abstractly and in general, that what doesn't kill us makes us stronger (Nietzsche 1998, 5). But it simply doesn't follow that the moral value of compassion is thereby refuted.

5
To Clear Our Minds of Selfish Care

> What is the value of preserving and strengthening this sense of awe and wonder, this recognition of something beyond the boundaries of human existence? Is the exploration of the natural world just a pleasant way to pass the golden hours of childhood or is there something deeper? I am sure there is something much deeper, something lasting and significant. Those who dwell, as scientists or laymen, among the beauties and mysteries of the Earth are never alone or weary of life. Whatever the vexations or concerns of their personal lives, their thoughts can find paths that lead to inner contentment and to renewed excitement in living. Those who contemplate the beauty of the earth will find reserves of strength that will endure as long as life lasts.
> — Rachel Carson, *The Sense of Wonder: A Celebration of Nature for Parents and Children*

In this chapter, I want to describe a philosophical insight about the management of our attention and mental energy—about a kind of *practice of attention*—from which I believe the anxious sufferer stands to benefit. The insight originates in the work of Irish-born novelist and philosopher Iris Murdoch and culminates in a therapeutic conclusion about the peace that can be afforded by directing one's attention toward a certain kind of good in a certain kind of way.

At the heart of Murdoch's insight is the encouragement to "give attention to nature in order to clear our minds of selfish care"

(Murdoch 1971, 82). I will try to make sense of this in what follows, and also to reflect on what Murdoch's insight reveals about the formidable therapeutic properties of the natural world, about the peace and inner tranquility that time spent in nature can sometimes provide. If I'm right, Murdoch's insight is explanatorily valuable in a broader way, too. It helps explain why some of the activities we know to be helpful for diminishing anxiety (meditation, a hike in the woods, reading, listening to music, a few miles of running, and so on) have the therapeutic attributes that they do. The insight describes the wisdom behind the therapy. It gives an account of what's going on when we discover (all of a sudden or in a more gradual way) that our worried, anxious state has been replaced by a more present-minded, calmer one.

Iris Murdoch was born in the summer of 1919, in Dublin. Her father was a civil servant who grew up in a family of sheep farmers in County Down, in Northern Ireland. Her mother came from a middle-class Anglican Dublin family. The Murdoch family was Anglo-Irish and Protestant, and so it made sense in the midst of the political turmoil of those years ("with the Troubles, the introduction of martial law, and then the civil war looming") for them to relocate to London around the time the Irish Free State was established in 1921 (Conradi 2001a, 27).

Despite confiding in a letter to Phillipa Foot in 1978 that she felt "unsentimental about Ireland to the point of hatred," and despite the occasional whiff of British superiority about the Irish that wafted into her letters and conversations, the biographical consensus seems now to be that Murdoch took pride in her Irish roots (Rowe 2019, 101). Her 1965 novel *The Red and the Green* is set in Dublin and follows the events leading up to the 1916 Easter Rebellion. Frances Bellman, the novel's most sympathetically pro-Irish character, remarks at one point that "Being a woman is like being Irish; everyone says you're important and nice, but you take second place all the time" (Murdoch 1965, 36).

Murdoch was a rare figure in twentieth-century philosophy for her ability to read appreciatively across the so-called analytic-continental divide. As a long-serving professor at Oxford, she was conversant in the latest trends in Anglophone philosophy, although this kind of work frequently left her cold and uninspired. Even much earlier, as an undergraduate, Murdoch would complain about what she regarded as a stiff and narrow intellectual climate at Oxford, bemoaning both the logical positivism and the "shallow stupid milk & water 'ethics' of English 'moralists' like Ross and Pritchard" that seemed to hold all the philosophers there in its sway. As she grumbled to a friend in a 1946 letter: "anyone interested in psychology, history, or religion is regarded as 'romantic' & ergo unsound. Sartre is mentioned only with derision & no one reads Kierkegaard" (Conradi 2001a, 216; 253).

Murdoch's appreciation for the writings of Schopenhauer, Kierkegaard, Sartre, and Heidegger is well known. Sartre's existentialism in particular was integral to her intellectual development. The twenty-six-year-old Murdoch was clearly starstruck when she met Sartre in Brussels, in 1945. "I am busily reading everything of his I can lay my hands on," she recounted in a letter from that time, "The excitement—I remember nothing like it since the days of discovering Keats & Shelley & Coleridge when I was very young" (Conradi 2001a, 215).

Murdoch was a prolific and wide-ranging writer. In their introduction to a collection of her letters, Avril Horner and Anne Rowe provide a summary of her output.

> She produced twenty-six novels, a body of philosophical writing which included a study of Sartre, two Platonic dialogues, over thirty essays and two seminal philosophical tracts, *The Sovereignty of Good*... and *Metaphysics as a Guide to Morals*.... She also wrote six plays, three of which were adaptations of her novels, a radio play and some poetry, of which only a small proportion has been published. (Horner and Rowe 2015, xiii)

Murdoch was probably most prolific as a writer of letters, spending hours each day keeping up on her vast correspondence. Biographers have speculated that writing and receiving letters were for Murdoch a way to achieve a sort of intimacy without the high emotional stakes of sexual encounters—a sort of "romance by correspondence" (Conradi 2001a, 79).

Murdoch's hankering for romance of one sort or another (with men and women alike) sometimes seemed unquenchable. In a 1967 letter she confessed, "I can't divide friendship from love or love from sex—or sex from love etc. If I care for somebody I want to caress them" (Horner and Rowe 2015, 347). As Benjamin Lipscomb tells the story, "Murdoch's capacity for friendship and for passionate devotion fused in a remarkable number of love affairs already during her first year at Oxford."

> After graduation, sharing a flat in London with Philippa Bosanquet [Bosanquet was the maiden name of Phillipa Foot, world-famous moral philosopher and one of Murdoch's closest, lifelong friends] they agreed one night to tell one another about the proposals of marriage they'd each received. Bosanquet went first, then Murdoch. As Murdoch's list went on and on, Bosanquet asked, annoyed, whether perhaps it would save time to list the men who had *not* proposed to her. The length of the list is partly a reflection of circumstance; she was surrounded her first year by men about to be called away, perhaps to their deaths. But it is partly too an index of Murdoch's capacity to display and inspire devotion. (Lipscomb 2022, 34)

Although her name and standing as a philosopher is undeniable, Murdoch is remembered most of all for her work as a novelist. (She won the Booker Prize in 1978 for her novel *The Sea, the Sea*, and was made a Dame by Queen Elizabeth for her services to literature in 1987.) Murdoch was one of the first thinkers of recent vintage to emphasize not only the important role that literature can play *in* philosophical reflection, but also to insist upon the superiority of literature *to* philosophy. If one could only have one or the other, Murdoch was sure that philosophy needed to take a back seat to literature. "For both the collective and the individual salvation of the human race," she wrote, "art is doubtlessly more important than philosophy, and literature most important of all" (Murdoch 1997, 362).

Murdoch was formally diagnosed with Alzheimer's disease in 1997, but cognitive decline ("sailing away into darkness," as she once grimly described it) had already been occurring for some time before that. As Lipscomb writes, her final journal entries from that period "reflect both the tenderness and fear that accompanied her decline" (Lipscomb 2022, 256).

> *1 August 1993.* My friends, my friends, I say to the teacups and spoons. Such intense love for Puss—more and more.
>
> *1 July 1995, of a peaceful Thames swim.* Indescribable. Holiness. Only one yacht quietly passed.
>
> *October 1995. The Cloud of Unknowing* in the which [sic] a soul is oned with God.
>
> *November 1995.* Dorothy Thompson writes, Edward has died. (And Frank—).
>
> *February 1996.* At last, and continuously, snow. Poor little birds. *Astonishing.*
>
> *Among her final entries, on 8 June 1996.* We swam in the Thames, in our usual secret place, for the first time this year. Ducks, geese, swans—a delightful man comes swimming in—we talked—no one else in the whole huge area. He swimmed by, swimmed off, conversation, beautiful. The area: immense field, river, another immense field, no one, no sign of the road on the other side, cows wander. Poor cows! (Conradi 2001a, 588–589)

"Unselfing"

In *The Sovereignty of the Good*, Murdoch says that, "We are anxiety-ridden animals. Our minds are continually active, fabricating an anxious, usually self-preoccupied, often falsifying *veil* which partially conceals the world" (Murdoch 1971, 82). Instead of letting our attention be dictated by what she calls our "fat relentless ego" (a major source of moral and spiritual delusion on her view), Murdoch thinks that we can achieve a modicum of relief from worry and inner turmoil by turning our attention outward, away from the self. This is an activity she calls "unselfing." Here is a key passage:

> I am looking out of my window in an anxious and resentful state of mind, oblivious of my surroundings, brooding perhaps on some damage done to my prestige. Then suddenly I observe a hovering kestrel. In a moment everything is altered. The brooding self with its hurt vanity has disappeared. There is nothing now but kestrel. And when I return to thinking of the other matter it seems less important. And of course this is something which we may also do deliberately: give attention to nature in order to clear our minds of selfish care. (Murdoch 1971, 51; 82)

Unselfing is not merely an activity of leisure or a handy trick designed to bring about relief from anxious suffering. Much more grandiosely, Murdoch regards it as part of a moral and spiritual pilgrimage toward truth and goodness. A "pilgrimage from appearance to reality" (Murdoch 1977, 80). Attention to the self is a source of error, of failing to see things as they really are. "We are blinded by the self," Murdoch writes. "The self, the place where we live, is a place of illusion." Turning away from the self gets us closer to the truth, letting us "join the world as it really is" (Murdoch 1997, 376–382).

Unselfing is depicted as both an activity and an achievement, but otherwise the concept is left purposely vague. There is no detailed account of how exactly unselfing occurs. Nor is there a set of necessary and sufficient conditions for having done it successfully. Despite such vagueness, the basic idea remains simple and striking. At bottom, unselfing involves directing our attention away from the misrepresentations of the self and attending to a world of beautiful beings and things.[1] It's the attempt to turn off auto-pilot, to disrupt the unreflectively self-centered flow of thought and attention. We're trying to "detach" from the "greedy organism of the self" which gives us a false, distorted picture of reality and perceive and engage with the world as it really is. Murdoch explains:

> This exercise of *detachment* is difficult and valuable whether the thing contemplated is a human being or the root of a tree or the vibration of a colour or a sound. Unsentimental contemplation of nature exhibits the same quality of detachment: selfish concerns vanish, nothing exists except the things which are seen. ... The direction of attention is... outward, away from self which reduces all to a false unity, towards the great surprising variety of the world. (Murdoch 1971, 64)

Such detachment is difficult, because our naturally "greedy" self is always trying to be the center of attention. It's valuable, in turn, because it brings us closer to reality, because our attention becomes "fixed upon the real situation" (Murdoch 1997, 375).

But who or what is this "unselfed" self? When we turn away from ourselves and "give attention to nature," *who* or *what* exactly is performing this activity? If the self on Murdoch's account is "the place where we live," then who or what is this *we* that supposedly lives there? Murdoch has plenty to say about the self in her work. It's an abiding theme in much of her philosophical writing, and in a good portion of her fiction, too. But it can be challenging to pin down precisely what Murdoch takes the self to be. Much more time is spent saying what the self is *not* (a kind of substance, a transcendental subject, a "unified" Cartesian knower whose ideas are fully transparent to itself) than is spent saying what it *is*. Murdoch's more important claim here is that the self is a concept that we would be loath to do without in philosophy, an idea we discard at our peril. We need to posit the existence of a conscious self with a rich "inner life" not because it is metaphysically fundamental or real necessarily, but because we wouldn't be able to make sense of our lives and experience without it. "It is one thing to present sound anti-Cartesian critical arguments," she says, "it is quite another to sweep aside as irrelevant a whole area of our private reflections, which we may regard as the very substance of our soul and being, as somehow unreal, otiose, without relevant *quality* or *value*" (Murdoch 1992, 150; 157).

The sense of self Murdoch thinks we need to retain has to do with a person's "inner life" and experience, their private consciousness and subjectivity. She's interested in something like what Michel Foucault has called "*le rapport à soi*," the kind of relationship one has with oneself (Foucault 1994, 263). On this way of thinking, what we call the "self" includes, "Our present moment, our experiences, our flow of consciousness, our indelible moral sense" and the further awareness that all of these are "essentially linked together" in a coherent whole (Murdoch 1992, 153). All of this requires a sense of what things are like on the inside, so to speak. But the mere subjectivity of experience will not be enough for full-fledged selfhood. The self also has a vital moral or evaluative dimension. It requires that a person be oriented in relation to what they recognize as good and valuable.[2] Charles Taylor, whose magisterial work on the modern self is heavily indebted to Murdoch's thinking, expresses the general idea like this:

> [There is an] essential link between identity and a kind of orientation. To know who you are is to be oriented in moral space, a

space in which questions arise about what is good or bad, what is worth doing and what not, what has meaning and importance for you and what is trivial and secondary... one of the most basic aspirations of human beings... [is]... the need to be connected to, or in contact with, what they see as good, or of crucial importance, or of fundamental value.... The fact that we have to place ourselves within a space which is defined by these qualitative distinctions cannot but mean that where we stand in relation to them must matter to us....We have to be rightly placed in relation to the good. (Taylor 1989, 28; 42; 44)

Taylor and Murdoch agree that we won't be able to make good sense of our lives—won't be able to get a grip on the question of *who we are*—without this explicitly moral-evaluative vocabulary. Any coldly amoral and naturalistic account of the self (what Murdoch sometimes called "the scientific self") will be for that reason deficient and incomplete (Murdoch 1997, 362). But notice that if selfhood has an inescapably moral dimension, as Murdoch and Taylor both contend, a certain realism or cognitivism is the upshot. For we see that we can sometimes be mistaken about what matters, about what has fundamental value. We see that we are capable of taking a wrong turn, of misidentifying or overlooking what is good and worthwhile and valuable. We sometimes get things wrong. And we see also that we can sometimes correct these mistakes and get back on the right path, as it were. To sum up, there is more to the self than an interior experiential life coupled with some profile of wants and desires. Selfhood also presupposes that there are higher moral impulses—a transcendent and "sovereign" Good—in relation to which we understand ourselves, toward which we strive, and about which we are sometimes in error.[3]

Trying to live one's life oriented toward the good is hard work. "It is difficult to look at the sun," Murdoch says, with obvious allusions to Plato (Murdoch 1997, 382).[4] Orienting oneself toward the good entails the use of a wide range of our capacities—intellectual, imaginative, artistic, and moral. As Murdoch explains, in a beautiful passage:

> The world is not given to us "on a plate," it is given to us as a creative task. It is impossible to banish morality from this picture. We *work*, using or failing to use our honesty, our courage, our truthful imagination, at the interpretation of what is present to us, as we of necessity shape it and "make something of it." We help it to be. We work at the meeting point where we deal with a world which is other than ourselves. This transcendental barrier is more like a band than a line. Our ordinary consciousness is a deep continuous working of values, a *continuous present and presence* of perceptions, intuitions, images, feelings, desires, aversions, attachments. It is a matter of what we "see things as," what we let, or make, ourselves think about, how by innumerable movements, we train our instincts and develop our habits and test our methods of verification. Imagery, metaphor, has its deep roots and origins in this self-being, and an important part of human learning is an ability both to generate and to judge and understand the imagery which helps us to interpret the world. (Murdoch 1992, 215)

Is the self really a place of fantasy and misapprehension, as Murdoch claims? Must turning inward always be a source of illusion and moral failure? Is it always better to be a person who, as Roger Crisp nicely puts it, "looks out rather than in"? (Crisp 2012, 287). I am skeptical. It's obviously true that the self can sometimes deceive or lead us astray. Many of the moral vices (self-aggrandizement, self-absorption, self-centeredness, self-interestedness, selfishness, and the list goes on) arise specifically because the self looms too large. But that's not always or necessarily so. There are a thousand ways to get things wrong, and only some of these involve paying too much attention to the self (Blackburn 2014, 86). Even more, as Christopher Mole argues, sometimes virtuousness demands that we take a long, hard look at ourselves.

In order to know whether we are acting as the virtuous agent we would need to know which aspects of our character we are exercising. It is not enough to know that we are hurting others, or that we are benefitting them. We need also to know whether we are being callous or manipulative. To know these things we must, it seems, pay close attention to ourselves. And that is precisely what Murdoch has told us we must not do. (Mole 2007, 75)

In sum, if the question is whether the self is a source of illusion or truth, vice or moral virtue, the correct answer must be something like: *Well, it depends. Sometimes the self is at the root of delusion and moral blindness. But sometimes turning inward is integral to seeing things clearly and correctly. And sometimes—probably most often—paying attention to ourselves is just boringly innocuous. Neutral from an ethical and epistemic point of view.*

Murdoch's account of "unselfing" helps us appreciate that anxiety is a fundamentally inward-facing, self-centered mental state. Some of the adjectives Murdoch uses to describe anxiety include, "egoistic," "self-indulgent," "obsessive," and "selfish" (Murdoch 1997, 455; 29). Anxiety focuses its sights in the direction of the self, and the self is where anxiety lives and thrives. More generally, anxiety involves the capacity to *worry* in a special kind of self-focused, inwardly directed way. As Joseph LeDoux argues, "Anxiety (worry, dread, apprehension, trepidation, angst . . .) involves a particular kind of conscious thought. It is all about the self." It wouldn't be possible to experience anxiety without the ability to place ourselves in the past and in the future, to conceive of earlier and later versions of ourselves. In order for anxiety to really get its grip on us, we need the capacity to conceive of counterfactual situations—"possible worlds" in which we fare better or worse, in which things turn out well or badly. (How else could we concoct wild, improbable scenarios that stretch off far into the future, as many of our anxious fears do?) Merely being conscious and having desires will not be enough for anxiety to arise. What's required, LeDoux maintains, is an "episodic, autonoetic self."

> a self that can be projected into the future, a contemplation of what the future self will be like if bad things happen—not just to it but also to those the self cares about, whether they are biologically related or not, whether they are a person or a pet, whether they are known personally or only as an idol or hero, as these are all psychologically part of our extended self. (LeDoux 2016, 258)

"Fear and anxiety . . . both involve the self," LeDoux concludes. "[T]o experience anxiety is to worry about whether future threats may harm YOU. This involvement of the self in fear and anxiety is a defining feature of these and other human emotions" (Ledoux 2016, 11). In short, suffering with anxiety requires not only that we have first-order thoughts about what we want and want to avoid. We also need a second-order concept of ourselves, a metacognitive self-consciousness and self-awareness.

If anxiety is all about the self, it follows that achieving some distance from the self will almost always redound to a more calm and peaceful state of mind. Turning away from the "noisy ego" will result in a shrinking of anxiety. "When . . . the noisy ego is silenced," Murdoch writes, "we are freed from possessive selfish desires and anxieties and are one with what we contemplate, enjoying a unique unity with something which is itself unique" (Murdoch 1992, 59). This is what unselfing is fundamentally about. What we are trying to do, recall, is shift our attention away from the "fat relentless ego" toward something outside of ourselves. To the extent that we are successful in this redirection of attention, an anxiety-diminishing "forgetfulness" of the self will be the happy consequence.

How does unselfing work as a form of anti-anxiety therapy? What is happening to us in such moments when, as Murdoch says, "everything is altered"? And what is it about nature in particular (about birds, trees, rivers, and mountains) that provides comfort and peace to so many anxious sufferers? Two closely related ideas are important here. One of them has to do with nature's capacity to initiate a calming forgetfulness of the self—what Murdoch calls a "self-forgetful pleasure." The other is connected to the observation that time spent in nature provokes a more contemplative state of mind and occasionally inspires feelings of awe and wonder.

Murdoch is careful to distinguish unselfing from the different idea that attention to nature can be an occasion for what she calls "exalted self-feeling" (Murdoch 1971, 83). She attributes that idea to the "lesser" of the great Romantics. And while we're left to guess who specifically these "lesser" Romantics might be, it's easy to imagine that Murdoch might have had William Wordsworth's (melodramatic?) celebration of "natural piety" in mind. As Wordsworth memorably wrote in 1802:

> My heart leaps up when I behold
> A rainbow in the sky:
> So was it when my life began;
> So is it now I am a man;
> So be it when I shall grow old,
> Or let me die!
> The Child is father of the Man;
> And I could wish my days to be
> Bound each to each by natural piety. (Wordsworth 2008, 246)

Beholding rainbows might occasionally make our hearts metaphorically leap up, but more important for Murdoch is our capacity to "take a self-forgetful pleasure in the sheer alien pointless independent existence of animals, birds, stones and trees," a capacity she connects with the early Wittgenstein's unforgettable claim that it is not *how* the world is, but *that* it is, which is the source of wonder and mysticism (Murdoch 1971, 83). It's not only nature's splendor that can provide comfort to the anxious sufferer (the beauty of a mountain landscape, the mesmeric sounds of birds or rushing water nearby, the fresh odors of trees, the moist, healthy soil). Moments of nature-induced "self-forgetfulness" can also be profound experiences of spontaneity, immediacy, and attention. These are experiences of temporarily becoming wrapped up in something else, of turning our mental gaze elsewhere (Olsson 2018). In such moments we lose track of ourselves. We forget momentarily about the anxious worries that our minds have been roiling with. Our attention is now anchored in the present. Turned outward, away from the self. Toward the beauty of the natural world. Anxiety is diminished. Panic and fear recede.

It's interesting that Murdoch's description of unselfing draws on the experience of spotting a bird—a "hovering kestrel"—outside her window. My sister, an ornithologist and avid birdwatcher, has told me that part of what she finds so captivating about bird-watching is a soothing reminder that virtually always accompanies the activity: about the existence of an ancient and intricate world (elusive songs and sounds, vibrant colors and patterns, elaborate nests, migration routes many thousands of years old, a world quite literally of the dinosaurs) to which human beings are normally more or less oblivious, and that, by deliberate focus of attention (early in the morning, tramping through the woods, crisp air in the lungs, binoculars dangling around the neck) one can get a brief glimpse of this world and share, to some small extent, in its business and happenings. This is what unselfing is all about. Not inattentiveness or mere daydreaming, but attention deliberately steered away from the self. Not absent-mindedness but present-mindedness someplace else.[5] Immersion in *Bird World* means that we are no longer attending to the anxious, worrying self. A calming forgetfulness is stimulated. What Murdoch calls the "anxious avaricious tentacles of the self" are temporarily pacified (Murdoch 1997, 385). We're no longer focused on the anxiety that had us in its grip just a little while earlier.

Consider two short poems that depict, if not unselfing as such, something very much in the same neighborhood. Here is Wendell Berry's well-known poem "The Peace of Wild Things."

> When despair for the world grows in me
> and I wake in the night at the least sound
> in fear of what my life and my children's lives may be,
> I go and lie down where the wood drake
> rests in his beauty on the water, and the great heron feeds.
> I come into the peace of wild things
> who do not tax their lives with forethought
> of grief. I come into the presence of still water.
> And I feel above me the day-blind stars
> waiting with their light. For a time
> I rest in the grace of the world, and am free. (Berry 2018, 25)

Mary Oliver's "On Meditating, Sort Of" movingly describes a similar kind of experience.

> Meditation, so I've heard, is best accomplished
> If you entertain a certain strict posture.
> Frankly, I prefer to just lounge under a tree.
> So why should I think I could ever be successful?
>
> Some days I fall asleep, or land in that
> even better place—half asleep—where the world,
> Spring, summer, autumn, winter—
> flies through my mind in its
> hardy ascent and its uncompromising descent.
>
> So I just lie like that, while distance and time
> reveal their true attitudes: they never
> heard of me, and never will, or ever need to.

> Of course I wake up finally
> thinking, how wonderful to be who I am,
> made out of earth and water,
> my own thoughts, my own fingerprints—
> all that glorious, temporary stuff. (Oliver 2017, 22)

Following Murdoch's celebration of unselfing, my argument is that part of what explains the therapeutic power of nature is the opportunity for "self-forgetfulness" that it affords. The beauty of the natural world takes us out of ourselves. We become engrossed with something else. Our minds can rest for a moment, and we can take a break from the regular churning of anxious worry.

If anxiety is centrally about the self, it seems to follow that the "self-forgetfulness" Murdoch celebrates will figure prominently in *all* techniques of anxiety relief, not only the particular variety associated with nature. Think of the various activities that we know have a tendency to diminish anxiety. A typical list of such activities might include: vigorous physical exercise, meditation, reading or listening to music, playing or watching sports, painting or drawing, going for a walk, even the consumption of drugs and alcohol. This list of activities is obviously not exhaustive. And different people will have their own idiosyncratic additions. (One activity that tends to make me feel less anxious, for instance, is preparing a meal by following a recipe. I relish the feeling of being bound to a recipe's serialized instructions. And I enjoy the concentration all of it requires: the back-and-forth of reading, gathering ingredients, measuring quantities, and executing steps.) These and other activities allow us to temporarily "lose ourselves," to get some distance from the anxious self. The activities all encourage in their different ways the "self-forgetful pleasure" that is at the core of unselfing.

Consider some popular examples. Millions of people run to help manage their anxiety. Many of us know firsthand that a few miles of running can cut through the tightness of an anxious mind and body. I think this is largely explained by the fact that long-distance running tends to produce a kind of self-forgetful, trance-like mental state.[6] In his memoir, *What I Talk About When I Talk About Running*, Haruki Murakami describes the serene forgetfulness brought about by long-distance running.

> I just run. I run in a void. Or maybe I should put it the other way: I run in order to *acquire* a void. But as you might expect, an occasional thought will slip into this void. People's minds can't be a complete blank. Human beings' emotions are not strong or consistent enough to sustain a vacuum. What I mean is, the kinds of thoughts and ideas that invade my emotions as I run remain subordinate to that void. Lacking content, they are just random thoughts that gather around that central void. The thoughts that occur to me while I'm running are like clouds in the sky. Clouds of all different sizes. They come and they go, while the sky remains the sky as always. The clouds are mere guests in the sky that pass away and vanish, leaving behind the sky. The sky both exists and doesn't exist. It has substance and at the same time doesn't. And we merely accept that vast expanse and drink it in. (Murakami 2008, 17)

For a different example, consider the widely celebrated therapeutic properties of meditation. There is no single practice or technique that the term "meditation" picks out. Still, the power that mediation has to diminish anxiety, which is widely corroborated, is largely explained by its capacity to disrupt the normal flow of anxious, self-centered thinking. To move our thoughts and mental energy elsewhere. To forget temporarily about the anxious self. The forgetfulness of self that Murdoch celebrates can even help explain the anxiety-blunting power of drugs and alcohol. It's difficult to disagree with William James when he said that, "Half the thirst for alcohol that exists in the world exists simply because alcohol acts as a temporary anaesthetic and effacer to all these morbid feelings. . . ." (James 1962, 101).[7] In short and to sum up, wherever there is genuine self-forgetfulness there will be a waning of anxiety, too. And inversely, whenever we catch ourselves feeling more peaceful and less anxious, there's a good chance that having achieved some distance from the self, whether knowingly or inadvertently, played an important role in bringing that happier state about.

Wonder in Nature and the Nature of Wonder

I am visiting Muir Woods, just north of San Francisco, home to dozens of coastal redwood trees (*Sequoia sempervirens*). The oldest known coastal redwood is about 2,500 years old, having taken root in the California soil hundreds of years before Jesus of Nazareth was born. The giant redwoods in Muir Woods are younger than that: the most ancient of them is about 1,200 years old (or so I am told by a friendly woman wearing the beige uniform and wide-brimmed hat of the U.S. National Park Service). She tells me that the particular giant Sequoia I am gazing up at is nearly one thousand years old. And suddenly, a sequence of deep and calming thoughts begin to toddle gently through my mind. This giant tree—this incredible *living organism*—was already many centuries old when Columbus landed in the Bahamas and when Shakespeare wrote *Hamlet*. It has been right here, on this very spot, for about thirty human generations—photosynthesizing, emitting oxygen into the atmosphere, braving the elements, living and thriving. It was standing right here when Genghis Kahn led the Mongol invasions of Eurasia and when Joan of Arc was burned at the stake. It might have already been a fledgling sapling during the Norman conquest of England. I find this sequence of thoughts moving and calming. I feel inexplicably lighter in the midst of these beautiful trees, suffused with a vague yet unmistakable sense of harmony and oneness with the world. Somehow these giant trees are communicating with me, comforting me, whispering in my ear. I'm prompted to think about my own miraculous (yet brief and puny) place in the order of things. About how improbable and wonderful it is that I am here—that *this* consciousness exists at all—having these thoughts and experiences. I think I now understand what Robert Nozick meant when he wrote, in a beautiful passage, that it's possible to feel a sense of "solidarity with all our comrades in existing."

> I see people descended from a long sequence of human and animal forebears in an unnumbered train of chance events, accidental encounters, brutal takings, lucky escapes, sustained efforts, migrations, survivings of wars and disease. An intricate and improbable concatenation of events was needed to yield each of us, an immense history that gives each person the sacredness of a redwood, each child the whimsy of a secret. It is a privilege to be a part of the ongoing realm of existing things and processes. When we see and conceive of ourselves *as* a part of those ongoing processes, we identify with the totality and, in the calmness this brings, feel solidarity with all our comrades in existing. (Nozick 1989, 302)

By all accounts, what I am experiencing in the midst of these incredible trees is a sense of awe or wonder. Awe and wonder make for powerful, poignant experiences. Yet there is something elusive about these emotional states. What are they exactly? How and in response to what do they arise? And what is it about natural and wilderness environments in particular that tend to bring about such strong feelings of lightness and calm—feelings of profundity, of harmony and oneness with the whole world?[8]

In *The Passions of the Soul* (from 1649), René Descartes categorized wonder (*l'admiration*) as the first of his six irreducible, "primitive" passions. The basic building blocks out of which all other emotions are constructed. Wonder is the "first of all the passions" for Descartes because, unlike other emotional states, it does not have a built-in direction of motion. All the other passions strike as either appetitive or aversive—they either attractive or repel—depending on how a person evaluates their objects. But wonder is more basic and primordial than that. It strikes before we know whether an object is "suitable to us or not"—before we form any judgment about whether something might be useful or harmful. Wonder also apparently "has no opposite." The absence of wonder is not itself any emotional state according to Descartes. Such a state is "without passion," an emotional blank (Descartes 1989, 52).

I have doubts that wonder is "primitive" in the sense Descartes claims. Experience tells us that it is a complex, hybrid affective state, containing elements of several other emotions and feelings—surprise, contemplation, reverence, curiosity, imagination, joy, and peace. The complexity and hybridity of wonder seems to be confirmed in Descartes's very own definition: "a sudden surprise of the soul which makes it tend to consider attentively those objects which seem to it rare and extraordinary" (Descartes 1989, 56). If Descartes is right—and here he seems to be on more solid ground—wonder only ever fastens onto "rare" and "extraordinary" things as its objects. It sparks as a response to something striking, out of the ordinary—something "novel and unexpected" (Fuller 2006, 33).

Adam Smith wrote in 1795 that, "We wonder . . . at all the rarer phaenomena of nature, at meteors, comets, eclipses, and singular plants and animals" (Smith 1980, 33). Jesse Prinz tells that the discovery of "extraordinary facts" causes him to experience awe and wonder. "I was enthralled to learn," he writes, "that, when arranged in a line, the neurons in a human brain would stretch the 700 miles from London to Berlin" (Prinz, 2013). Rare and extraordinary things may be the most obvious catalysts for awe and wonder, especially when our experience is intervallic, linked with a specific time, place, or stimulus. But we also sometimes speak of a more general "sense of wonder," understood as a cultivated ability to see and respond to the world in a certain way. Men and women with this cultivated ability do not need to see comets and eclipses for feelings of awe and wonder to arise. They will be able to experience these powerful emotions in the mundane business of everyday living. In a beautiful passage, Zen master Thich Nhat Hanh brings this possibility into focus.

> I like to walk alone on country paths, rice plants and wild grasses on both sides, putting each foot down on the earth in mindfulness, knowing that I walk on the wondrous earth. In such moments, existence is a miraculous and mysterious reality. People usually consider walking on water or in thin air a miracle. But I think the real miracle is not to walk either on water or in thin air, but to walk on earth. Every day we are engaged in a miracle which we don't even recognize: a blue sky, white clouds, green leaves, the black, curious eyes of a child—our own two eyes. All is a miracle. (Hanh 1975, 12)

Hanh feels moved to reflect on "the wondrous earth" not because anything unusual or extraordinary has taken place. Quite the contrary, his sense of wonder arises when he reflects on the "miracle which we don't even recognize" and the feeling that "existence is a miraculous and mysterious reality."[9]

Feelings of awe and wonder are frequently stirred in me by what Oliver Sacks has called "the sense of deep time" that communion with nature sometimes brings about. In *The Island of the Colorblind,* Sacks recounts a visit to Micronesia.

> I find myself walking softly on the rich undergrowth beneath the trees, not wanting to crack a twig, to crush or disturb anything in the least—for there is such a sense of stillness and peace that the wrong sort of movement, even one's very presence, might be felt as an intrusion... The beauty of the forest is extraordinary—but "beauty" is too simple a word, for being here is not just an esthetic experience, but one steeped with mystery, and awe.

And, he continues:

> The sense of deep time brings a deep peace with it, a detachment from the timescale, the urgencies, of daily life. Seeing these volcanic islands and coral atolls, and wandering, above all, through this cycad forest on Rota, has given me an intimate feeling of the antiquity of the earth, and the slow, continuous processes by which different forms of life evolve and come into being. Standing here in the jungle, I feel part of a larger, calmer identity; I feel a profound sense of being at home, a sort of companionship with the earth. (Sacks 1996, 197–198)

There is something profound and therapeutic about the contemplation of long stretches of time. This kind of perspective offers relief from the churning of everyday anxious worry. Matt Haig expresses similar thoughts about the "therapeutic majesty of the night sky" and is worth quoting at length.

> I often wondered, and still wonder, why the sky, especially the night sky, had such an effect. I used to think it was to do with scale. When you look up at the cosmos you can't help but feel miniscule. You feel the smallness of yourself not only in space but also in time. Because, of course, when you stare into space you are staring up at ancient history. You are staring at stars as they *were*, not as they *are*. Light travels ... at 186,000 miles per second... which... means that light from the closest star to Earth (after the sun) took over four years to get here. But some of the stars visible to the naked eye are over 15,000 light years away. Which means that the light reaching your eye began its journey at the end of the Ice Age. Before humans knew how to farm land. ... When looking at the sky, all our 21st-century worries can be placed in their cosmic context. The sky is bigger than emails and deadlines and mortgages and internet trolls. It is bigger than our minds, and their illnesses. It is bigger than names and nations

and dates and clocks. All of our earthly concerns are quite transient when compared to the sky. Through our lives, throughout every chapter of human history, the sky has always been the sky. (Haig 2018, 273–275)

It's difficult to feel the bite of panic and anxiety when immersed in a sense of awe or wonder, contemplating a living organism that is thousands of years old or a constellation of stars many billions of years old. Taking a long view of things helps put anxiety in its proper place, helps shrink and neutralize it. Juxtaposing our own anxious thoughts and feelings with something prehistoric can have a calming effect. What are those worries about my job or health, about that tightness in my chest or those wobbly agoraphobic legs, compared to the seventy-million-year lifespan of the Grand Canyon, a site ancient enough to have been observed by the dinosaurs? What are those surges of panic that give my body an electric zap when measured against the "deep time" of a thousand-year-old California redwood? What's the significance of my nervous stomach or tight muscles viewed from the perspective of geological time? Placed next to something very old (and nothing is older than nature), the anxiety we suffer with can come to look smaller, trivial, innocuous even.

Some of these observations help explain how considering anxiety from an evolutionary perspective can sometimes provide a modicum of comfort to the anxious sufferer. Trying to imagine how anxious feelings may have played a valuable role in the lives of our distant relatives makes them, somehow, less formidable. Consider William James's musings on a "strange symptom" associated with agoraphobia, which was first diagnosed in 1876.

> The patient is seized with palpitation and terror at the site of any open space or broad street which he has to cross alone. He trembles, his knees bend, he may even faint at the idea. Where he has sufficient self-command he sometimes accomplishes the

object by keeping safe under the lee of a vehicle going across, or joining himself to a knot of other people. But usually he slinks round the sides of the square, hugging the houses as closely as he can. This emotion has no utility in a civilized man, but when we notice the chronic agoraphobia of our domestic cats, and see the tenacious way in which many wild animals, especially rodents, cling to cover, and only venture on a dash across the open as a desperate measure ... we are strongly tempted to ask whether such an odd kind of fear in us be not due to the accidental resurrection, through disease, of a sort of instinct which may in some of our ancestors have had ... a useful part to play? (James 2007b, 421–422)[10]

I suffer from a mild form of what James describes. When these uncomfortable agoraphobic feelings strike, as they invariably do when I cross a "broad street" or find myself in a large open space, I sometimes conjure thoughts of my ancient ancestors—wild haired, clad in animal pelts, half naked—inhabiting a world in which human beings were both predator and prey. I imagine them cautiously tiptoeing through a field, nervously aware that being exposed in this way, physically out in the open, makes them vulnerable to attack. I can occasionally even muster a vague sense of gratitude that these distant men and women were responsive to this kind of fear. Being afraid in this way helped keep my prehistoric grandmothers and grandfathers safe. It enabled them to ward off attack, to survive, to muddle through, to have babies, and ultimately to become *my* ancestors.

Reflection on the "deep time" of the natural world may not spark feelings of awe or wonder in everyone. But part of what Murdoch's doctrine of unselfing suggests, even if she does not quite express it in these terms, is that awe and wonder are powerful antidotes to anxiety, and that anxious sufferers will reap the benefit if they can manage to inspire these emotions once in a while. Wonder and awe are essentially non-selfish affective states. They naturally point us away from ourselves. As philosopher Helen De Cruz writes, awe and wonder "make you aware that there is a lot you don't know. You feel small, insignificant and part of something bigger. In this way, awe is a *self-transcendent* emotion because it focuses our attention away from ourselves and toward our environment..." (De Cruz, 2020). In short, awe and wonder are catalysts for unselfing. Instead of having our attention turned inward, toward the anxious self, awe and wonder naturally steer our attention outward, toward a world of independently existing things. Whereas anxiety is a selfish, inward-facing emotion, wonder and awe are unselfish and world-directed.[11]

Murdoch is certainly not alone in celebrating the anxiety-diminishing power of awe and wonder. A similar line of argument can be found in Lisa Feldman Barrett's fascinating book, *How Emotions Are Made: The Secret Life of the Brain*. Barrett argues that "cultivating and experiencing awe"—which she plausibly describes as "the feeling of being in the presence of something vastly greater than yourself"—can help a person achieve some distance from their self, which in turn can help ease unpleasant emotions like anxiety (Barrett 2017, 193). Barrett's argument is that the development of "an awe-inspired concept" can equip a person with the vocabulary to re-describe their unpleasant feelings and thus help them master their emotions in the moment. Her idea involves the "deconstruction" of our mental-psychological experience into physical sensations. Such deconstruction allows for the "recategorization" of anxious thoughts and feelings. "When you feel bad," she says, "treat yourself like you have a virus, rather than assuming that your unpleasant feelings mean something personal" (Barret 2017, 194). Re-categorization lets us put a less-threatening gloss on our anxious thoughts. The goal is to tell ourselves a more compelling story about what these thoughts and feelings are and what they really mean. Here is an important passage from Barrett's book. (As you read it, take note that "body budget" is Barrett's metaphor for how the brain allocates energy resources within the body, and "affective niche" refers to anything that bears on a person's body budget at a given time).

I experienced these benefits firsthand when my family spent a few summer weeks at a beach house in Rhode Island. A symphony of crickets surrounded us each evening, resonating with an intensity I'd never heard before. I hadn't paid much attention to crickets before that, but now they entered my affective niche. I began to look forward to them every evening and to find their song comforting while falling asleep. When we returned from our vacation, I discovered that I could hear crickets through the thick walls of my home if I lay quietly enough. Now, whenever I wake in the middle of a summer night, feeling anxious after a stressful day . . . the crickets help me drift back to sleep. I developed an awe-inspired concept of being enveloped within nature and feeling like a tiny speck. This concept helps me change my body budget whenever I want. I can notice a tiny weed forcing its way through a crack in the sidewalk, proving yet again that nature cannot be tamed by civilization, and employ the same concept to take comfort in my insignificance. You can experience similar awe when hearing ocean waves crash against rocks on the beach, gazing at the stars, walking under storm clouds in the middle of the day, hiking deep into uncharted territory, or taking part in spiritual ceremonies. (Barrett 2017, 194)

The conclusion, Barrett says, is that, "When you categorize something as 'Not About Me,' it exits your affective niche and has less impact on your body budget" (Barrett 2017, 192).

I confess that something feels off about *instrumentalizing* awe and wonder as Barrett apparently seems to be doing. As if these powerful feelings were nothing more than "life hacks" that we might deploy to help us deal with anxiety or stress or burnout. As if feelings of awe and wonder were merely "critical tools" for coping with unpleasant emotions. And yet, viewed from a sufficiently great height, Barrett and Murdoch are clearly in agreement. Both rightly regard the self as the place where anxiety happens. And crucially, they share the view that temporarily escaping or getting some distance from the self, therefore, is fundamental to anxiety relief.

Whereas Barrett's therapeutic recommendation might be something like: *Cultivate an "awe-inspired concept." It will enable you to "re-categorize" unpleasant anxious feelings, to see them as nothing more than constructions,* I imagine that Murdoch might have preferred something simpler and less mechanical, something like: *Finding ways to spark feelings of awe and wonder in your life will help you feel less anxious.* But maybe these are ultimately just differences of temperament and emphasis and not really worth fussing over. If Barrett's formulation strikes me as a little bit cold and unfeeling, perhaps what I have been suggesting here on Murdoch's behalf would inversely strike her as unscientific and mushy. Either way, it should be clear that the imperative at the heart of Murdoch's doctrine of unselfing—*viz.*, "give attention to nature in order to clear our minds of selfish care"—is one that we anxious sufferers would do well to take seriously.

6
Never Let the Future Disturb You

> The first step: Don't be anxious. Nature controls it all. And before long you'll be no one, nowhere—like Hadrian, like Augustus.
>
> The second step: Concentrate on what you have to do. Fix your eyes on it. Remind yourself that your task is to be a good human being; remind yourself what nature demands of people. Then do it, without hesitation, and speak the truth as you see it. But with kindness. With humility. Without hypocrisy.
>
> — Marcus Aurelius, *Meditations*

In the whole history of Western philosophy, it is probably Stoicism that best exemplifies the ideal of philosophy as a form self-help. No other philosophical movement or school (perhaps with the exception of Stoicism's contemporaneous rival, Epicureanism) more explicitly celebrates a conception of philosophy as a kind of *therapy*, a practice designed to help people better manage unnecessary worry and dread, to help them move through their lives with more peace and tranquility. Stoicism is a philosophical "school" in the more conventional sense, to be sure. It offers a wide-ranging view of the world—a *Weltanschauung*, as the Germans say—complete with a metaphysics, epistemology, ethics, moral psychology, physics, cosmology, and logic, along with an account of how these different elements hang together in a coherent whole. But the Stoics were also adamant that philosophy is and should be a comprehensive way of life, not merely a set of true beliefs (Hadot 1995). The value of philosophy on this view is properly explained in terms of its practical upshot: philosophy can help us become more rational, more grounded and level-headed, and ultimately happier and more virtuous. Marcus Aurelius says that, at its best, philosophy is like a "soothing ointment, a warm lotion" (Aurelius 2002, 57). It can help us achieve a kind of emotional mastery (*apatheia*) from which will follow a corresponding inner peace and tranquility (*ataraxia*).

In this chapter, I consider what the Stoic philosophers might teach us about the nature of anxiety, along with some of the strategies and techniques by which they thought it could be eradicated, or at least more effectively managed. I borrow selectively from Stoic thought in what follows, accentuating what is useful for these purposes and passing over what is not. Readers interested in a more comprehensive, scholarly overview of Stoic philosophy are urged to consult different sources.[1] I also more or less ignore the formidable group of philosophers colloquially known as the "old Stoics." That group includes Zeno of Citium himself (Stoicism's official founder, who first established the Stoic school in a public "stoa" or portico near the central marketplace in Athens, about a century after the death of Socrates), but also Cleanthes, the onetime boxer who eventually succeeded Zeno as the second head (or "scholarch") of the Stoic school in Athens. Cleanthes in turn was the teacher of Chrysippus, who is widely regarded as the "greatest and most systematic" of the old Stoic philosophers (Cooper 2012 150). I focus instead on a trio of well-known Stoic philosophers from the Roman Imperial period: Seneca (tutor and advisor to Nero, the infamously extravagant fifth emperor of the Roman Empire who allegedly "fiddled" while Rome burned), Epictetus (the freed slave and Stoic teacher), and Marcus Aurelius (the last emperor of the *Pax Romana*).

A common stereotype is that Stoicism in the Roman era was watered down and philosophically uncreative. As one commentator points out, most of the surviving work from this period consists of "exercises in practical moralizing based on ideas mapped out centuries before." According to a fairly common kind of story, it is precisely this lack of ingenuity which helps account for Stoicism's eventual supplanting by a revived Platonism and a form of Christianity that was increasingly more sophisticated and theoretically aware (Gill 2003, 33). There is probably some truth in this story. It's impossible to deny, for instance, that Roman Stoicism places a strong emphasis on ethics (in the famous Socratic sense of that term), and that the metaphysical and theoretical elements of the Stoic system are correspondingly less well developed. But I'm inclined to regard this as a virtue of the work rather than a shortcoming. Practical wisdom about how human beings can live with more happiness and peace is at the very center of the Stoic philosophical mission, and it's not a blunder that this should be the primary focus for Stoicism in the Roman period.

Even more, insofar as Stoic philosophy is animated by an importantly anti-elitist and democratic spirit—insofar as Stoicism was always intended to be a guide for ethical and happy living which is clear and accessible to any and every rational individual—there are good reasons for thinking that that spirit burns brightest in the Roman Imperial period.[2] As Pierre Hadot explains,

> Since technical and theoretical discussions were matters for specialists, they could be summed up—for the benefit of beginners and students who were making progress—in a small number of formulas which were tightly linked together and which were essentially rules for practical life. In this respect, such philosophies coincided with the "missionary" and "popular" spirit of Socrates. Whereas Platonism and Aristotelianism were reserved for an elite which had the "leisure" to study, carry out research, and contemplate ... Stoicism [and Epicureanism] were addressed to everyone: rich and poor, male and female, free citizens and slaves. Whoever adopted the Epicurean or Stoic way of life and put it into practice would be considered a philosopher,

even if he or she did not develop a philosophical discourse, either written or oral. (Hadot 2002, 107–108)

In short, if what makes philosophies like Stoicism and Epicureanism unique is their "popular and missionary character," there is reason to believe that this character is best exemplified, in the case of Stoicism at least, in the three Roman Imperial thinkers (Seneca, Epictetus, and Marcus Aurelius) whose work will be our primary guide in what follows.

Controlling Fear with Reason

The idea of rationally controlling and mitigating fear is at the very heart of Stoic philosophy. The Stoics all maintained that reason is our best weapon against anxiety. Nothing diminishes anxiety more effectively than logical, clear-headed, non-emotional thinking. Seneca is explicit about the anxiety-diminishing power of reason, writing in his famous *Epistulae Morales ad Lucilia*, "There is no such thing as 'peaceful stillness' except where reason has lulled it to rest." Only reason can deliver genuine peace. Only clear, rational thinking can bring about "true serenity." "Night does not remove our worries," Seneca continues, "it brings them to the surface. All it gives us is a change of anxieties. For even when people are asleep they have dreams as troubled as their days. The only true serenity is the one which represents the free development of a sound mind" (Seneca 1969, 111). The Stoics believed that reason, properly deployed, helps us distinguish the real from the illusory. It helps us partition what is actually dangerous from what is merely unsettling. Most vital of all, it helps us differentiate what is properly within our control from what we are powerless to change.

Epictetus begins his *Discourses* with a discussion "Concerning what is in our power and what is not" (Epictetus 2008, 5). This is the starting point for large swaths of Stoic wisdom. Using reason to control and diminish anxiety begins with sound inventory taking: with a proper accounting of how things actually are, and with an accurate division between what is internal to us and therefore within our control and what is external to us and therefore not. According to Epictetus, people are only ever really anxious about what is external to them (e.g., the involuntary operations of "the body, material possessions, our reputation, status"). We never feel anxiety about what is within us (e.g., "our judgment, our impulse, our desire, aversion and our mental faculties in general") (Epictetus 2008, 221). This is how he puts the point:

> "We are anxious for our bit of a body, for our bit of property, for what Caesar will think, but are not anxious at all for what is within us. Am I anxious about not conceiving a false thought? No, for that depends on myself. Or about indulging an impulse contrary to nature? No, not about this either" (Epictetus 1940, 306).

On Epictetus's view, anxiety is fundamentally irrational and misplaced: it only ever arises when we desire something external to ourselves, something over which we have no control. He has his readers consider the example of a musician who is not nervous at all when playing by himself, but who suddenly becomes anxious at the prospect of having to perform in front of an audience.

> When I see a man in a state of anxiety, I say, What can this man want? If he did not want something which is not in his power, how could he still be anxious? It is for this reason that one who sings to the lyre is not anxious when he is performing by himself, but when he enters the theatre, even if he has a very good voice and plays well: for he not only wants to perform well, but also to win a great name, and that is beyond his control. (Epictetus 1940, 305)

The Stoics all agree that it is fundamentally irrational and pointless to be anxious about what is beyond our control. What purpose is served by worrying about something that we are powerless to change? And yet, so much of our anxiety fixes on precisely these kinds of occurrences. We're anxious about whether people like or admire us. About whether that little twinge of pain in the chest is the beginning of a heart attack. About whether we will be able to fall asleep. About how some farfetched sequence of events will culminate in destitution or death. About what tomorrow will bring. According to the Stoics, such anxieties are the result of a cognitive mistake (albeit an extremely common one). The good news is that we can correct the mistake by learning how to better control ourselves. We can achieve, over time, a kind of emotional self-mastery (what the Greeks called *apatheia*, or "impassivity") that will enable us to stop our feelings from, in Epictetus's words, "carrying us away" (Epictetus 1940, 473).[3]

According to Epictetus, a person's primary desire—the overarching desire that should inform and shape all other desires—is to not be frustrated by forming desires one will not be able to fulfill. We should learn to "despise what is not in our power" (Epictetus 1940, 472). All of a person's other desires should conform to this "meta-desire" about the kinds of desires one should and should not ideally have. If a person finds themselves forming desires the fulfillment of which lie outside their own control, they should try to extirpate them. If they are successful in extirpating those unworthy desires, such a person will no longer experience anxiety about whether or not they get what they want. They will be completely insulated from the pain of unfulfilled desire. In fact, Epictetus thinks that if a person cannot be made upset by anything not under their control, they will then become "invincible"—impervious to anxious worry. If you refuse to enter contests "where victory is not in your power," you are guaranteed never to lose a contest (Epictetus 1940, 257; 472).

Montaigne once wrote that, for Epictetus, "Man has nothing properly his own except his opinions" (Montaigne 2003, 544). There is nothing "intrinsically evil in the world" (Epictetus 1940,

475). Brute facts are only brute facts, evaluatively neutral taken on their own. Nothing external to us is good or bad as such. Everything depends on the view we take of them. As Seneca says, "Everything hangs on one's thinking."

> Provided that one's thinking has not been adding anything to it, pain is a trivial sort of thing. If by contrast you start giving yourself encouragement, saying to yourself, "it's nothing—or nothing much, anyway—let's stick it out, it'll be over presently," then in thinking it a trivial matter you will be ensuring that it actually is.... A man is as unhappy as he has convinced himself he is. (Seneca 1969, 134)

"What disturbs men's minds is not events but their judgments on events," writes Epictetus in the *Enchiridion*, his "handbook" or "manual" of Stoic ethical advice. "Remember that foul words or blows in themselves are no outrage, but your judgment that they are so. So when any one makes you angry, know that it is your own thought that has angered you" (Epictetus 1940, 469; 472). "External things are not the problem," says Marcus Aurelius, echoing both Seneca and Epictetus. "It's your assessment of them. Which you can erase right now."

> If the problem is something in your own character, who's stopping you from setting your mind straight? And if it's that you're not doing something you think you should be, why not just do it?—But there are insuperable obstacles. Then it's not a problem. The cause of your inaction lies outside you.... Choose not to be harmed—and you won't feel harmed. Don't feel harmed—and you haven't been. (Aurelius 2002, 110; 39)

The corresponding thought is that if we could exercise what the Greeks call *prohairesis*—the faculty that endows us with the power to choose, to exert our will, the power to rationally oversee our raw emotional responses—that would change how we feel about the object of our anxiety. How the world just happens to be is not something over which we exercise any control, and it's pointless therefore to feel any anxiety about it. What is rightly within our power is what *we* choose to do and refrain from doing, how *we* decide emotionally to respond. Epictetus puts the point like this:

> Ask not that events should happen as you will, but let your will be that events should happen as they do, and you shall have peace. Sickness is a hindrance to the body, but not to the will, unless the will consent. . . . Say this to yourself at each event that happens, for you shall find that though it hinders something else it will not hinder you. (Epictetus 1940, 470)

The Stoics all agree that this kind of emotional partitioning is something we can become more skilled at over time. We can develop a rational mastery over our will first by distinguishing between those things that are in our power (*prohairetic* things) and those things that are not in our power (*aprohairetic* things) and then by training ourselves to focus on the former while cultivating a peaceful indifference to the latter. *Don't worry about how the world just happens to be. Accept that things are as they are.* "Welcome with affection what is sent by fate" (Aurelius 2002, 34). *Focus instead only on what is within you, on what you can control.*

In short, if anxiety only ever arises because we desire something which is not under our power, it follows that the best way to obviate anxiety would be to learn how to avoid desiring anything that others control. The therapeutic conclusion, as Epictetus writes, is this: "If . . . nothing beyond our will's control is either good or evil, and everything within our will's control depends entirely on ourselves, so that no one can take any such thing away from us or win it for us against our will, what room is left for anxiety?" (Epictetus 1940, 306)

But is anxiety really always controllable through the careful exercise of reason? If firsthand experience is any guide, anxiety is sometimes just dumbly there, neither against nor by permission of anyone's will or choice. The Stoics would have agreed that primal flashes of panic and anxiety (what Seneca would have counted among the "involuntary motions of the soul" and what earlier Stoics called "proto-emotions" or *propatheiai*) are not themselves under anyone's control (Knuuttila 2004, 64). But their guidance concerns how a person should respond to the emotions that visit them, not about whether the visitation of the emotions should have occurred in the first place. Epictetus for instance grants that the arrival of certain feelings is not under anyone's control. They involuntarily "strike a person's mind" and "impose themselves" seemingly with a "will of their own."

> Impressions . . . , striking a person's mind as soon as he perceives something within range of his senses, are not voluntary or subject to his will, they impose themselves on people's attention almost with a will of their own. But the act of assent . . . which endorses these impressions *is* voluntary and a function of the human will. Consequently, when a frightening noise comes from heaven or in consequence of some accident, if an abrupt alarm threatens danger, or if anything else of the kind happens, the mind even of a wise man is inevitably shaken a little, blanches and recoils—not from any preconceived idea that something bad is about to happen, but because certain irrational reflexes forestall the action of the rational mind. (Epictetus 2008, 212)

The brute fearful stimulus is not within our control. We are visited by "frightening mental images" through no fault or choice of our own. What is within our control—and this is the key Stoic insight—is whether to "spurn and reject" these frightening thoughts. The question is whether we let the thoughts have power over us. Whether we feed and sustain them by taking them seriously, by giving them authority and influence (Epictetus 2008, 212). Don't be "overwhelmed by what you imagine," writes Marcus

Aurelius (Aurelius 2002, 64). *There is no reason to accept as true the first thought or impression that pops uninvited into one's head. Just because a thought or impression occurs doesn't mean that we must take it seriously.* We should not let impressions "knock us off our feet" without rationally scrutinizing them first. Before giving credence to a thought that flashes before our mind we should say to it: "Hold on a moment; let me see who you are and what you represent. Let me put you to the test" (Epictetus 2008, 123). After all, asks Epictetus, why should you "trust your mind to the chance comer...?" (Epictetus 1940, 475).

There is obviously a lot of important wisdom in these Stoic reflections. But I think the contrast between what is internal to us and what is external—between what is within our control and what not—might sometimes be drawn too sharply. At least from the point of view of the experience of anxiety, these might be more porous distinctions than the Stoics seemed to allow. From the perspective of what it feels like on the inside for the anxious sufferer, anxiety is not always responsive to a clear partitioning between mind and world—between private affective states, on the one hand, and how things are factually in the world, on the other. It frequently involves a blending together, sometimes indecipherably, of that which "depends on myself" and that which "depends on others."

Consider Richard Sorabji's observation that the "ups and downs of life" are Stoic therapy's main area of competence. Stoic cognitive techniques can help a person cope more effectively with concrete situations: worries about health, the pressures of work and travel, stress in relationships, road rage, and so on. But this kind of therapy will be less successful at treating "moods which are not directed to a particular situation, but which, like depression, fasten themselves on whatever situation comes to hand" (Sorabji 2000, 2). Similarly, when anxiety is unspecific and diffuse rather than object-directed, Stoic cognitive therapies will be less effective. This gives us reason to think that the distinction that the Stoics draw between the *prohairetic* and the *aprohairetic* is often blurrier than they took it to be. When anxiety has propositional content—when it is *about* something identifiable and specific—the Stoic distinction between internal and external, between what we can control and what we cannot, will be sharper. But when anxiety is just there—nebulous, diffuse, unspecific, "a shapeless unease"—the Stoic distinction holds up less well (Harvey 2020).

A charitable reply is that the Stoics were not really attempting to systematically catalog all the different modalities of anxious suffering. More centrally, they were offering a kind of practical therapy that sometimes helps people feel better. They were urging something like: *when you feel anxious, try to separate all of those things that you can do, which are in your control, and those things you cannot, which are out of your control. Performing this little "spiritual exercise" will help you better manage anxious worry. Like other cognitive-therapeutic techniques, it will allow you to more clearly locate the source of your anxiety and to respond to it in a more rational and clearheaded way. This can help you feel better* (Hadot 1995). Probably not every single time and no matter what. No therapy is one hundred percent effective. But frequently and significantly enough to make a noticeable difference in our lives. Once again, Sorabji sums it up eloquently and is worth quoting at length:

> Stoicism can be very helpful in dealing with counter-productive emotion. But it is not a matter of gritting your teeth. It is about seeing things differently, so that you do not need to grit your teeth. This may require you to say things to yourself. It involves a rather intellectual approach to coping with emotions, and it contrasts, for example, with such non-intellectual techniques as diet, gymnastics, and music, not to mention breathing, posture, the reciting of mantras, or the taking of drugs.... [Stoic cognitive therapy] ... involves a habit of mind of questioning appearances by saying things to yourself, and this habit can be exercised all the time in daily life, for the many little ups and downs that occur. You can apply it to yourself, and you need no therapist

other than yourself, once you have taken in the system. I believe that practicing Stoic thoughts will show how often they are effective even though they will not always be so. This belief is an encouraging one. If we believed, erroneously, that the amygdala's reactions could not be countered by taking thought, this despairing attitude would become self-fulfilling by leading us not to make the effort. (Sorabji 2000, 1; 165)

Past, Present, and Future

When Marcus Aurelius enjoined his readers to never be "disturbed" by the future, to live always in the present moment, to calmly welcome whatever fate sends one's way, he was giving voice to an important set of Stoic ideas. The Stoics recognized that anxiety is a fundamentally forward-looking emotion, always fastened on the future. Seneca says that anxiety arises when we project our thoughts "far ahead of us instead of adapting ourselves to the present." Anxiety is caused by "looking into the future," Seneca writes. Whereas "Wild animals run from the dangers they actually see, and once they have escaped them worry no more. We . . . are tormented alike by what is past and what is to come" (Seneca 1969, 38).

The Stoics had plenty to say about the attitude we should ideally adopt toward the future. That attitude has two central elements. On the one hand, it requires that we refrain from worrying about the future, that we try to "live immediately," as Seneca puts it. The recommendation is to be calm and present-minded, focused on the task at hand. Not to let our minds get carried away. "For the only safe harbour in this life's tossing, troubled sea is to refuse to be bothered about what the future will bring and to stand ready and confident, squaring the breast to take without skulking or flinching whatever fortune hurls at us" (Seneca 1969, 190). On the other hand, the Stoics also suggest that meditation on the future in a more abstract and general way can serve as a reminder of the impermanence of things, of the "change and flux" which "constantly remake the world" (Aurelius 2002, 71). This kind of meditation can help a person achieve what the Stoics called *ataraxia* (a state of tranquility and inner peace). It can help them appreciate that how things are in the present moment is no indication of how they will be at another time in the future. Everything changes. Nothing is permanent. The sun is new each day. The "world is continually renewed" (Aurelius 2002, 89). The Stoic imperative, then, is to *live in the moment, but simultaneously to recognize that the moment is ephemeral. To be present-minded yet also cognizant that everything is in motion and subject to change. To never be disturbed by the future, rather to be comforted by the fundamental transience of things.*

The Stoics were constantly emphasizing the importance of the present moment. Seneca rhetorically asks: "What's the good of dragging up sufferings which are over, of being unhappy now just because you were then?" (Seneca 1969, 134–135). As it is with sufferings "which are over," so is it with sufferings which are yet to come. Seneca is not denying that bad things sometimes happen. Rather, he is questioning the value of worrying about such things in advance. It's foolish, he says, to "make yourself wretched now just because you are going to be wretched some time in the future" (Seneca 1997, 87). We should neither feel bad about the past nor worried about the future. "The greatest obstacle to living is expectancy," Seneca writes, "which hangs upon tomorrow and loses today. You are arranging what lies in Fortune's control, and abandoning what lies in yours. What are you looking at? To what goal are you striving? The whole future lies in uncertainty: live immediately" (Seneca 1997, 68). As Marcus Aurelius puts the same point, "remind yourself that past and future have no power over you. Only the present—and even that can be minimized" (Aurelius 2002, 110; 32; 108).

The past is irretrievably gone. The future is abstract and illusive. The present moment is all there is. In a passage aimed at taking the sting out of the fear of death, Marcus Aurelius puts it like this:

> Even if you're going to live three thousand more years, or ten times that, remember: you cannot lose another life than the one you're living now, or live another one than the one you're losing. The longest amounts to the same as the shortest. The present is the same for everyone; its loss is the same for everyone; and it should be clear that a brief instant is all that is lost. For you can't lose either the past or the future; how could you lose what you don't have? . . . the longest-lived and those who will die soonest lose the same thing. The present is all that they can give up, since that is all you have, and what you do not have, you cannot lose. (Aurelius 2002, 21–22)

Why is it a mistake to let the future disturb us? Because there really is no such thing as "the future." There is only the present moment, which Marcus Aurelius describes as a "gift." "Each of us lives only now, this brief instant. The rest has been lived already, or is impossible to see" (Aurelius 2002, 32). The future is always just out of reach, just around the corner. There is only an ever-flowing stream of immediately vanishing present moments. Time is like a river, Marcus Aurelius says, "a violent current of events, glimpsed once and already carried past us, and another follows and is gone" (Aurelius 2002, 46). It is always and continuously the present moment. And each moment is full and complete in its own right.

What we call the future is a nebulous blob. In reality, we live out our lives in a stream of moments. Consider these lines from Phillip Larkin's short poem "Days":

> What are days for?
> Days are where we live.

> They come, they wake us
> Time and time over.
> They are to be happy in:
> Where can we live but days? (Larkin 2003, 98)

Larkin's poem reminds us that the future never springs upon us all at once. Tomorrow will be a new day. We'll wake up and try to accomplish various things, big and small, some more urgent than others. If the past is a reliable guide, it's likely that we will be partially successful, achieving some of the things we attempt and failing to achieve others. Some days will be better than others in this regard. *And so it goes. The world turns. Another day will follow this one. Life goes on. One day at a time.* The point is that the future will be less overwhelming if it can be trimmed down into manageable chunks. "Don't let your imagination be crushed by life as a whole," Marcus Aurelius counsels his readers. "Don't try to picture everything bad that could possibly happen. Stick with the situation at hand" (Aurelius 2002, 108). The implication is that there is no terrifying monster called "the future" that we must confront. Only our various tasks and projects, big and small, one thing at a time. And once we see that there is nothing more to "the future" than the next set of things to do, we are in a position to be reassured, as the Stoics are constantly reassuring us, about how tough and resilient we are. About how much we have already handled and how far we've already come. "Consider all that you've gone through, all that you've survived" (Aurelius 2002, 63). Just as we were able to use our intelligence and grit to navigate through past episodes of fear and anxiety, so, too, will we navigate future episodes. Just as we were able to muddle through in the past, we will be able to cope with what comes next. "When and if [the future comes], you'll have the same resources to draw on" (Aurelius 2002, 86).

The Stoics spent a lot of time trying to neutralize the anxiety-generating power of the future, trying to make the future look less ominous and daunting. But they also frequently invoked the vastness and uncertainty of the future as a source of peace and tranquility. The universe is perpetually in a state of flux. "Constant alteration." Nothing is permanent. *Panta rhei.* Everything flows. "None of us have much time," Marcus Aurelius writes. "And yet you act as if things were eternal—the way you fear and long for them" (Aurelius 2002, 102; 142).

> Keep in mind how fast things pass by and are gone—those that are now, and those to come. Existence flows past us like a river; the "what" is in constant flux, the "why" has a thousand variations. Nothing is stable, not even what's right here. The infinity of past and future gapes before us—a chasm whose depths we cannot see. (Aurelius 2002, 61)

And again:

> Frightened of change? But what can exist without it? What's closer to nature's heart? Can you take a hot bath and leave the firewood as it was? Eat food without transforming it? Can any vital process take place without something being changed? Can't you see? It's just the same with you—and just as vital to nature. (Aurelius 2002, 88)

The Stoics believed that there was tranquility and comfort to be had in this way of thinking. There's something calming about taking the long, cosmic view of things, about reflecting on our puny lives from the point of view of an ever-fluctuating universe. What appears burning and exigent at one moment will come to look trivial and small at another moment. In a beautiful passage from her first novel, *Under the Net*, Iris Murdoch expresses the idea like this:

> Events stream past us like these crowds and the face of each is seen only for a minute. What is urgent is not urgent for ever but

only ephemerally. All work and love, the search for wealth and fame, the search for truth, life itself, are made up of moments which pass and become nothing. Yet through this shaft of nothings we drive onward with that miraculous vitality that creates our precarious habitations in the past and the future. So we live; a spirit that broods and hovers over the continual death of time, the lost meaning, the unrecaptured moment, the unremembered face, until the final chop that ends all our moments and plunges that spirit back into the void from which it came. (Murdoch 2002, 275)

If all our lives are "made up of moments which pass and become nothing," it follows that "what is urgent is not urgent forever but only ephemerally." The Stoics maintained that a proper appreciation for the deep impermanence of things brings about a sense of acceptance and tranquility. It's a mistake to "feel self-importance or distress. Or any indignation, either. As if the things that irritate us lasted" (Aurelius 2002, 61). *Everything is in flux. Change is constant. This too shall pass.*[4]

An appreciation for the impermanence of things also brings the possibility of improvement and healing into sharper focus. Sometimes, anxiety and psychic suffering just go away, as suddenly and mysteriously as they arrived in the first place. If change is a constant, after all, it's always possible that things may change for the better. Here is Samantha Harvey, writing about the end of a brutal bout of insomnia, sounding very much like Marcus Aurelius from the *Meditations*. "This is the cure of insomnia: no things are fixed. Everything passes, this too. One day, when you're done with it, it will lose its footing and fall away, and you'll drop each night into sleep without knowing how you once found it impossible" (Harvey 2020, 175). This is one hopeful implication of the Stoic worldview and its bearing on psychic suffering: The present moment is fleeting. It doesn't represent the deep, unalterable truth about who we are, about how things must be for us. How things feel for us in this moment is not indicative of how they will feel for us at a later moment. As Seneca says, "Many of the things that have caused terror during the night ... [have] been turned into matters of laughter with the coming of daylight" (Seneca 1969, 191). Nothing is permanent. Sometimes our mental health just improves, on its own, for no good or even discernable reason. Brains change. Old cognitive and behavioral habits are loosened, while fresh patterns of thought gradually, imperceptibly replace old ones. In short, one day we just feel better, and we look back with disbelief at how it ever could have been so bad before. As Seneca reminds us, quoting Virgil from the *Aeneid*, there is comfort to be had in taking the long view of things: "There may be pleasure in the memory / Of even these events one day" (Seneca 1969, 135).

Stoicism and Modern-Day Psychotherapy

A lot of Stoic wisdom about anxiety has by now seeped into the popular culture. This is confirmed by all the commonsense aphorisms and bits of folk wisdom that extol quintessentially Stoic ideas. *Worrying about it won't help. Life is short. Nothing lasts forever. Let go of what you can't control. Live in the moment. This too shall pass.* Yet Stoic wisdom about anxiety also figures prominently in various forms of psychotherapy, especially cognitive behavioral therapy (CBT) and acceptance-commitment therapy (ACT).[5] While the Stoic elements in these and other forms of therapy are unmistakeable, it would be a mistake to assume that there is a single form of modern therapy that best or most closely corresponds with Stoicism. As we'll see, it's better to think of Stoicism as offering the anxious sufferer a variegated toolbox of different strategies and techniques. The tools are of multiple kinds, and, like all tools, there is no general or necessary hierarchy among them. Some tools are more effective than others for the accomplishment of particular tasks, in particular contexts, for particular people.

The main issue on which practitioners of CBT and ACT are usually thought to diverge—an issue on which the Stoics themselves were sometimes divided—is about whether *confrontation* or *acceptance* is the therapeutically optimal response to anxiety. Is it better to rationally *confront* anxious worry or merely to *accept* that one is having certain thoughts and experiences? If ACT is usually thought to involve *accepting* anxious thoughts, trying simply to observe them as if from a safe distance, CBT is usually understood to recommend more or less the opposite: fighting back, going toward and interrogating false beliefs, "putting the lie to them," as psychiatrist David Burns (2006) has it. Describing the contrast between CBT and ACT in terms of the distinction between *confrontation* and *acceptance* is rough and stylized.[6] I carve things up in this way only to fix ideas and to help us appreciate how both of these strategies have analogues in Stoic philosophy.

On the one hand, the Stoics frequently recommended going toward and fighting against anxious fear. The goal, as we have seen, is to use reason to refute anxiety. As Seneca says, we must "look hard at our fears, and it will soon be obvious how short-lived, uncertain and reassuring they are" (Seneca 1997, 101). This kind of strategy is particularly prominent in Epictetus, who invites his readers to scrutinize the "impressions" that show up uninvited into their minds. As if he were the author of a modern-day CBT workbook extolling the importance of overcoming "negative self-talk," Epictetus instructs his readers literally to talk back to anxious thoughts. We are urged to say: "An impression is all you are" and then to "test and assess" the impression by asking whether its object is something under our control or not. If not, we are then urged to say, "Then it's none of my concern" (Epictetus 2008, 221–222).

On the other hand, the Stoics sometimes appear more closely aligned with practitioners of ACT than CBT. On such occasions, they appear more committed to a strategy of acceptance rather than confrontation. Mindfulness is accentuated over vigilance. Rather than standing on-guard against our anxiety, armed with logic and reason, ready to engage in battle, we simply accept that we are having certain thoughts and experiences. One exercise which has become a staple of ACT—"leaves on a stream"—brings the core idea into focus. Psychologist Steven Hayes explains it this way:

> Imagine that you are watching a quietly flowing brook with large leaves on it floating by. Each thought that comes into your mind, place it on a leaf and watch it float downstream. If it reappears, that is fine—just put the second version on a leaf too. The goal is to stay by the stream, watching your thoughts. If you discover you've stopped doing the exercise and your mind has gone elsewhere, which is common, try to catch what led your mind astray. Almost inevitably, what happened was cognitive fusion with a thought. Something popped into your head and instead of placing it on the leaf you started engaging with its content, and it triggered your automatic thought processes. After noting how the "fusion trigger" worked, get right back to watching the brook and begin again (Hayes 2019, 156).

As Hayes elaborates, the goal is to watch our thoughts "from a distance with a sense of open curiosity." We are attempting to "direct attention in an intentional way . . . noticing what is present here and now, inside us and out" (Hayes 2019, 23). Such present-mindedness and acceptance is at the very heart of ACT. We're not trying to parse our thoughts as true or false, worthy or unworthy, appropriate or inappropriate. We're not interested in rendering a judgment about our thoughts. We're simply observing them, as if from a third-person point of view. Present-minded. At peace with the knowledge that these are just mental events—merely thoughts—and that they pose no danger to us.

Whatever their other differences, there is broad agreement among proponents of CBT and ACT about the therapeutic importance of *exposure*. And here, too, there are important affinities with Stoicism. Exposure therapy is premised on an extremely simple and intuitive idea: A person grows accustomed to something frightening by facing or exposing themselves to it. This can happen in vivo or in the imagination; incrementally, step-by-step, or more drastically all at once. Here is John Locke, writing in 1693 about the anxiety-reducing benefits of exposure therapy.

> If your child shrieks and runs away at the sight of a frog, let another catch it and lay it down at a good distance from him; at first accustom him to look upon it; when he can do that, to come nearer to it and see it leap without emotion; then to touch it lightly, when it is held fast in another's hand; and so on, until he can come to handle it. (Locke 1996, 88)

Just as a horror movie tends to become less frightening with each viewing, just as certain phobias can be overcome by gradual exposure to the feared stimuli, the bite of anxiety can be diminished by continually confronting and attending to it. A monster becomes less forbidding if it can be met head-on, if it can be looked at squarely in the face. Exposure dulls the fear.

When my anxiety was at its ugliest, crossing the street felt like an impossible undertaking. I have a vivid recollection of being frozen on the curb one day, head spinning, body buzzing with agoraphobic fear, literally unable to put one foot in front of the other, completely dumfounded that something like this was actually happening. I don't have a clear memory about how I got home that particular day, but for weeks afterward I carefully planned my walking routes, avoiding any larger streets I might have to cross. This is textbook PDA (or "panic disorder with agoraphobia"). In his magisterial work on anxiety disorders, David Barlow describes PDA as "panic disorder as anxiety focussed on somatic sensations associated with panic attacks, and agoraphobia as a strategy for coping with panic attacks by avoiding unsafe situations where attacks might occur" (Barlow 2004, 328).[7] Many of us are intimately acquainted with this sequence of thinking: A person has a panic attack, say, while riding in an elevator. Riding in an elevator becomes the object of intense fear. The person becomes convinced that riding in an elevator will trigger another attack, which leads to a phobic avoidance of elevators. (This need not happen immediately or all at once. Phobic avoidance can take root more slowly and progressively.) The person may feel privately ashamed about their inability to do this mundane thing. They may think to themselves: *What kind of a person can't ride in an elevator? What's wrong with me?* But the behavioral grooves of avoidance are already in place and growing deeper all the time.

The doctor I was seeing at the time gave some extremely helpful advice, which was paradigmatically about exposure. He urged me to really push myself to cross the street, maybe a smaller, narrower street at first. Just cross in a square, from north to south, south to west, west to north, and north to east. Just keep doing it, he said, until (I remember his words) "it becomes boring." Crossing the street became my main project. On the first day I found a small intersection in a quiet, residential area, and just crossed the street, in a square, for about an hour. (I feel a little twinge of anxiety now as I wonder whether anyone was watching me that day, thinking to themselves: *Who is this crazy man who keeps crossing the street at this little intersection? Why on earth is he doing that?*) The next day I found a broader street, with more traffic. And then a broader, more-traffic-filled one the day after. I spent several hours one day just crossing the street at a busy intersection. The whole episode was extremely unpleasant. I remember the rickety wobble of my agoraphobic legs and the electric jolts of panic firing through my body. But it became incrementally less difficult, and eventually, just as my doctor had suggested, it became "boring." That's the essence of exposure therapy.[8]

The reverse side of the same coin, of course, is that avoidance is an inefficient and possibly dangerous way to respond to anxiety. Just as anxious fear is weakened by exposure, so is it inversely strengthened and reinforced by avoidance. Avoidance behavior can feel like a rational response to anxiety in the moment: *If you burn your hand whenever you touch a hot stove, it's a good piece of advice which says don't touch hot stoves.* So too with the vicious cycle of anxiety. If doing certain things or going certain places makes you anxious, then you should avoid them. Exposure demands courage, while avoidance is the path more easily taken, at least in the short run. The trouble is that, despite whatever temporary relief it affords, avoidance does not ultimately help alleviate anxiety. On the contrary, as the habitual ruts of avoidance grow deeper, the corresponding anxiety tends to become bigger and more formidable.

It's interesting that both exposure and avoidance have their analogues in Stoic thought. One prominent variety of cognitive exposure therapy in the Stoic tradition is the *premeditatio malorum* (roughly translated, "the premeditation of evils"). The Stoics believed that anxiety can be reduced by engaging in a sort of negative visualization, by deliberately bringing into mind the objects of one's anxiety. In Seneca's words, "If an evil has been pondered beforehand, the blow is gentle when it comes" (Seneca 2016, 212). Here is a "negative visualization" that Marcus Aurelius recommends for early in the morning:

> When you wake up in the morning, tell yourself: The people I deal with today will be meddling, ungrateful, arrogant, dishonest, jealous, and surly. They are like this because they can't tell good from evil. But I have seen the beauty of good, and the ugliness of evil, and have recognized that the wrongdoer has a nature related to my own—not of the same blood or birth, but the same mind, and possessing a share of the divine. And so none of them can hurt me. No one can implicate me in ugliness. Nor can I feel angry at my relative, or hate him. We were born to work together like feet, hands, and eyes, like the two rows of teeth, upper and lower. To obstruct each other is unnatural. To feel anger at someone, to turn your back on him: these are obstructions. (Aurelius 2002, 17)

The *premeditatio malorum* is equivalent to what practitioners of CBT sometimes call "decatastrophization" or "cognitive flooding." As Seneca writes, in words that could have easily been plucked from a modern-day CBT self-help manual, "If you want to be rid of all anxiety, suppose that anything you are afraid of happening is going to happen in any case, then mentally calculate all the evil involved in it and appraise your own fear: you will undoubtedly come to realize that what you fear is either not great or not long-lasting" (Seneca 1997, 87). And again:

> Everyone faces up more bravely to a thing for which he has long prepared himself, sufferings, even, being withstood if they have been trained for in advance. Those who are unprepared, on the other hand, are panic-stricken by the most insignificant happenings. We must see to it that nothing takes us by surprise. And since it is invariably unfamiliarity that makes a thing more formidable than it really is, this habit of continual reflection will ensure that no form of adversity finds you a complete beginner. (Seneca 1969, 198)

Despite their emphasis on attention (*prosochê*) and a continuously vigilant presence of mind—despite the emotional discipline they always preached—the Stoics also recognized that learning to cope with anxiety should involve more than constantly confronting fear (Hadot 1995, 84).While the Stoics were champions for the therapeutic value of exposure, they also saw the benefit in a modicum of healthy diversion and escapism, even in the short-term comfort that distraction and avoidance can sometimes provide. Not all the time, certainly, but now and again. This line of argument is prominent in Seneca, who recommends all of the diversions and distractions that typically give respite to an anxious mind. "The mind should not be kept continuously at the same pitch of concentration, but given amusing diversions," he says (Seneca 1997, 56). Sometimes the best way to combat "the turmoil of a restless mind" is to take a nap, go for a walk, or to enjoy a glass of wine (Seneca 1997, 34). In his famous dialogue, "On Tranquility of Mind," Seneca stresses the benefits of good sleep, noting that one's mind will always "rise better and keener after a rest." He commends going for walks in nature "so that the mind can be strengthened and invigorated by a clear sky and plenty of fresh air." He similarly recommends the excitement of traveling to new places, the delights of "fond and loyal friendship," and the value of virtuous participation in civic and political life. Seneca is also explicit about the benefits of moderate wine drinking. "There is a healthy moderation in wine," he insists. At one point, he even acclaims the value of drunkenness: "occasionally we should even come to the point of intoxication, sinking into drink but not being totally flooded by it; for it does wash away cares, and stirs the mind to its depths, and heals sorrow" (Seneca 1997, 57–58). Finally, there are the more general imperatives to be realistic about one's goals, to abandon "those things which are impossible or difficult to attain," and also to "make ourselves flexible, so that we do not pin our hopes too much on our set plans." Obstinacy is "hostile to tranquility" and brings "wretchedness and anxiety." Much better to cultivate a light and easygoing attitude, to loosen up and roll with the punches (Seneca 1997, 46; 52).

In general, Seneca's encouragement involves keeping oneself busy "with pursuits of the right nature" (Seneca 1969, 111). But one implication of this view is that a person's anxiety will be diminished if they are not always absorbed with the goal of diminishing their anxiety. Anxiety will be managed more effectively if we can make space in our lives for activities that are not centrally concerned with the management of anxiety. It follows that what Seneca calls tranquility (what the Greeks called *euthymia*) is at least to some extent a "self-effacing" good. The kind of good which is obtained, not by pursuing it directly, but circuitously, as a consequence of pursuing something else (Parfit 1984). Some good things in life are only ever acquired indirectly, by deliberately taking aim at something different. Happiness might be a good of this kind, as Plato and Aristotle both famously theorized. Similarly, we typically achieve inner peace not by taking direct aim at inner peace itself (whatever that might come to, exactly). Rather, we turn our attention to other valuable activities, we cultivate other habits, we pursue other virtues, and inner peace will or may come as the welcome byproduct. If inner peace is to some degree self-effacing, it follows that effective therapy for anxiety will involve the vital principle that not everything is therapy for anxiety. The best treatment for anxiety, in short, will be mindful of its own limits.

If all of this is correct, it follows that a certain impatient, grouchy kind of thought is sometimes justified. *This endless dwelling on anxiety is pointless and exhausting. Everyone feels anxious sometimes. It's completely normal. Take a deep breath and get on with things. Stop obsessing about every tiny detail and get on with the business of living your life.* There is a nugget of truth in this kind of impatient, grouchy thought, which is not to deny that it can be taken too far. Taken too far, the thought suggests a dismissiveness about the reality of mental health struggle. At its extreme, it can even culminate in outright denial about the fact that, sometimes, people are in genuine distress and in need of help.

A more plausible version of this grouchy complaint is simply that there is much too much talking and obsessing about anxiety in our culture. It's everywhere we look. Health food stores selling "mood boosting" vitamins and dietary supplements. The weighted blankets and meditation apps. Essential oils and online Mindfulness training seminars. Adult coloring books, salt lamps, stress-relief toys, emotional support animals. An endless stream of self-help books. A million things to help us fall and stay asleep: melatonin pills, therapeutic pillows, soothing teas infused with valerian, white noise machines, CBD oil. Everywhere we look there are products and services promoted under the ambit of "wellness" and "self-care". Anxiety is big business. And business—no one can deny it—is booming.[9]

It's easy to be skeptical of this vast anti-anxiety infrastructure. Still, I believe that a popular culture in which mental health struggle is attended to too much is probably better, all things considered, than one in which it is attended to too little. Excess is probably better than deficiency in this area. Either way, if the Stoics were right that inner peace and mental tranquility are at least to some degree self-effacing goods—that they are achieved, in part, by taking aim at other things—it follows that excessiveness is a genuine possibility.

We have seen that the Stoic approach to the management of anxiety is an amalgam of different strategies and therapies. It features elements of cognitive therapy, exposure, acceptance and mindfulness, and even a drop of healthy escapism and avoidance. Sometimes, the Stoics encourage their followers to battle against unpleasant, anxious thoughts. To scrutinize and rationally dismantle them. On other occasions, they recommend present-mindedness and acceptance, urging followers to calmly watch their anxious thoughts, without judgment, as if from the outside and from a safe distance. The Stoics frequently encourage us to be brave, but they also concede that metaphorically running for cover has its proper time and place.

In the end, the Stoics probably would have denied that there is always a best or fundamental therapy for anxiety. No single approach can or should be allowed to command the field. Nor is there a general formula or fixed set of principles to which we can turn. In the end, the most promising therapeutic path involves experimentation and testing. We figure out how best to proceed, always tentatively and imperfectly, through a process of trial and error—experimenting with one kind of therapy, then giving another one a whirl, and so on. We slowly accumulate knowledge about the comparative effectiveness of this or that strategy. About what is more or less likely to work for us in different circumstances. And we gradually piece together for ourselves a toolbox of more and less effective strategies, fully cognizant of the fact that some of them will work differently, and with different degrees of success, in different contexts. There are no silver bullets or magical cures. Only a set of tools that we can slowly, more carefully hone over time.

Notes

Introduction

1. Kieran Setiya recollects that it was both "a sense of wonder, and an undertow of worry" that ultimately made him a philosophical person. "I remember staring at the corrugated trunks of trees in the playground at recess," he writes, "stunned by the fact that there was anything at all. The thought that there might not have been induced a lurch of anxiety I now recognize as Jean-Paul Sartre's 'nausea': alarm at the brute facticity of things, their sheer contingency, their blank resistance to reason.... Wonder and worry, anxiety and awe: these feelings are what led me to philosophy" (Setiya 2022, 147–148).
2. According to the most recent 5th edition of the *Diagnostic and Statistical Manual of Mental Disorders*, there are eleven different diagnoses that fall within anxiety's larger ambit.
3. On the epistemic and moral benefits of anxiety, see de Sousa 2008, Goldie 2004, Hookway 1998, Kurth 2015 and 2024, Maibom 2022, Munch-Jurisic 2021, Vazard 2019 and 2024, and Vazard and Kurth 2022. The introduction to Rondel and Chopra 2024 is also germane.
4. For more on emotions and natural kinds, see Barrett 2006, de Sousa 1987, Griffiths 1997, Prinz 2004 (chapter 4), Rorty 2004, and Scarantino 2009. See also Rorty 1980, in which it is claimed that emotions like anxiety "do not form a natural class." Such emotions cannot be "shepherded together under one set of classifications as active or passive; thought-generated and thought-defined or physiologically determined; voluntary or nonvoluntary; functional or malfunctional; corrigible or not corrigible by a change in beliefs. Nor can they be sharply distinguished from moods, motives, attitudes, character traits" (Rorty 1980, 1). On the prospect of anxiety as a unified category, see Kurth 2018 and Prinz 2024.
5. A widely held view is that the difference between the *emotion* of anxiety and the *mood* of anxiety is that the former is always directed at something, whereas the latter is more generalized and diffuse (see Kurth 2018, 9–11). This general view about the difference between emotions and moods is endorsed by Goldie 2000, Solomon 1993, Nussbaum 2001, and Flanagan 2021. Nussbaum maintains, for example, that emotions always have an object, even if only a vague one, whereas moods do not. The consequence, she notes, is that, "In reality it is very difficult to distinguish an emotion with a vague or highly general object from a mood" (Nussbaum 2001, 133). Understood in these terms, the emotion/mood distinction looks to be tightly yoked with the belief dependence/independence distinction. See Ben-Ze'ev 2000 (chapter 4), Price 2006, and Prinz 2004 (182–88) for further valuable discussion.
6. A small sample of important work on recalcitrant emotions includes: Benbaji 2013, Brady 2009, D'Arms and Jacobson 2003, Döring 2015, Grzankowski 2020, Helm 2015, and Thomason 2022.
7. As Christine Tappolet writes, emotions like anxiety "can be assessed in terms of their appropriateness. We are prone to assess our emotions with respect to how they appear to fit evaluative states of affairs. We criticize someone's fear when it bears

on something that is not fearsome, such as an innocuous little spider.... Thus, fear appears to have correctness conditions in much the same way as the visual experience of poppies as blue has correctness conditions" (Tappolet 2016, 20). On the appropriateness or fittingness of the emotions, some important work includes: Ballard 2021, Brady 2008, D'Arms and Jacobson 2000, and Deonna and Teroni 2012. On the fittingness of anxiety in particular, see Fritz 2021.
8. Similar claims can be found in Roberts 2013 (especially chapters 3 and 4).
9. The approach I'm defending mirrors the one found in Thomason 2024.

Chapter 1

1. See for instance Grøn 2008 and Marino 1998.
2. Franz Kafka remarked in 1913 that Kierkegaard and he were "on the same side of the world" and that Kierkegaard "bears me out like a friend" (Kafka 1972, 230).
3. Among the massive secondary literature on Kierkegaard, Beabout 2009, Dupré 1963, Gouwens 1996, and Hampson 2013 all give the explicitly religious elements in Kierkegaard's treatment of anxiety their full due. Bergo 2021 (chapter 3) is also a useful source.
4. Whether and to what extent Kierkegaard's numerous pseudonyms should be understood as communicating Kierkegaard's own views remains a subject of scholarly controversy. We get some of Kierkegaard's own feelings on this issue at the very end of his *Concluding Unscientific Postscript*. "Therefore," he writes, "if it should occur to anyone to want to quote a particular passage from the books, it is my wish, my prayer, that he will do me the kindness of citing the respective pseudonymous author's name, not mine—that is, of separating us in such a way that the passage femininely belongs to the pseudonymous author, the responsibility civilly to me" (Kierkegaard 1992, 627).
5. Here is Scott Stossel arguing for essentially the same conclusion: "Animals have no abstract concept of the future; they also have no abstract concept of anxiety, no ability to worry about their fears. An animal may experience stress-induced 'difficulty in breathing' or 'spasms of the heart' (as Freud put it)—but no animal can *worry* about that symptom or *interpret* it in any way. An animal cannot be a hypochondriac. Also, an animal cannot fear death. Rats and marine snails are not abstractly aware of the prospect of a car accident, or a plane crash, or a terrorist attack, or nuclear annihilation—or of social rejection, or diminishment of status, or professional humiliation, or the inevitable loss of people we love, or the finitude of corporeal existence. This, along with our capacity to be consciously aware of the sensations of fear, and to cogitate about them, gives human experience of anxiety an existential dimension that the 'alarm response' of a marine snail utterly lacks" (Stossel 2013, 56–57).
6. I concede that we are largely in the dark about what the cognitive-emotional repertoire of other animals is like. Primatologist Frans de Waal is right to say about other animals that, strictly speaking, "we cannot know what they feel" (de Waal 2014). Perhaps we humans are not the only spiritual creatures. Perhaps dolphins also have the capacity to reflect on what matters to them, to ask themselves how they should be spending their time, etc. If so, then dolphins would be spiritual creatures too.
7. How exactly to characterize the difference between despair and anxiety in Kierkegaard is a thorny issue best left for another time. Kierkegaard himself sometimes seems to use the terms interchangeably, as when he writes: "[I]n the remote depths, in the most inward parts, in the hidden recesses of happiness, there dwells also the anxious dread which is despair" (Kierkegaard 2013, 25). Hägglund similarly notes that Kierkegaard "defines despair as encompassing all forms of anxiety, ranging from the smallest worry to the most severe existential breakdown"

(Hägglund 2019, 158). Beabout 2009 (especially in chapter 6) gives the clearest account of the differences between anxiety and despair in Kierkegaard that I have been able to find. Hannay 1998 and Theunissen 2005 are also excellent sources.
8. Reflecting on his conversion to Christianity, Augustine wrote, "It was as if a light of relief from all anxiety flooded into my heart. All the shadows of doubt were dispelled" (Augustine 1991, 153).
9. William James echoes these sentiments when he says that religion offers "peace and rest" to its devotees—a "paradise of inward tranquility"—because it promises a future and a world in which everything works out happily. Religion tells us that we do not need to be afraid. It promises "security against the bewildering accidents of so much finite experience" (James 2000, 128). As a result, James says (and as Kierkegaard would enthusiastically concur) that religious believers, "are never anxious about the future, nor worry over the outcome of the day" (James 1982, 285; 289).
10. Interestingly, Joseph LeDoux thinks that recent brain science more or less corroborates the view that Kierkegaard and Freud share. He writes, "fear states occur when a threat is present or imminent; states of anxiety result when a threat is possible but its occurrence is uncertain." He goes on to argue that "somewhat different brain mechanisms are engaged when the state is triggered by an objective and present threat as opposed to an uncertain event that may or may not occur in the future. An immediately present stimulus that is itself dangerous, or that is a reliable indicator that danger is likely to soon follow, results in fear. Anxiety may well also be present, but if the initial state is triggered by a specific stimulus, it is a state of fear. However, when the state in question involves worry about something that is not present and may never occur, then the state is anxiety. Fear can, like anxiety, involve anticipation, but the nature of the anticipation in each is different: In fear the anticipation concerns if and when a present threat will cause harm, whereas in anxiety the anticipation involves uncertainty about the consequences of a threat that is not present and may not occur" (LeDoux 2016, 10–11).
11. Thanks to Jake Jackson for this formulation.
12. See Baumgartner, Pieters, and Bagozzi 2008. See also Elpidorou 2020, 125–126.
13. And similarly: "It is fear that I am most afraid of" (Montaigne 2003, 83).
14. Quotations from Kierkegaard in Carlisle's passage are all taken from the fifth chapter of *The Concept of Anxiety*—"Anxiety as Saving Through Faith." See Kierkegaard 1980, 155–162.
15. As Pascal noted in his *Pensées*: "If our condition were truly happy, we should not have to divert ourselves from thinking about it" (Pascal 1995, 26).
16. The reverse side of the same coin is that equanimity gives us more freedom than we would otherwise have without it. After all, equanimity just is, definitionally, freedom from dread and disquiet. The very freedom that anxiety steals away from its sufferer.
17. Here is the full passage from Nietzsche's *Human, All Too Human*: "At the waterfall. When we see a waterfall, we think we see freedom of will and choice in the innumerable turnings, windings, breakings of the waves; but everything is necessary; each movement can be calculated mathematically. Thus it is with human actions; if one were omniscient, one would be able to calculate each individual action in advance, each step in the progress of knowledge, each error, each act of malice. To be sure the acting man is caught in his illusion of volition; if the wheel of the world were to stand still for a moment and an omniscient, calculating mind were there to take advantage of this interruption, he would be able to tell into the farthest future of each being and describe every rut that wheel will roll upon. The acting man's delusion about himself, his assumption that free will exists, is also part of the calculable

mechanism" (Nietzsche 1986, 74). I cannot witness a waterfall without this passage immediately springing into mind. And of course, if the determinism expressed in Nietzsche's passage is correct, the very fact that thoughts about Nietzsche's waterfall passage flash through David Rondel's mind whenever he sees a waterfall is also wholly determined.

18. Even higher-order thought theorists who maintain that a person's beliefs can dramatically alter their phenomenology will have to admit that the feeling of our own agency is impressively impervious to beliefs about the truth of determinism. Even the most passionate and "iron-clad" determinists (to use a phrase from William James) still feel as though they have the ability to decide and to act voluntarily.

19. As Heidi Maibom notes, "Emotions are seldom felt in isolation, particularly in isolation from related emotions" (Maibom 2014, 7). This suggests that spontaneous freedom will rarely (if ever) be experienced as a pure specimen. It's much more likely to arise in a package with other kinds of emotions, moods, and feelings.

20. The fourth edition of the *Diagnostic and Statistical Manual of Mental Disorders* cites "an important loss of freedom" as a possible defining feature of mental disorder. It's fascinating that this language no longer appears in the DSM's most current fifth edition. See Cooper 2018. Meynen 2010 also features an insightful discussion about some of the connections between mental disorder and free will. The essays collected in King and May 2022 also address these connections.

21. Havi Carel argues that injury or illness can bring about a feeling she calls "bodily doubt"—a loss of faith in one's body, a tacit uncertainty about what our bodies are capable of. It's undeniable that "bodily doubt" can be interpreted as a species of unfreedom. When it takes hold, the natural, unreflective confidence a person has in one's bodily abilities is "displaced by a feeling of helplessness, alarm, and distrust [in one's body]" (Carel 2016, 93).

22. Some of these observations about depression are corroborated by Cvetkovich 2012, Radden 2014, Ratcliffe 2008 and 2015, Andrew Solomon 2001, and Styron 1992.

23. If feeling out of control is distressing, the inverted version of the same idea is that feeling as though one was "in charge" of one's actions and behavior commonly produces a sense of peace and safety. As St. Augustine asked rhetorically many centuries ago in his *De libero arbitrio*: "What greater security could there be than to have a life in which nothing can happen to you that you do not will?" (Augustine 1993, 69).

24. One of the most effective therapeutic techniques I've found for dealing with anxiety is Cognitive Flooding, a type of exposure therapy commonly used in cognitive-behavioral therapy (or CBT). David Burns explains: "When you use Cognitive Flooding, you visualize your worst fear.... Try to make yourself as anxious as possible and endure the anxiety for as long as you can.... Picture the thing you fear as vividly as possible. If you become panicky, don't fight it! Instead, try to make it even worse. Eventually the anxiety will burn itself out" (Burns 2006, 269). What I like about this therapy, among other things, is that we are intentionally trying to stir up anxious feelings. The anxiety does not just arrive out of nowhere, as normally is the case. Instead, in a way, we are the ones in control.

Chapter 2

1. Richard M. Gale gets it exactly right when he writes: "The best way to characterize the philosophy of William James is to say that it is deeply rooted in the blues. It is the soulful expression of someone who has 'paid his dues,' someone who, like old wagon wheels, has been through it all. Whereas its immediate aim is to keep him sane and nonsuicidal—'to help him make it through the night'—its larger one is to help him find his way to physical and spiritual health" (Gale 1999, 1).

2. The term "neurasthenia" was first introduced by neurologist George Miller Beard in his 1881 *American Nervousness: Its Causes and Consequences*. Fatigue, anxiety, headaches, and impotence were some of its major symptoms. Beard believed that a major impetus for neurasthenia was modern urbanization and the corporate, workaholic ethos to which it gave rise. Neurasthenia was sometimes half-seriously referred to as "Americanitis"—a nickname supposedly popularized by James himself. For more on the young William James's mental health struggles, two highly readable sources are Croce 2018 and Feinstein 1984.

3. Whether James was a proponent of the doctrine philosophers call "value pluralism" is not worth fussing about here. He was certainly a proponent of something with the same "tragic" upshot. Following Berlin's famous articulation of the doctrine, value pluralism is usually understood as a species of moral realism. For Berlin, values are objective, but there are also impassable conflicts among values. He was a realist about value, in other words, who thought that certain objectively real values are inescapably at odds with one another. I can't imagine James endorsing this kind of moral realism. As Scott Aiken and Robert Talisse correctly point out, "Whereas Berlin holds that goods are quasi-Platonic objects, James held that goods are *psychological* states" (Aiken and Talisse 2018, 172). Technicalities aside, Berlin and James agree that all good things cannot be simultaneously realized, and that agonizing choices are "an intrinsic, irremovable element in human life" (Berlin 1969, 167).

4. This general view is eloquently defended by Lucy Foulkes: "there isn't a clear boundary between the everyday and the pathological," she writes. "All symptoms—mood, worry, disordered eating, self-harm, delusions—everything exists on a spectrum. Along each spectrum, every psychological problem shifts gradually from being mild and controllable to something that can entirely take over your life. There is no sudden change, no distinct shift on any graph that indicates mental illness has begun. In addition, the processes that make a person susceptible to mental illness in the first place—genetic vulnerabilities, stressful life events, coping styles—are the very same ones that make a person susceptible to experiencing non-pathological distress as well" (Foulkes 2021, 164). James would have enthusiastically agreed with every word of this passage. See also Alessandri (2023, 145), who points out that, "The distinction between 'normal' and 'disordered' anxiety buckles once it says that 30 percent of us have an anxiety disorder. One in three may not constitute a majority, but it seems awfully close to normal."

5. In the 1895 essay "Is Life Worth Living?," James argues that we have much to learn from those who end their own lives. We need to take the suicidal point of view seriously. "That life is not worth living the whole army of suicides declare," James writes. "We, too, as we sit here in our comfort, must 'ponder these things' . . . for we are of one substance with these suicides, and their life is the life we share . . . the simplest manliness and honor, forbid us to forget their case" (James 2000, 223). James himself struggled terribly with suicidal thoughts as a younger man, and concluded, in an 1870 letter to the philosopher and poet Benjamin Paul Blood, "no man is educated who has never dallied with the thought of suicide" (Townsend 1996, 32).

6. The subsequent discussion draws from some of my previous work on William James and habit. See Rondel 2017, 2018, 2021a, and 2021b.

7. Later on in the *Varieties*, James again suggests a version of the same thought experiment. But in the *Varieties* version he seems to be using the term "emotion" as coextensive with "mood" or "overall affective orientation to the world." The truth is that James used words like "emotion" and "feeling" to refer to different kinds of things, and he was not always as clear as he could have been in distinguishing different kinds of mental states. Here is the passage from *Varieties*: "Conceive yourself, if

possible, suddenly stripped of all the emotion with which your world now inspires you, and try to imagine it *as it exists*, purely by itself, without your favorable or unfavorable, hopeful or apprehensive comment. It will be almost impossible for you to realize such a condition of negativity and deadness. No one portion of the universe would then have importance beyond another; and the whole collection of its things and series of its events would be without significance, character, expression, or perspective. Whatever of value, interest, or meaning our respective worlds may appear endued with are thus pure gifts of the spectator's mind. The passion of love is the most familiar and extreme example of this fact. If it comes, it comes; if it does not come, no process of reasoning can force it. Yet it transforms the value of the creature loved as utterly as the sunrise transforms Mont Blanc from a corpse-like gray to a rosy enchantment; and it sets the whole world to a new tune for the lover and gives a new issue to his life. So with fear, with indignation, jealousy, ambition, worship. If they are there, life changes" (James 1982, 150).

8. We human beings are, after all, a certain kind of primate. And it shouldn't be surprising that the physical manifestations of fear among animals, products of evolution just like us, are strikingly similar to our own. In an 1872 work called *The Expression of the Emotions in Man and Animals*, Charles Darwin, himself a sufferer of debilitating agoraphobia and panic attacks, describes fear of attack in animals with his characteristic lucidity. "With all or almost all animals, even with birds, terror causes the body to tremble. The skin becomes pale, sweat breaks out, and the hair bristles. The secretions of the alimentary canal and of the kidneys are increased, and they are involuntary voided, owing to the relaxation of the sphincter muscles, as is known to be the case with man, and as I have seen with cattle, dogs, cats, and monkeys. The breathing is hurried. The heart beats quickly, wildly, violently; but whether it pumps the blood more efficiently through the body may be doubted, for the surface seems bloodless and the strength of the muscles soon fails. In a frightened horse I have felt through the saddle the beating of the heart so plainly that I could have counted the beats. The mental faculties are much disturbed. Utter prostration soon follows, and even fainting. A terrified canary-bird has been seen not only to tremble and to turn white about the base of the bill, but to faint: and I once caught a robin in a room, which fainted so completely, that for a time I thought it dead" (Darwin 1872, 77). For more on Darwin's struggles with anxiety and panic, see Barloon and Noyes 1997.

9. Many of our affective states, James says, are "non-logical and beyond our control." They are, for better or for worse, "gifts to us." As James asks rhetorically: "How can the moribund old man reason back to himself the romance, the mystery, the imminence of great things with which our old earth tingled for him in the days when he was young and well?" (James 1982, 151). In short, sometimes we are just stuck with how we feel.

Chapter 3

1. Death anxiety (or *thanatophobia*, after Thanatos, the ancient Greek mythological version of the Grim Reaper) is not classified as a stand-alone mental disorder. It typically occurs as a feature of other disorders, particularly anxiety and hypochondriasis disorders. I don't use the term *thanatophobia* to describe the death anxiety that is my subject here, because I'm not interested in a clinical diagnosis per se, just the regular sense, which I assume is widespread, of fear and trepidation regarding the prospect of death.

2. This is what Heidegger means when he says that, "Anxiety is anxious in the face of the 'nothing' of the world" (Heidegger 1962, 393). Thomas Nagel echoes Heidegger's idea when he writes that there is something that can be called "the

expectation of nothingness, and though the mind tends to veer away from it, it is an unmistakeable experience, always startling, often frightening, and very different from the familiar recognition that your life will go on for only a limited time—that you probably have less than thirty years and certainly less than a hundred" (Nagel 1986, 225-226). Similar views are found in Baillie 2013, Behrendt 2010, and Amélie Rorty's classic article, "Fearing Death" (Rorty 1983). Philip Larkin's famous death poem—"Aubade"—is another source for this kind of view.

3. Rorty writes, "Heidegger watched his Jewish colleagues being dismissed from their jobs, and then watched them disappear to a fate about which he could have easily learned if he had thought it worth the trouble. That silence is also what makes Heidegger different from the general run of antiegalitarians. Many eminent twentieth-century writers have mistrusted democracy, but he was the only one to have remained unmoved by the Holocaust" (Rorty 1999, 593).

4. As far as I can tell, the term "Heideggerese" was first used in print in L.A. Garrard's 1959 essay, "What Is Christianity? A Linguistic Inquiry" (published in Twin 1959). There is a Twitter user who goes by the name "Jy Houston" to whom thanks are owed for hunting this reference down.

5. A small sample of excellent work on Heidegger's thinking about death and anxiety includes Blattner 1994, Carel 2006, Dreyfus 1993, Edwards 1975, Polt 1999, and Ratcliffe 2008.

6. We can hope to achieve a greater sense of composure and acceptance as time goes by and death gets nearer. Or perhaps we can hope that we'll be too confused and incoherent to really understand what's going on when our time comes. Julian Barnes, who makes no bones about his intense fear of death, lays out a terrifying possibility in his 2008 memoir, *Nothing to Be Frightened Of*. "What you—I—will be clinging on to is not a few more minutes in a warm baronial hall with the smell of roast chicken and the cheery noise of fife and drum, not a few more days of real living, but a few more days and hours of breathing decrepitude, mind gone, muscles wasted, bladder leaking. . . . And yet—and worse—imagine this failing body now even more fearful of oblivion than when it was healthy and strong and could divert itself from contemplation of that oblivion by physical and mental activities, by social usefulness and the company of friends. . . . All that is left—the last bit of the engine still with stoking power—is the compartment that makes us fear death. Yes, that little bit of brain activity will keep going strong, puffing out the panic, sending the chill and the terror coursing through the system. They will give you morphine for your pain . . . but there is nothing they can give you to stop this grim cluster of brain cells scaring you shitless . . . until the very end. Then we might find ourselves regretting that we ever thought, with Renard, 'Please, God, don't make me die too quickly'" (Barnes 2008, 111-112).

7. It's also central in *The Death of Ivan Illyich*, in which Tolstoy describes Ivan's movement in thought from the abstract proposition, "men are mortal," to the personal recognition that he, Ivan, now terminally ill, will soon die (Tolstoy 1981, 79). In a brief footnote in *Being and Time*, Heidegger acknowledges the connection to Tolstoy's novella. See Heidegger 1962, 495, n. xii.

8. See Blattner 1994, 60-62 and Drefyus 1993, 178-180.

9. In "What is Metaphysics?" Heidegger argues that anxiety need not be experienced as distressing or unpleasant. It need not be "accompanied by sweating, crying, or wringing of the hands" (Dreyfus 1993, 180-181). Heidegger actually suggests that it's possible for anxiety to be pervaded with "a peculiar kind of calm" (Heidegger 1993, 100). I'm not sure how this claim can be fully squared with Heidegger's observation that we have a tendency to flee the mood of anxiety, but that is for another time and place. I think Heidegger would grant that, in the overwhelming majority

of cases, the mood of anxiety is experienced as something unpleasant. See Blattner 1994, 60.
10. The form this reaction takes involves what Heidegger calls "the Falling" . . . (*das Verfallen*). See Heidegger 1962, 219–224.
11. An "ownmost" perspective also brings death's "non-relational character" into view (Heidegger 1962, 308). As Safranski explains: "Although everyone is affected by death, we each have to die our own death. We are not helped by the thought of the universality of this fate. Death individualizes, even though dying takes place in huge numbers" (Safranski 1998, 164). I respectfully disagree with Heidegger about this. I *am* sometimes comforted by the thought of the universality of our fate. It can be soothing to remember that death is the great leveller, that we are all equal members in what Nietzsche beautifully called "a brotherhood of death" (Nietzsche 2001, 158).
12. In a passage with which Heidegger would have agreed completely, Thomas Nagel puts the core idea like this: "Like the contingency of our birth, the inevitability of our death is easy to grasp objectively, but hard to grasp from within. Everyone dies; I am someone, so I will die. But it isn't just that TN will be killed in a plane crash or a holdup, have a stroke or a heart attack or lung cancer, the clothes going to the Salvation Army, the books to the library, some bits of the body to the organ bank and the rest to the crematorium. In addition to these mundane objective transitions, my world will come to an end, as yours will when you die. That's what's hard to get hold of: the internal fact that one day this consciousness will black out for good and subjective time will simply stop. My death as an event in the world is easy to think about; the end of my world is not" (Nagel 1986, 225).
13. This brings to mind a few lines from Phillip Larkin's poem *The Mower*:

> "The first day after a death, the new absence
> Is always the same; we should be careful
> Of each other, we should be kind
> While there is still time" (Larkin 2003, 194).

14. Larkin's phrase comes from the poem "The Old Fools," some lines of which include the following:

> "At death, you break up: the bits that were you
> Start speeding away from each other for ever
> With no one to see. It's only oblivion, true:
> We had it before, but then it was going to end,
> And was all the time merging with a unique endeavor
> To bring to bloom the million-petalled flower
> Of being here. Next time you can't pretend
> There'll be anything else" (Larkin 2003, 131).

15. Thanks to Sterling Hall for help in deciphering the provenance of this passage.
16. Antonio Damasio provides some useful context for Spinoza's view. "I do not believe Spinoza had any difficulty in seeing the darkness in nature, having experienced its effects himself," Damasio says. "But he refused to *accept* darkness and to let it dominate the individual as a bad passion. He saw darkness as a part of existence and prescribed ways with which it can be minimized. Spinoza was resilient and courageous rather than naturally cheerful. He *strived* to be cheerful. He worked hard at cancelling the feelings of fear and sorrow that nature inspires, with feelings of joy based on the discovery of nature. That discovery, almost perversely, included nature's cruelty and indifference" (Damasio 2003, 281–282).

Chapter 4

1. "But let us merely look at it; this world of constantly needy creatures who continue for a time merely by devouring one another, pass their existence in anxiety and want, and often endure terrible afflictions, until they fall at last into the arms of death" (Schopenhauer 1966a, 349).
2. Though, see Bettina Bergo's (2021) massive philosophical history of anxiety, in which Schopenhauer's work figures prominently.
3. "The dog," Schopenhauer wrote in one of his aphorisms, "is rightly the symbol of loyalty" (Schopenhauer 1970, 235). And elsewhere: "To anyone who needs lively entertainment for the purpose of banishing the dreariness of solitude, I recommend a dog, in whose moral and intellectual qualities he will almost always experience delight and satisfaction" (Schopenhauer 1974, 82).
4. At the beginning of *Seeing Clearly: A Buddhist Guide to Life*, Nicolas Bommarito summarizes the central "problem" to which Buddhism offers a kind of solution like this: "You achieve a goal or have some good luck. But there's still a slight buzz just underneath the sound of celebration—a kind of anxiety that the success, whatever it is, is fleeting. You now have to protect against losing what you've won. People will expect you to replicate or even better it. For some achievements, you feel a target on your back—people now have the goal of taking you down, of bettering you. Though it's not always apparent, each success brings with it new problems and new goals that pop up like weeds" (Bommarito 2020, 3–4). It's impossible to deny that this sounds an awful lot like Schopenhauer.
5. If the opposite of depression is vitality, we might say that anxiety is vitality run amok. If depression conveys to the depressed person a sense of futility, of hopelessness, an exhausted resignation about even the most mundane tasks, anxiety conveys to the anxious person the need to remain always on high alert. If depression can make a simple task like preparing lunch or replying to an email feel like scaling a mountain, anxiety can make a simple task feel like a four-alarm fire. And yet, despite these obvious differences, anxiety and depression have a tendency to arise together. Robert Burton claimed all the way back in 1621 that fear and sorrow were "continual companions" (Burton 2001, 261). Andrew Solomon writes: "Much depression incorporates anxiety symptoms. It's possible to read anxiety and depression separately, but according to James Ballenger of the Medical College of South Carolina, a leading expert in anxiety, 'they're fraternal twins'" (Solomon 2001, 65). "Anxiety is the partner of depression," notes Matt Haig. "It accompanies half the cases of depression. Sometimes it triggers depression. Sometimes depression triggers anxiety. Sometimes they simply coexist, like a nightmare marriage. Though of course it is perfectly possible to have anxiety minus depression, and vice versa. Anxiety and depression are an interesting mix. In many ways they are opposite experiences, and yet mix them together and you don't get a happy medium. Quite the opposite. Anxiety, which often bubbles up into panic, is a nightmare in fast-forward" (Haig 2015, 189).
6. This brings to mind Ron Padgett's poem "Poet as Immortal Bird":

> A second ago my heart thump went
> and I thought, "This would be a bad time
> to have a heart attack and die, in the
> middle of a poem," then took comfort
> in the idea that no one I have ever heard
> of has ever died in the middle of writing
> a poem, just as birds never die in mid-flight.
> I think. (Padgett 2013, 450)

7. The basic distinction supposedly goes back at least to Aristotle, whose division between *kinesis* and *energeia* maps neatly onto the difference between the sorts of actions that are amenable to completion and those that are not. For painstaking analysis of Aristotle's distinction, see Burnyeat 2008.
8. Ronald Pursur has argued recently that Buddhist mindfulness practices have been "coopted" by a hyper-competitive, capitalist, self-obsessed, neoliberal order. He calls this cooption "McMindfulness." Mindfulness has become "a form of capitalist spirituality," he says, "perfectly attuned to maintaining the neoliberal self." "No wonder Wall Street traders and hedge fund managers now use the practice to fine-tune their brains, up their game and gain an edge" (Pursur 2019, 29). In *Why I am Not a Buddhist*, Evan Thompson agrees that what Buddhists call "Right mindfulness" is "incompatible with greed and that it is wrong to market mindfulness as a commodity for personal or corporate enhancement." Yet he also maintains that many critiques of what he calls "mindfulness mania" are "superficial," because the idea of "authentic Buddhism" is unhelpful (Thompson 2020, 119).
9. Another good thing about compassion for Schopenhauer is that non-human animals "are also taken under its protection." Like many of the Hindu and Buddhist thinkers that inspire him, Schopenhauer defends "a deeply felt, universal compassion for every living thing." "Tastes differ," he writes, "but I know of no finer prayer than the one which ends old Indian dramas. . . . It runs: 'May all living beings remain free from pain'" (Schopenhauer 1995, 175; 192; 173). I think Schopenhauer is right to argue that compassion as such is not interested in the human/non-human distinction. But compassion for every living thing also seems excessive. Are feelings of compassion stirred in us by the misfortunes of single-celled organisms and bacteria? Should they be? Are we falling short somehow if we find ourselves unmoved by the fate of the amoebas?
10. I'm skeptical that moral motivation is as pure and uniform as Schopenhauer takes it to be. This focus on the motivational purity of compassion seems to me an unfortunate residue of Kantian thinking. The truth is, in a wide range of cases, what Schopenhauer calls our "incentives" for acting or refraining draw from a range of different reasons and considerations. In the real world, moral motivation is multifarious and messy, which is not to deny that compassion is sometimes part of the story here, too. I'm grateful to Christopher Williams for helpful discussion on this point.
11. To say that such questions are less important is not to say that Schopenhauer never asks them. Christopher Janaway notes that Schopenhauer "tends to speak . . . in the vocabulary of value, asking whether life is a business which covers its costs, whether the world is bankrupt, whether this world is the best, or the worst, possible" (Janaway 1999, 318). These are highly abstract questions, posed from a thirty-thousand-foot point of view. Schopenhauer sometimes adopts this more abstract point of view in his writings, as when he reflects upon "the sum total of distress, pain and suffering of every kind which the sun shines upon" (Schopenhauer 1970, 47). But more often, I think, he chooses a perspective which is closer to the ground, to the hard facts of lived lives. For Schopenhauer, it's more important to accentuate the concrete individual sufferer than it is the nebulous fact of suffering.
12. See Bloom 2016, D'Arms 2000, Maibom 2009 and 2014, and Prinz 2011.
13. The first part of the slogan corresponds with the virtue of justice (*Gerechtigheit*), the second part with loving kindness (*Menschenliebe*), both of which are ultimately derived from compassion.
14. And inversely: "In solitude the wretch feels the whole of his wretchedness" (Schopenhauer 1974, 419).

15. For Richard Rorty, this kind of compassion is achieved not by inquiry or theory, but, in his words, by "increasing our sensitivity to the particular details of the pain and humiliation of other, unfamiliar sorts of people." It is "the imaginative ability to see strange people as fellow sufferers" that does the heavy, compassion-building work here. Such increased sensitivity "makes it more difficult to marginalize people different from ourselves by thinking, 'They do not feel it as *we* would,' or 'There must always be suffering, so why not let *them* suffer?' (Rorty 1989, xvi).
16. Here is Kierkegaard remarking on the "hidden inwardness" of his own mental suffering: "It is frightful to think for a single moment of the kind of life I have led in my most hidden inwardness, literally never a word about it spoken to a single human being, of course, not even daring to write down the least thing about it—and then that I have been able to encase that life in an exterior existence of zest for life and cheerfulness" (Kierkegaard 1980, 172).
17. Émile Durkheim similarly claims "... the way he braves pain is the best indication of the greatness of man" (Durkheim 2001, 234).
18. See Brady 2018 for a rich and sophisticated discussion of suffering and its various connections to growth, wisdom, and the virtues.

Chapter 5

1. Following Plato in the *Phaedrus*, Murdoch says that the most "obvious thing in our surroundings which is an occasion for 'unselfing' is beauty" (Murdoch 1971, 82). I will be focusing mainly on the therapeutic properties of the natural world in this chapter, but Murdoch's main idea generalizes to other beautiful things, like human beings or works of art. Patricia J. O'Connor speculates (and I agree) that one of the main differences between the experience of beauty in nature and in art for Murdoch "is that while the first may surprise us into selflessness [remember the "hovering kestrel"] the second almost always requires deliberate, detached attention before it can be perceived." (O'Connor 1996, 89–90). Murdoch herself claims that, "Art is less accessible than nature" and "When we move from beauty in nature to beauty in art we are already in a more difficult region" (Murdoch 1971, 83–84).
2. Peter J. Conradi explains that Murdoch integrates a Freudian "mechanical model of the psyche" with a Platonic "moral" one (Conradi 2001b, 96). This "marriage" of Freud and Plato gives rise to an odd, tension-filled pair of claims (Meszaros 2016, 140). Plato's contribution to the marriage requires a *moral* concept of the self, a self that understands itself as oriented toward a sovereign good. The Freudian contribution requires conceding that the self is frequently a source of error and illusion. "We are largely mechanical creatures," Murdoch writes in a more Freudian moment, "the slaves of relentlessly strong selfish forces of nature of which we scarcely comprehend" (Murdoch 1997, 381). I have misgivings about whether the marriage between Plato and Freud is ultimately viable, but such is the richness and complexity of Murdoch's work.
3. For more on Murdoch's unique brand of moral realism, see Antonaccio 2000 (especially chapter 2) and Widdows 2005 (especially chapter 4). Gomes 2022 and Mason 2023 are also excellent sources.
4. Fergus Kerr helpfully notes that Murdoch wants to retain the Platonic idea of "the image of the Good as the sun, in the light of which we can see things with lucidity, diminishingly self-centered attention, and a kind of compassionate love" (Kerr 2004, 98).
5. I borrow this wording from a story about William James recounted by Jacques Barzun. James is walking on the campus of Harvard University with a student when they notice "an imposing figure coming toward them." The figure is disheveled and

talking to himself. The student reflects that he is "the epitome of the absent-minded professor," to which James replies: "What you really mean to say . . . is that he is present-minded somewhere else" (Barzun 1983, 6).

6. As Matt Haig nicely points out, running also mimics many of the physical symptoms of panic and anxiety ("the racing heart, the problematic breathing, the sweating"). This means that, while running, we are less likely to be worried about a racing heart, problematic breathing, or sweating, because these physical symptoms are explained away by the very fact that we are running (Haig 2015, 152).

7. See Flanagan 2020 for moving, personal corroboration of James's claim—though, as Flanagan points out, once alcohol addiction reaches a more advanced stage, drinking tends to no longer produce the effects that initially drew the addict to alcohol. Flanagan writes: "My first drink at the age of thirteen produced a flash-bulb memory of feeling safe; a vivid experience of being not scared, which prior to that experience I did not know I was. Later, I consciously used alcohol to achieve that goal, as well as several others. . . . By the time I was in the grip of addiction to alcohol, drinking itself was phenomenologically center stage, not any of the original reasons for drinking. By late addiction, I was in a familiar state as reported by many alcoholics, namely, the drinking no longer worked to produce any of the effects I originally loved it for. I did not feel safe and less anxious (the opposite). I was not cool and socially adept (the opposite). It did not make women like me (the opposite) . . . " (Flanagan 2020, 245–246). See also Flanagan 2011. Interestingly, James's philosophy had a powerful influence on Bill Wilson (or Bill W), co-founder of Alcoholics Anonymous. As Wilson recounts of his reading James's *Varieties of Religious Experience*: "The book was not easy reading, but I kept at it all day. By nightfall, this Harvard professor, long in his grave, had, without anyone knowing it, become a founder of Alcoholics Anonymous" (W, Bill. 2000, 151). For more on James's influence on Wilson and the development of Alcoholics Anonymous, see Walle 1992.

8. One possibility worth considering is that natural environments represent something like a standard, default setting, which turn out to be a calming and welcome relief from the disharmonious *unnatural* environments—fluorescent lights, recycled air, the tedious, blue glow of a computer screen—in which so many of us regularly spend our time. It's not that natural environments are special as such. It's that non-natural environments are such an aberration. On this kind of view, nature is powerful more for what it *isn't* than for what it *is*. I'm skeptical about this thesis. It seems farfetched to think that such feelings can be wholly explained by the emergence of our modern living and working spaces. Ralph Waldo Emerson never knew artificial lights and work cubicles, yet still maintained that there is "no disgrace, no calamity . . . which nature cannot repair" (Emerson 2000, 6). Aristotle never stared at a computer monitor or had to breathe stale, recycled office air yet still believed that, "In all natural things there is something marvelous" (Aristotle 2001, 14). The scientific literature detailing the array of positive psychological effects of exposure to nature is too voluminous to lay out here. Zhang et al. (2014) provides a useful starting place and guide. Williams and Harvey 2001 is also a valuable resource. Thanks to Carlos Mariscal for illuminating discussions on these issues.

9. The awe and wonder we experience in nature need not be triggered only by grand displays— a giant sequoia or a majestic mountain range, say. Concentrating on something small can be equally powerful. As Emerson wrote, "All natural objects make a kindred impression, when the mind is open to their influence" (Emerson 2000, 5). Emerson's view about the power of even small, common natural objects is beautifully captured in a journal entry from 1838: "At night I went out into the dark and saw a glimmering star and heard a frog, and Nature seemed to say, Well do not

these suffice? Here is a new scene, a new experience. Ponder it, Emerson, and not like the foolish world, hanker after thunders and multitudes and vast landscapes, the sea of Niagara" (Emerson 1995, 127).
10. Just before the term "agoraphobia" was coined in the late 1800s, the same condition was given the German name *platzschwindel*, which refers to the sensation of dizziness in public spaces. As David Barlow notes, because it highlights the "attempt to avoid internal physical sensations associated with panic, and dizziness is indeed one of the primary symptoms of panic," *platzschwindel* might actually convey a more accurate conception of this disorder than the now widely accepted "agoraphobia" (Barlow 2004, 329).
11. Some of these claims are corroborated by Brewer 2021, 165–167.

Chapter 6

1. Bobzien 1998, Brennan 2005, Graver 2007, Nussbaum 2009, Sellars 2006, and Sorabji 2000 are excellent places to begin, as are the essays in Inwood 2003. For more widely accessible books on Stoic philosophy, see Irvine 2009 and Pigliucci 2017. There has been an explosion of interest in Stoicism in recent years, culminating in uncountably many public-facing articles, books, and podcast interviews. One criticism frequently leveled against some of this popular work is that it seems to reduce complex philosophical issues into a series of "hacks." Everything from mental health to virtuousness is simplistically boiled down into little nuggets of wisdom and pithy aphorisms. Personal discipline and self-control turn out to be the answers to all of life's problems. As one recent critic put it, "The conviction that self-control is a conduit to virtue recurs so often among the salesmen of the modern Stoic movement that it appears less a motif than an unhealthy obsession" (O'Brien 2020). The new Stoicism is a hyper-individualistic brand of self-improvement literature designed to help people become tougher, more resilient, and ultimately more efficient. My quick two cents: I readily concede that Stoic ideas, much like elements of Buddhism, are ripe for neoliberal appropriation, but also, such ripeness should not lead anyone to overlook what is correct and valuable in Stoicism and Buddhism.
2. As Seneca says, "Truth lies open to everyone. There has yet to be a monopoly of truth" (Seneca 1969, 81).
3. Note that *apatheia* for the Stoics does not have the negative connotations that its modern English derivative—"apathy"—sometimes has. Whereas "apathy" can connote a lack of interest, perhaps even laziness, Stoic *apatheia* is a cultivated, deliberate indifference to the vicissitudes of the emotions. *Apatheia* is a virtuous and praiseworthy achievement. The ideal of *apatheia* helps explain, in turn, where the colloquial valence of the term "Stoic"—solid, upright, unmoved, impervious to emotional ebbs and flows—comes from.
4. "Human lives are brief and trivial. Yesterday a blob of semen; tomorrow embalming fluid, ash" (Aurelius 2002, 48).
5. See Marguia and Kim 2015, Pigliucci 2024, and Robertson 2019.
6. My colleague at the University of Nevada, Steven Hayes (who is, incidentally, the founder of ACT and the "Relational Frame Theory" upon which it is based), put it to me like this in an email: "Cognitive reappraisal was thought to work by challenging and changing thoughts. We now know that is incorrect. Cognitive reappraisal works by creating more cognitive distancing and defusion (the original name for ACT in the 80's was 'comprehensive distancing') which fosters greater cognitive flexibility. You still have the same whacky thoughts but you take a step back, behave differently with regard to them, and permit a wider variety of thoughts. Voila. ACTified CBT." If this is right, ACT and CBT are much closer than implied above.

7. Barlow reports that "PDA has become... one of the most widely recognized and publicized anxiety disorders.... [T]he central problem in PDA is anxiety focussed on the symptoms of panic; hence the well-known and commonly accepted characterization of agoraphobia as 'fear of fear'.... We know that individuals with this disorder focus on and attempt to avoid internal physical sensations associated with panic" (Barlow 2004, 328–329).

8. There is a passage from Claire Weekes's 1969 self-help classic, *Hope and Help for Your Nerves*, that strongly resonated with me in those difficult days: "But here again I whisper, 'Jelly legs will still get you there if you will let them. It is only a feeling. Not a true weakness. Don't be bluffed by jelly legs. And don't add more adrenalin by being afraid of them. Let them wobble. They'll get you across the street whether they wobble or not. And don't think you have to hold tensely on to yourself to keep yourself from collapsing. It's the holding on that exhausts, not the letting go. So let your legs wobble. It's only a feeling, not a true muscular weakness'" (Weekes 1969, 62).

9. A different but related idea has to do with the steady lowering, over the course of decades and even centuries, of the threshold for emotional pain that people are inclined to tolerate. Recall Nietzsche's quip from *The Genealogy of Morals*, that, in earlier times, "pain did not hurt so much as it does nowadays" (Nietzsche 2003, 43). Many commentators have observed that what would have once been regarded as everyday worry or commonplace sorrow have been, through complex processes of "medicalization" and "biologization," transformed into distinctively medical diagnoses. Historian Ian Dowbiggin is illuminating on this point. He writes: "Reports of anxiety, including shyness and stage fright, stretch back to classical antiquity, but before the nineteenth century the majority view was that most social anxiety was normal and even an asset in some situations that called for vigilance. Within cultures that prized bashfulness as a mark of modesty, shyness was widely praised in women. It may be a little consolation for people wracked with anxiety, for whom it is a genuinely painful experience, to learn how history has affected the public perception of anxiety, but the fact remains that over time everyday feelings have been transformed into symptoms of illness. The same goes for commonplace sorrow, which now is defined as depression. In this process of medicalization, more and more people have concluded that life is impossible without the guidance of state-certified experts" (Dowbiggin 2011, 3). Similar arguments can be found in Scull 2015 and Davis 2020. Gipps 2022 is also germane. The suggestion is not that people these days are wimpier than they used to be—although that's one way this kind of argument is often received. No one is claiming that the pain and suffering associated with anxiety is contrived or illusory. The conclusion we should draw from this analysis is that, psychiatrically speaking, it behooves us to tread carefully. If what counts as mental illness and wellness is determined to a large extent by contingent historical circumstance, this should encourage epistemic humility about our various diagnoses, thresholds, and courses of treatment.

Bibliography

Aho, Kevin. 2020. "Temporal Experience in Anxiety: Embodiment, Selfhood, and the Collapse of Meaning." *Phenomenology and the Cognitive Sciences* 19: 259–270.
Aiken, Scott F., and Robert B. Talisse. 2018. *Pragmatism, Pluralism, and the Nature of Philosophy*. New York: Routledge.
Alessandri, Mariana. 2023. *Night Vision: Seeing Ourselves Through Dark Moods*. Princeton, NJ: Princeton University Press.
Allen, Barry. 2004. *Knowledge and Civilization*. Boulder, CO: Westview Press.
American Psychiatric Association. 2013. *Diagnostic and Statistical Manual of Mental Disorders*, 5th edition. Arlington, VA: American Psychiatric Association Publishing.
Antonaccio, Maria. 2000. *Picturing the Human: The Moral Thought of Iris Murdoch*. New York: Oxford University Press.
Aristotle. 2001. *On the Parts of Animals*. Translated by James G. Lennox. New York: Oxford University Press.
Auden, W.H. 1976. *W.H. Auden: Collected Poems*. Edited by Edward Mendelson. New York: Vintage Books.
Augustine, Saint. 1991. *Confessions*. Translated by Henry Chadwick. New York: Oxford University Press.
Augustine, Saint. 1993. *On Free Choice of the Will*. Translated by Thomas Williams. Indianapolis, IN: Hackett.
Aurelius, Marcus. 2002. *Meditations*. Translated by Gregory Hays. New York: Modern Library.
Auster, Paul. 2012. *Winter Journal*. London: Faber & Faber.
Baillie, James. 2013. "The Expectation of Nothingness." *Philosophical Studies* 166 (1): 185–203.
Ballard, Brian Scott. 2021. "Content and the Fittingness of Emotion." *The Philosophical Quarterly* 71 (4): 845–863.
Barloon, Thomas, and Noyes, Russell, Jr. 1997. "Charles Darwin and Panic Disorder." *Journal of the American Medical Association* 277 (2): 138–141.
Barlow, David. H. 2000. "Unraveling the Mysteries of Anxiety and its Disorders from the Perspective of Emotion Theory." *The American Psychologist* 55 (11): 1247–1263.
Barlow, David H. 2004. *Anxiety and its Disorders: The Nature and Treatment of Anxiety and Panic*. 2nd edition. New York: Guilford Press.
Barnes, Julian. 2008. *Nothing to Be Frightened Of*. New York: Random House.
Barrett, Lisa Feldman. 2006. "Are Emotions Natural Kinds?" *Perspectives on Psychological Science* 1 (1): 28–58.

BIBLIOGRAPHY

Barrett, Lisa Feldman. 2017. *How Emotions Are Made: The Secret Life of the Brain*. New York: Houghton Mifflin Harcourt.
Barzun, Jacques. 1983. *A Stroll with William James*. Chicago: University of Chicago Press.
Baumeister, Roy F., and Dianne M. Tice. 1990. "Anxiety and Social Exclusion." *Journal of Social and Clinical Psychology* 9 (2): 165–195.
Baumgartner, Hans, Pieters Rik, and Richard P. Baggozzi. 2008. "Future-Oriented Emotions: Conceptualization and Behavioral Effects." *European Journal of Social Psychology* 38 (4): 685–696.
Beabout, Gregory, R. 2009. *Freedom and Its Misuses: Kierkegaard on Anxiety and Despair*. Milwaukee, WI: Marquette University Press.
Beard, George Miller. 1881. *American Nervousness: Its Causes and Consequences*. New York: G.P. Putnam's Sons.
Behrendt, Kathy. 2010. "A Special Way of Being Afraid." *Philosophical Psychology* 23 (5): 669–682.
Benbaji, Hagit. 2013. "How Is Recalcitrant Emotion Possible?" *Australasian Journal of Philosophy* XCI (3): 577–599.
Ben-Ze'ev, Aaron. 2000. *The Subtlety of Emotions*. Cambridge, MA: MIT Press.
Bergo, Bettina. 2021. *Anxiety: A Philosophical History*. New York: Oxford University Press.
Berlin, Isaiah. 1969. *Four Essays on Liberty*. Oxford: Oxford University Press.
Berlin, Isaiah. 1990. *The Crooked Timber of Humanity*. Edited by H. Hardy. Princeton, NJ: Princeton University Press.
Berman, David. 1995. "Introduction." In Arthur Schopenhauer's *The World as Will and Idea*, xvii–xxxix. London: Everyman.
Berry, Wendell. 2018. *The Peace of Wild Things and Other Poems*. New York: Penguin.
Blackburn, Simon. 2014. *Mirror, Mirror: The Uses and Abuses of Self-Love*. Princeton, NJ: Princeton University Press.
Blattner, William D. 1994. "The Concept of Death in *Being and Time*." *Man and World* 27: 49–70.
Bloom, Paul. 2016. *Against Empathy: The Case for Rational Compassion*. New York: Harper Collins.
Bobzien, Susanne. 1998. *Determinism and Freedom in Stoic Philosophy*. New York: Oxford University Press.
Bommarito, Nicolas. 2020. *Seeing Clearly: A Buddhist Guide to Life*. New York: Oxford University Press.
Bourne, Edmund J. 2010. *The Anxiety & Phobia Workbook*. 5th edition. Oakland, CA: New Harbinger.
Boyd, Richard. 1991. "Realism, Anti-Foundationalism, and the Enthusiasm for Natural Kinds." *Philosophical Studies* 61: 127–148.
Brady, Michael S. 2008. "Value and Fitting Emotions." *Journal of Value Inquiry* 42: 465–475.
Brady, Michael S. 2009. "The Irrationality of Recalcitrant Emotions." *Philosophical Studies* CXLV (3): 413–430.
Brady, Michael S. 2018. *Suffering and Virtue*. New York: Oxford University Press.
Brady, Michael S. 2024. "Anxiety's Allure." In *The Moral Psychology of Anxiety*, edited by David Rondel and Samir Chopra, 197–211. New York: Lexington.

Brennan, Tad. 2005. *The Stoic Life: Emotions, Duties, and Fate.* New York: Oxford University Press.
Brewer, Judson. 2021. *Unwinding Anxiety.* New York: Penguin Random House.
Burns, David, D. 2006. *When Panic Attacks: The New, Drug-Free Anxiety Therapy That Can Change Your Life.* New York: Harmony Books.
Burnyeat, M.F. 2008. "Kinesis versus Energeia: A Much Read Passage in (But Not Of) Aristotle's *Metaphysics*." *Oxford Studies in Ancient Philosophy* XXXIV: 219–292.
Burton, Robert. 2001. *The Anatomy of Melancholy.* New York: New York Review Books.
Carel, Havi. 2006. *Life and Death in Freud and Heidegger.* New York: Rodopi.
Carel, Havi. 2016. *Phenomenology of Illness.* Oxford: Oxford University Press.
Carlisle, Clare. 2019. *Philosopher of the Heart: The Restless Life of Søren Kierkegaard.* New York: Farrar, Straus and Giroux.
Carson, Rachel. 1956. *The Sense of Wonder: A Celebration of Nature for Parents and Children.* New York: Harper Collins.
Cartwright, David E. 2010. *Schopenhauer: A Biography.* New York: Cambridge University Press.
Cavell, Stanley. 2010. *Little Did I Know: Excerpts from Memory.* Stanford, CA: Stanford University Press.
Chamberlain, Jane, and Jonathan Rée. 2001. "Introduction: Becoming a Philosopher." In *The Kierkegaard Reader*, edited by Jane Chamberlain and Jonathan Rée, 1–12. Oxford: Blackwell.
Chopra, Samir. 2018. "The Usefulness of Dread." *Aeon.* February 21.
Conradi, Peter J. 2001a. *Iris Murdoch: A Life.* London: Harper Collins.
Conradi, Peter J. 2001b. *The Saint and the Artist: A Study of the Fiction of Iris Murdoch.* London: Harper Collins.
Cooper, John. 2012. *Pursuits of Wisdom: Six Ways of Life in Ancient Philosophy from Socrates to Plotinus.* Princeton, NJ: Princeton University Press.
Cooper, Rachel. 2018. "Understanding the DSM-5: Stasis and Change." *History of Psychiatry* 29 (1): 49–65.
Craske, Michelle G., and David H. Barlow. 2007. *Mastery of Your Anxiety and Panic.* New York: Oxford University Press.
Crisp, Roger. 2012. "Iris Murdoch on Nobility and Moral Value." In *Iris Murdoch, Philosopher*, edited by Justin Broackes, 275–292. New York: Oxford University Press.
Croce, Paul J. 2018. *Young William James Thinking.* Baltimore, MD: Johns Hopkins University Press.
Cvetkovich, Ann. 2012. *Depression: A Public Feeling.* Durham, NC: Duke University Press.
D'Arms, Justin. 2000. "Empathy and Evaluative Inquiry." *Chicago-Kent Law Review* 74 (4): 1467–1500.
D'Arms, Justin, and Daniel Jacobson. 2000. "The Moralistic Fallacy: On the 'Appropriateness' of the Emotions." *Philosophy and Phenomenological Research* LXI (1): 65–90.
D'Arms, Justin, and Daniel Jacobson. 2003. "The Significance of Recalcitrant Emotion (or, Anti-quasijudgmentalism)." *Royal Institute of Philosophy Supplement* LII: 127–146.

Darwin, Charles. 1872. *The Expression of the Emotions in Man and Animals.* London: John Murray.
Davis, Joseph E. 2020. *Chemically Imbalanced: Everyday Suffering, Medication, and Our Troubled Quest for Self-Mastery.* Chicago: University of Chicago Press.
De Cruz, Helen. 2020. "The Necessity of Awe." *Aeon.* July 10.
Deonna, Julien A., and Fabrice Teroni. 2012. *The Emotions: A Philosophical Introduction.* New York: Routledge.
Descartes, René. 1989. *The Passions of the Soul.* Translated by Stephen Voss. Indianapolis, IN: Hackett.
de Sousa, Ronald. 1987. *The Rationality of Emotion.* Cambridge, MA: MIT Press.
de Sousa, Ronald. 2004. "Emotions: What I Know, What I'd Like to Think I Know, and What I'd Like to Think." In *Thinking About Feeling: Contemporary Philosophers on Emotions*, edited by Robert C. Solomon, 61–75. New York: Oxford University Press.
de Sousa, Ronald. 2008. "Epistemic Feelings." In *Epistemology and Emotions*, edited by George Brun, Ulvi Douoglu, and Dominique Kuenzle, 185–203. New York: Routledge.
de Waal, Frans. 2014. Interviewed by Edwin Rutsch at the Center for Building a Culture of Empathy. http://cultureofempathy.com/references/Experts/Frans-de-Waal.htm.
Dewey, John. 1957. *Reconstruction in Philosophy.* Boston: The Beacon Press.
Dickinson, Emily. 1960. *The Complete Poems of Emily Dickinson.* Edited by Thomas H. Johnson. New York: Little, Brown and Company.
Dickinson, Emily. 1982. *Collected Poems of Emily Dickinson.* New York: Avenel Books.
Döring, Sabine A. 2015. "What's Wrong with Recalcitrant Emotions? From Irrationality to Challenge of Agential Identity." *Dialectica* 69 (3): 381–402.
Dowbiggin, Ian. 2011. *The Quest for Mental Health: A Tale of Science, Medicine, Scandal, Sorrow, and Mass Society.* New York: Cambridge University Press.
Dreyfus, Hubert L. 1993. *Being-in-the-World: A Commentary on Heidegger's Being and Time, Division I.* Cambridge, MA: MIT Press.
Du Bois, W.E.B. 1968. *Autobiography of W.E.B. Du Bois: A Soliloquy on Viewing My Life from the Last Decade of its First Century.* New York: International.
Du Bois, W.E.B. 1994. *The Souls of Black Folk.* New York: Dover.
Dupré, Louis K. 1963. *Kierkegaard as Theologian.* New York: Sheed & Ward.
Durkheim, Émile. 2001. *The Elementary Forms of Religious Life.* Translated by Carol Cosman. New York: Oxford University Press.
Edwards, Paul. 1975. "Heidegger and Death as 'Possibility.'" *Mind* 84: 548–566.
Elpidorou, Andreas. 2020. *Propelled: How Boredom, Frustration, and Anticipation Lead Us to the Good Life.* New York: Oxford University Press.
Emerson, Ralph Waldo. 1995. *The Heart of Emerson's Journals.* Edited by Bliss Perry. New York: Dover.
Emerson, Ralph Waldo. 2000. *The Essential Writings of Ralph Waldo Emerson.* Edited by Brooks Atkinson. New York: Modern Library.
Epictetus. 1940. *The Discourses of Epictetus* and *the Manual of Epictetus.* In *The Stoic and Epicurean Philosophers.* Edited by Whitney J. Oates, 223–490. New York: The Modern Library.

Epictetus. 2008. *Discourses and Selected Writings.* Translated and edited by Robert Dobbin. London: Penguin.
Epicurus. 1940. "Letter to Menoeceus." In *The Stoic and Epicurean Philosophers.* Edited by Whitney J. Oates, 30–34. New York: The Modern Library.
Feinstein, Howard M. 1984. *Becoming William James.* Ithaca, NY: Cornell University Press.
Flanagan, Owen. 2011. "What Is It Like to Be an Addict?" In *Addiction and Responsibility,* edited by Jefferey Poland and George Graham, 269–292. New York: MIT Press.
Flanagan, Owen. 2020. "The Disunity of Addictive Cravings." *Philosophy, Psychiatry, & Psychology* 27 (3): 243–246.
Flanagan, Owen. 2021. *How to Do Things with Emotions: The Morality of Anger and Shame Across Cultures.* Princeton, NJ: Princeton University Press.
Foucault, Michel. 1994. *Ethics: Subjectivity and Truth. The Essential Works of Foucault, 1954– 1984.* Edited by Paul Rabinow. New York: The New Press.
Foulkes, Lucy. 2021. *Losing Our Minds: What Mental Illness Really Is and What It Isn't.* London: Penguin.
Freeman, Daniel, and Jason Freeman. 2012. *Anxiety: A Very Short Introduction.* Oxford: Oxford University Press.
Freud, Sigmund. 1924. *Collected Papers, Vol. 1.* London: Hogarth Press.
Freud, Sigmund. 1952. *A General Introduction to Psychoanalysis.* New York: Washington Square Press.
Freud, Sigmund. 1959. *Inhibitions, Symptoms and Anxiety.* Translated by Alix Strachey. New York: W.W. Norton.
Freud, Sigmund. 1963. *The Problem of Anxiety.* New York: WW. Norton.
Freud, Sigmund. 1989. *The Freud Reader.* Edited by Peter Gay. New York: W.W. Norton & Co.
Freud, Sigmund. 2005. *On Murder, Mourning and Melancholia.* Translated by Shaun Whiteside. New York: Penguin.
Freud, Sigmund. 2018. *Reflections on War and Death.* Translated by Gabriela Guzman. *CreateSpace* Independent Publishing.
Fritz, James. 2021. "Fitting Anxiety and Prudent Anxiety." *Synthese* 199: 8555–8578.
Fuller, Robert C. 2006. *Wonder: From Emotion to Spirituality.* Chapel Hill: University of North Carolina Press.
Gale, Richard M. 1999. *The Divided Self of William James.* New York: Cambridge University Press.
Geuss, Raymond. 2005. *Outside Ethics.* Princeton, NJ: Princeton University Press.
Geuss, Raymond. 2017. *Changing the Subject: Philosophy from Socrates to Adorno.* Cambridge, MA: Harvard University Press.
Gill, Christopher. 2003. "The School in the Roman Imperial Period." In *The Cambridge Companion to the Stoics,* edited by Brad Inwood, 33–58. Cambridge, UK: Cambridge University Press.
Gingerich, Jonathan. 2018. "Freedom and the Value of Games." *Canadian Journal of Philosophy* 48 (5): 831–849.
Gingerich, Jonathan. 2022. "Spontaneous Freedom." *Ethics* 133 (1): 38–71.
Gipps, Richard G.T. 2022. "I've Got Anxiety." *Journal of Philosophy of Education* 56: 124–128.

BIBLIOGRAPHY

Goldie, Peter. 2000. *The Emotions: A Philosophical Exploration.* Oxford, UK: Oxford University Press.

Goldie, Peter. 2004. "Emotion, Reason and Virtue." In *Emotion, Evolution, and Rationality,* edited by Dylan Evans and Pierre Cruse, 249–268. Oxford, UK: Oxford University Press.

Gomes, Anil. 2022. "Moral Vision." In *The Murdochian Mind,* edited by Silvia Caprioglio Panizza and Mark Hopwood, 142–155. New York: Routledge.

Gouwens, David J. 1996. *Kierkegaard as a Religious Thinker.* Cambridge, UK: Cambridge University Press.

Graver, Margaret R. 2007. *Stoicism and Emotion.* Chicago: University of Chicago Press.

Gray, John. 2020. *Feline Philosophy: Cats the Meaning of Life.* New York: Farrar, Straus and Giroux.

Griffiths, Paul. E. 1997. *What Emotions Really Are: The Problem of Psychological Categories.* Chicago: University of Chicago Press.

Griffiths, Paul E. 2004. "Is Emotion a Natural Kind?" In *Thinking About Feeling: Contemporary Philosophers on Emotions,* edited by Robert C. Solomon, 233–249. New York: Oxford University Press.

Grøn, Arne. 2008, *The Concept of Anxiety in Søren Kierkegaard.* Translated by Jeanette B.L. Knox. Macon, GA: Mercer University Press.

Grzankowski, Alex. 2020. "Navigating Recalcitrant Emotions." *Journal of Philosophy* 117 (9): 501–519.

Hadot, Pierre. 1995. *Philosophy as a Way of Life.* Translated by Michael Chase. Oxford: Blackwell.

Hadot, Pierre. 2002. *What Is Ancient Philosophy?* Translated by Michael Chase. Cambridge, MA: Harvard University Press.

Hägglund, Martin. 2019. *This Life: Secular Faith and Spiritual Freedom.* New York: Pantheon Books.

Haig, Matt. 2015. *Reasons to Stay Alive.* New York: Penguin.

Haig, Matt. 2018. *Notes on a Nervous Planet.* Edinburgh, UK: Canongate Books.

Hampson, Daphne. 2013. *Kierkegaard: Exposition and Critique.* Oxford, UK: Oxford University Press.

Hanh, Thich Nhat. 1975. *The Miracle of Mindfulness.* Translated by Mobi Ho. Boston: Beacon Press.

Hanh, Thich Nhat. 1999. *The Heart of the Buddha's Teaching.* New York: Harmony Books.

Hannay, Alastair. 1998. "Kierkegaard and the Variety of Despair." In *The Cambridge Companion to Kierkegaard,* edited by Alastair Hannay and Gordon D. Marino, 329–348. Cambridge, UK: Cambridge University Press.

Hannay, Alastair. 2001. *Kierkegaard: A Biography.* Cambridge, UK: Cambridge University Press.

Harvey, Samantha. 2020. *The Shapeless Unease: A Year of Not Sleeping.* London: Penguin.

Hayes, Steven. 2019. *A Liberated Mind: How to Pivot toward What Matters.* New York: Avery.

Heidegger, Martin. 1962. *Being and Time.* Translated by John Macquarrie and Edward Robinson. New York: Harper & Row.

Heidegger, Martin. 1993. *Martin Heidegger: Basic Writings*. Edited by David Farrell Krell. New York: Harper Collins.

Helm, Bennett W. 2015. "Emotions and Recalcitrance: Reevaluating the Perceptual Model." *Dialectica* LXIX (3): 417-433.

Hobbes, Thomas. 1991. *Leviathan*. Edited by Richard Tuck. Cambridge, UK: Cambridge University Press.

Holloway, Richard. 2018. *Waiting for the Last Bus: Reflections on Life and Death*. Edinburgh, UK: Canongate Books.

Hookway, Christopher. 1998. "Doubt Affective States and the Regulation of Inquiry." *Canadian Journal of Philosophy* 24 (supplement): 203-225.

Horner, Avril, and Anne Rowe, eds. 2015. *Living on Paper: Letters from Iris Murdoch, 1934-1995*. Princeton, NJ: Princeton University Press.

Horwitz, Allan V. 2013. *Anxiety: A Short History*. Baltimore, MD.: Johns Hopkins University Press.

Hume, David. 2009. Selections from *An Enquiry Concerning Human Understanding*. In *Free Will*, edited by Derk Pereboom, 87-104. Indianapolis, IN: Hackett.

Inwood, Brad. 2003, ed. *The Cambridge Companion to the Stoics*. Cambridge, UK: Cambridge University Press.

Irvine, William. 2009. *A Guide to the Good Life: The Ancient Art of Stoic Joy*. New York: Oxford University Press.

Jacquette, Dale. 2005. *The Philosophy of Schopenhauer*. Montreal, CAN: McGill-Queen's University Press.

James, William. 1956. *The Will to Believe and Other Essays in Popular Philosophy*. New York: Dover.

James, William. 1961. *Psychology: The Briefer Course*. Edited by Gordon Allport. New York: Harper Torchbooks.

James, William. 1962. *Talks to Teachers on Psychology and to Students on Some of Life's Ideals*. Mineola, NY: Dover.

James, William. 1982. *The Varieties of Religious Experience*. Edited by Martin E. Marty. Harmondsworth, UK: Penguin.

James, William. 1996. *Essays in Radical Empiricism*. Lincoln: University of Nebraska Press.

James, William. 2000. *Pragmatism and Other Writings*. London: Penguin.

James, William. 2007a. *The Principles of Psychology*. Vol 1. New York: Cosimo.

James, William. 2007b. *The Principles of Psychology*. Vol 2. New York: Cosimo.

James, William. 2010. *The Heart of William James*. Edited by Robert Richardson. Cambridge, MA: Harvard University Press.

Jamison, Kay Redfield. 1995. *An Unquiet Mind: A Memoir of Moods and Madness*. New York: Vintage Books.

Janaway, Christopher. 1999. "Schopenhauer's Pessimism." In *The Cambridge Companion to Schopenhauer*, edited by Christopher Janaway, 318-343. Cambridge, UK: Cambridge University Press.

Kaag, John. 2020. *Sick Souls, Healthy Minds: How William James Can Save Your Life*. Princeton, NJ: Princeton University Press.

Kafka, Franz. 1972. *The Diaries of Franz Kafka*. Edited by Max Brod. New York: Penguin.

Kerr, Fergus. 2004. "The Self and the Good: Taylor's Moral Ontology." In *Charles Taylor*, edited by Ruth Abbey, 84–103. Cambridge, UK: Cambridge University Press.

Kierkegaard, Søren. 1980. *The Concept of Anxiety*. Edited and translated by Reidar Thomte. Princeton, NJ: Princeton University Press.

Kierkegaard, Søren. 1983. *Fear and Trembling* and *Repetition*. Edited and translated by Howard V. Hong and Edna H. Hong. Princeton, NJ: Princeton University Press.

Kierkegaard, Søren. 1992. *Concluding Unscientific Postscript to Philosophical Fragments*. Vol. 1. Edited and translated by Howard V. Hong and Edna H. Hong. Princeton, NJ: Princeton University Press.

Kierkegaard, Søren. 1996. *Papers and Journals: A Selection*. Translated by Alastair Hannay. London: Penguin.

Kierkegaard, Søren. 1997. *Christian Discourses: The Crisis and a Crisis in the Life of an Actress*. Edited and translated by Howard V. Hong and Edna H. Hong. Princeton, NJ: Princeton University Press.

Kierkegaard, Søren. 2013. *The Sickness Unto Death*. Translated by Walter Lowrie. Milwaukee, WI: Wiseblood Books.

King, Matt, and Joshua May, eds. 2022. *Agency in Mental Disorder: Philosophical Dimensions*. Oxford: Oxford University Press.

Knuuttila, Simo. 2004. *Emotions in Ancient and Medieval Philosophy*. Oxford: Clarendon Press.

Kurth, Charlie. 2015. "Moral Anxiety and Moral Agency." *Oxford Studies in Normative Ethics* 5: 171–195.

Kurth, Charlie. 2018. *The Anxious Mind: An Investigation into the Varieties and Virtues of Anxiety*. Cambridge, MA: MIT Press.

Kurth, Charlie. 2022. *Emotion*. New York: Routledge.

Kurth, Charlie. 2024. "Moral Anxiety: A Kantian Perspective." In *The Moral Psychology of Anxiety*, edited by David Rondel and Samir Chopra, 149–172. New York: Lexington.

Larkin, Philip. 2003. *Collected Poems*. Edited by Anthony Thwaite. London: Faber and Faber.

Lavine, T.Z. 1984. *From Socrates to Sartre: The Philosophic Quest*. New York: Bantam Books.

Law, Iain. 2009. "Motivation, Depression, and Character." In *Psychiatry as Cognitive Neuroscience: Philosophical Perspectives*, edited by Matthew Broome and Lisa Bortolotti, 351–364. Oxford, UK: Oxford University Press.

Lawrence, D.H. 1993. *The Complete Poems*. Edited by Vivian de Sola Pinto and F. Warren Roberts. New York: Penguin.

LeDoux, Joseph. 2016. *Anxious: Using the Brain to Understand and Treat Fear and Anxiety*. New York: Penguin.

Lipsomb, Benjamin J.B. 2022. *The Women Are Up to Something*. New York: Oxford University Press.

Locke, John. 1996. *Some Thoughts Concerning Education and of the Conduct of Understanding*. Edited by Ruth W. Grant and Nathan Tarcov. Indianapolis, IN: Hackett.

Lucretius. 1965. *On Nature*. Translated by Russell M. Greer. Indianapolis, IN: Bobbs-Merrill.
Machery, Edouard. 2009. *Doing without Concepts*. New York: Oxford University Press.
Maibom, Heidi. 2009. "Feeling for Others: Empathy, Sympathy, and Morality." *Inquiry* 52 (5): 483–499.
Maibom, Heidi. 2014. "Introduction: (Almost) Everything You Ever Wanted to Know About Empathy." In *Empathy and Morality*, edited by Heidi Maibom, 1–40. Oxford, UK: Oxford University Press.
Maibom, Heidi. 2022. "Don't Worry, Be Happy." *Synthese* 200 (67): 1–22.
Maier-Katkin, Daniel, and Birgit Maier-Katkin. 2007. "Love and Reconciliation: The Case of Hannah Arendt and Martin Heidegger." *Harvard Review* 32: 34–48.
Marguia, Edward, and Kim Diaz. 2015. "The Philosophical Foundations of Cognitive Behavioral Therapy: Stoicism, Buddhism, Taoism, and Existentialism." *Journal of Evidence-Based Psychotherapies* 15 (1): 37–50.
Marino, Gordon D. 1998. "Anxiety in *The Concept of Anxiety*." In *The Cambridge Companion to Kierkegaard*, edited by Alastair Hannay and Gordon D. Marino, 308–328. Cambridge, UK: Cambridge University Press.
Marks, Isaac. M. 1987. *Fears, Phobias, and Rituals: Panic, Anxiety, and Their Disorder*. New York: Oxford University Press.
Mason, Cathy. 2023. "Reconceiving Murdochian Realism." *Ergo* 10: 649–672.
May, Rollo. 1977. *The Meaning of Anxiety*. New York: W.W. Norton.
Meszaros, Julia T. 2016. *Selfless Love and Human Flourishing in Paul Tillich and Iris Murdoch*. Oxford, UK: Oxford University Press.
Meynen, Gerben. 2010. "Free Will and Mental Disorder: Exploring the Relationship." *Theoretical Medicine and Bioethics* 31 (6): 429–443.
Mole, Christopher. 2007. "Attention, Self and *The Sovereignty of the Good*." In *Iris Murdoch, A Reassessment*, edited by Anne Rowe, 72–84. New York: Palgrave MacMillan.
Montaigne, Michel. 2003. *The Complete Essays*. Translated by M.A. Screech. London: Penguin.
Munch-Jurisic, Ditte Marie. 2021. "Lost for Words: Anxiety, Well-Being, and the Costs of Conceptual Deprivation." *Synthese* 199: 13583–13600.
Murakami, Haruki. 2008. *What I Talk About When I Talk About Running: A Memoir*. Translated by Phillip Gabriel. New York: Vintage Books.
Murdoch, Iris. 1965. *The Red and the Green*. London: Vintage.
Murdoch, Iris. 1971. *The Sovereignty of Good*. London: Routledge.
Murdoch, Iris. 1977. *The Fire and the Sun: Why Plato Banished the Artists*. Oxford, UK: Oxford University Press.
Murdoch, Iris. 1992. *Metaphysics as a Guide to Morals*. London: Penguin.
Murdoch, Iris. 1997. *Existentialists and Mystics: Writings on Philosophy and Literature*. Edited by Peter J. Conradi. London: Penguin.
Murdoch, Iris. 2002. *Under the Net*. London: Vintage.
Nabokov, Vladimir. 1989. *Speak, Memory*. New York: Vintage Books.
Nadler, Steven. 2020. *Think Least of Death: Spinoza on How to Live and How to Die*. Princeton, NJ: Princeton University Press.

Nagel, Thomas. 1979. *Mortal Questions.* Cambridge, UK: Cambridge University Press.

Nagel, Thomas. 1986. *The View from Nowhere.* New York: Oxford University Press.

Nicholls, Moira. 1999. "The Influences of Eastern Thought on Schopenhauer's Doctrine of the Thing-in-Itself." In *The Cambridge Companion to Schopenhauer,* edited by Christopher Janaway, 171–212. Cambridge, UK: Cambridge University Press.

Nielsen, Kai. 1990. *Ethics without God.* Amherst, NY: Prometheus Books.

Nielsen, Kai. 2000. "Death and the Meaning of Life." In *The Meaning of Life,* edited by E.D. Klemke, 153–159. Oxford, UK: Oxford University Press.

Nietzsche, Friedrich. 1967. *The Will to Power.* Edited by Walter Kaufmann. Translated by Walter Kauffman and R.J. Hollingdale. New York: Vintage Books.

Nietzsche, Friedrich. 1986. *Human, All Too Human: A Book for Free Spirits.* Translated by Marion Faber and Stephen Lehmann. Omaha: University of Nebraska Press.

Nietzsche, Friedrich. 1997. *Untimely Meditations.* Edited by Daniel Breazeale. Translated by R.J. Hollingdale. Cambridge, UK: Cambridge University Press.

Nietzsche, Friedrich. 1998. *Twilight of the Idols.* Translated by Duncan Large. New York: Oxford University Press.

Nietzsche, Friedrich. 2001. *The Gay Science.* Edited by Bernard Williams. Cambridge, UK: Cambridge University Press.

Nietzsche, Friedrich. 2003. *The Genealogy of Morals.* Translated by Horace B. Samuel. Mineola, NY: Dover.

Nozick, Robert. 1989. *The Examined Life: Philosophical Meditations.* New York: Simon & Schuster.

Nussbaum, Martha C. 2001. *Upheavals of Thought: The Intelligence of the Emotions.* Cambridge, UK: Cambridge University Press.

Nussbaum, Martha C. 2009. *The Therapy of Desire: Theory and Practice in Hellenistic Ethics.* Princeton, NJ: Princeton University Press.

O'Brien, Hettie. 2020. "Grin and Bear It: On the Rise and Rise of Neo-Stoicism." *The Rambler.* October 28. https://thebaffler.com/latest/grin-and-bear-it-obrien

O'Connor, Patricia J. 1996. *To Love the Good: The Moral Philosophy of Iris Murdoch.* New York: Peter Lang.

Oliver, Mary. 2017. *Devotions: The Selected Poems of Mary Oliver.* New York: Penguin.

Olsson, Anna-Lova. 2018. "The Moment of Letting Go: Iris Murdoch and the Morally Transformative Process of *Unselfing.*" *Journal of Philosophy of Education* 52 (1): 163–177.

Padgett, Ron. 2013. *Collected Poems.* Minneapolis, MN: Coffee House Press.

Parfit, Derek. 1984. *Reasons and Persons.* Oxford, UK: Clarendon Press.

Pascal, Blaise. 1995. *Pensées and Other Writings.* Translated by Honor Levi. Oxford, UK: Oxford University Press.

Pigliucci, Massimo. 2017. *How to Be a Stoic.* New York: Basic Books.

Pigliucci, Massimo. 2024. "The Moral Psychology of Anxiety: A Stoic Perspective." In *The Moral Psychology of Anxiety,* edited by David Rondel and Samir Chopra, 13–28. New York: Lexington.

Polt, Richard. 1999. *Heidegger: An Introduction*. Ithaca, NY: Cornell University Press.
Price, Carolyn. 2006. "Affect without Object: Moods and Objectless Emotions." *European Journal of Analytic Philosophy* 2 (1): 49–68.
Prinz, Jesse. 2004. *Gut Reactions: A Perceptual Theory of Emotion*. New York: Oxford University Press.
Prinz, Jesse. 2011. "Against Empathy." *Southern Journal of Philosophy* 49: 214–243.
Prinz, Jesse. 2012. *Beyond Human Nature: How Culture and Experience Shape the Human Mind*. New York: W.W. Norton.
Prinz, Jesse. 2013. "How Wonder Works." *Aeon*. June 21.
Prinz, Jesse. 2024. "Generalized Anxiety Disorder: Natural, Normative, or Neither?" In *The Moral Psychology of Anxiety*, edited by David Rondel and Samir Chopra, 99–124. New York: Lexington.
Pursur, Ronald, E. 2019. *McMindfulness: How Mindfulness Became the New Capitalist Spirituality*. London: Repeater Books.
Puryear, Stephen. 2022. "Schopenhauer's Rejection of the Moral *Ought*." In *Schopenhauer's Moral Philosophy*, edited by Patrick Hassan, 12–30. New York: Routledge.
Putnam, Hilary. 2017. "Reconsidering Deweyan Democracy." In *Pragmatism and Justice*, edited by Susan Dieleman, David Rondel, and Christopher J. Voparil, 249–264. New York: Oxford University Press.
Radden, Jennifer. 2014. "The Self and Its Moods in Depression and Mania." In *Depression, Emotion and the Self*, edited by Matthew Ratcliffe and Achim Stephan, 59–78. Exeter, UK: Imprint Academic.
Ramsey, Frank. 1990. *Philosophical Papers*. Edited by D.H. Mellor. Cambridge, UK: Cambridge University Press.
Ratcliffe, Matthew. 2008. *Feelings of Being: Phenomenology, Psychiatry and the Sense of Reality*. Oxford, UK: Oxford University Press.
Ratcliffe, Matthew. 2015. *Experiences of Depression: A Study in Phenomenology*. Oxford, UK: Oxford University Press.
Ratcliffe, Matthew. 2017. *Real Hallucinations: Psychiatric Illness, Intentionality, and the Interpersonal World*. Cambridge, MA: MIT Press.
Rice, Anne. 1988. *The Queen of the Damned*. New York: Random House.
Roberts, Robert C. 2003. *Emotions: An Essay in Aid of Moral Psychology*. Cambridge, UK: Cambridge University Press.
Roberts, Robert C. 2013. *Emotions in the Moral Life*. New York: Cambridge University Press.
Robertson, Donald. 2019. *The Philosophy of Cognitive-Behavioral Therapy (CBT): Stoic Philosophy as Rational and Cognitive Psychotherapy*. 2nd edition. New York: Routledge.
Rockmore, Tom. 1996. "Heidegger and Holocaust Revisionism." In *Martin Heidegger and the Holocaust*, edited by Alan Milchman and Alan Rosenberg, 113–126. Atlantic Highlands, NJ: Humanities Press.
Rondel, David. 2017. "William James on Justice and the Sacredness of Individuality." In *Pragmatism and Justice*, edited by Susan Dieleman, David Rondel, and Christopher J. Voparil, 309–323. New York: Oxford University Press.

Rondel, David. 2018. *Pragmatist Egalitarianism*. New York: Oxford University Press.
Rondel, David. 2021a. "Strenuous Citizenship: William James and Political Action." In *The Jamesean Mind*, edited by Sarin Marchetti, 211–221. New York: Routledge.
Rondel, David. 2021b. "William James and the Metaphilosophy of Individualism." *Metaphilosophy* 52 (2): 220–233.
Rondel, David, and Samir Chopra, eds. 2024. *The Moral Psychology of Anxiety*. New York: Lexington.
Rorty, Amélie Oksenberg. 1980. "Introduction" In *Explaining Emotions*, edited by Amélie Oksenberg Rorty, 1–8. Los Angeles: University of California Press.
Rorty, Amélie Oksenberg. 1983. "Fearing Death." *Philosophy* 58 (224): 175–188.
Rorty, Amélie Oksenberg. 2004. "Enough Already with 'Theories of the Emotions.'" In *Thinking About Feeling: Contemporary Philosophers on Emotions*, edited by Robert C. Solomon, 269–278. New York: Oxford University Press.
Rorty, Richard. 1989. *Contingency, Irony, and Solidarity*. Cambridge, UK: Cambridge University Press.
Rorty, Richard. 1999. *Philosophy and Social Hope*. London: Penguin.
Rosenberg, Jay. 1983. *Thinking Clearly About Death*. Englewood Cliffs, NJ: Prentice-Hall.
Rousseau, Jean-Jacques. 1968. *Julie, or the new Eloise*. Translated by Judith H. McDowell. University Park: Pennsylvania State University Press.
Rowe, Anne. 2019. *Iris Murdoch*. Liverpool, UK: Liverpool University Press.
Sacks, Oliver. 1996. *The Island of the Colorblind*. New York: Penguin.
Safranski, Rüdiger. 1998. *Martin Heidegger: Between Good and Evil*. Translated by Ewald Osers. Cambridge, MA: Harvard University Press.
Sartre, Jean-Paul. 1956. *Being and Nothingness*. Translated by Hazel E. Barnes. New York: Washington Square Press.
Sartre, Jean-Paul. 1984. *War Diaries: Notebooks from a Phony War, 1939–1940*. Translated by Quintin Hoare. New York: Verso.
Scarantino, Andrea. 2009. "Core Affect and Natural Affective Kinds." *Philosophy of Science* 76 (5): 940–957.
Scarre, Geoffrey. 2007. *Death*. Montreal, CAN: McGill-Queen's University Press.
Schopenhauer, Arthur. 1966a. *The World as Will and Representation*. Vol. II. Translated by E.F.J. Payne. New York: Dover.
Schopenhauer, Arthur. 1966b. *The World as Will and Representation*. Vol. I. Translated by E.F.J. Payne. New York: Dover.
Schopenhauer, Arthur. 1970. *Essays and Aphorisms*. New York: Penguin.
Schopenhauer, Arthur. 1974. *Parerga and Paralipomena: Short Philosophical Essays*. Translated by E.F.J. Payne. Oxford, UK: Oxford University Press.
Schopenhauer, Arthur. 1988. *Manuscript Remains*. Translated by E.F.J. Payne. Vol. 4. Oxford: Berg.
Schopenhauer, Arthur. 1995. *On the Basis of Morality*. Translated by E.F.J. Payne. Indianapolis, IN.: Hackett.
Schopenhauer, Arthur. 1998. *The World as Will and Idea*. Edited by David Berman. Translated by Jill Berman. London: Everyman.

BIBLIOGRAPHY

Schopenhauer, Arthur. 2009. *The Two Fundamental Problems of Ethics*. Edited and translated by Christopher Janaway. Cambridge, UK: Cambridge University Press.

Scull, Andrew. 2015. *Madness in Civilization*. Princeton, NJ: Princeton University Press.

Sellars, John. 2006. *Stoicism*. Berkeley: University of California Press.

Seneca. 1969. *Letters from a Stoic*. Translated by Robin Campbell. Harmondsworth, UK: Penguin.

Seneca. 1997. *Dialogues and Letters*. Edited and translated by C.D.N. Costa. London: Penguin.

Seneca. 2016. *Seneca's Letter from a Stoic*. Edited by Richard Mott Gummere. New York: Dover.

Setiya, Kieran. 2017. *Midlife: A Philosophical Guide*. Princeton, NJ: Princeton University Press.

Setiya, Kieran. 2022. *Life Is Hard: How Philosophy Can Help Us Find Our Way*. New York: Riverhead Books.

Slote, Michael A. 1975. "Existentialism and the Fear of Dying." *American Philosophical Quarterly* 12 (1): 17–28.

Smith, Adam. 1980. *Essays on Philosophical Subjects*. Edited by W.P.D. Wightman, J.C. Bryce, and I.S. Ross. Oxford, UK: Oxford University Press.

Smith, Daniel. 2012. *Monkey Mind: A Memoir of Anxiety*. New York: Simon & Schuster.

Solomon, Andrew. 2001. *The Noonday Demon: An Atlas of Depression*. New York: Touchstone.

Solomon, Andrew. 2013. "Depression, Too, Is a Thing with Feathers." *Contemporary Psychoanalysis* 44 (4): 509–530.

Solomon, Robert C. 1993. *The Passions: Emotions and the Meaning of Life*. Indianapolis, IN: Hackett.

Solomon, Robert C. 1998. "Death Fetishism, Morbid Solipsism." In *Death and Philosophy*, edited by Jeff Malpas and Robert C. Solomon, 152–176. London: Routledge.

Solomon, Robert C. 2007. *True to Our Feelings: What Our Emotions Are Really Telling Us*. New York: Oxford University Press.

Sorabji, Richard. 2000. *Emotion and Peace of Mind: From Stoic Agitation to Christian Temptation*. New York: Oxford University Press.

Spinoza, Benedict. 2018. *Ethics: Proved in Geometrical Order*. Edited by Matthew J. Kisner. Translated by Michael Silverthorne and Matthew J. Kisner. Cambridge, UK: Cambridge University Press.

Stephen, James Fitzjames. 1874. *Liberty, Equality, Fraternity*. London: Smith, Elder.

Stossel, Scott. 2013. *My Age of Anxiety: Fear, Hope, Dread, and the Search for Peace of Mind*. New York: Vintage Books.

Strawson, P.F. 2008. *Freedom and Resentment and Other Essays*. New York: Routledge.

Strawson, Galen. 2018. *Things That Bother Me: Death, Freedom, the Self, etc*. New York: New York Review Books.

Styron, William. 1992. *Darkness Visible: A Memoir of Madness.* New York: Vintage Books.
Tappolet, Christine. 2016. *Emotions, Values, and Agency.* New York: Oxford University Press.
Taylor, Charles. 1989. *Sources of the Self: The Making of the Modern Identity.* Cambridge, MA: Harvard University Press.
Theunissen, Michael. 2005. *Kierkegaard's Concept of Despair.* Translated by Barbara Harshaw and Helmut Illbruck. Princeton, NJ: Princeton University Press.
Thomason, Krista K. 2022. "How Should We Feel about Recalcitrant Emotions?" In *Self-Blame and Moral Responsibility*, edited by Andreas Brekke Carlsson, 134–148. New York: Cambridge University Press.
Thomason, Krista K. 2024. *Dancing with the Devil: Why Bad Feelings Make Life Good.* New York: Oxford University Press.
Thompson, Evan. 2020. *Why I Am Not a Buddhist.* New Haven, CT: Yale University Press.
Tillich, Paul. 2014. *The Courage to Be.* New Haven, CT: Yale University Press.
Tolstoy, Leo. 1981. *The Death of Ivan Ilyich.* Translated by Lynn Solotaroff. New York: Bantam.
Townsend, Kim. 1996. *Manhood at Harvard: William James and Others.* New York: W.W. Norton.
Trigg, Dylan. 2017. *Topophobia: A Phenomenology of Anxiety.* London: Bloomsbury.
Twin, Kenneth, ed. 1959. *Essays in Unitarian Theology: A Symposium.* London: Lindsey Press.
Vazard, Juliette. 2019. "(Un)reasonable Doubt as Affective Experience: Obsessive-Compulsive Disorder, Epistemic Anxiety and the Feeling of Uncertainty." *Synthese* 198: 6917–6934.
Vazard, Juliette. 2024. "The Epistemic Virtue of Anxiety." In *The Moral Psychology of Anxiety*, edited by David Rondel and Samir Chopra, 173–196. New York: Lexington.
Vazard, Juliette, and Charlie Kurth. 2022. "Apprehending Anxiety: An Introduction to the Topical Collection on Worry and Well-Being." *Synthese* 200: 327.
W, Bill. 2000. *My First Forty Years.* Center City, MN: Hazelden Publishing.
Walle, A.H. 1992. "William James' Legacy to Alcoholics Anonymous: An Analysis and a Critique." *Journal of Addictive Diseases* 11 (3): 91–99.
Warren, James. 2004. *Facing Death: Epicurus and His Critics.* Oxford, UK: Oxford University Press.
Weekes, Claire. 1969. *Hope and Help for Your Nerves.* New York: Penguin.
Welchman, Alistair. 2017. "Schopenhauer." In *The Cambridge History of Moral Philosophy*, edited by Sacha Golob and Jens Timmerman, 448–458. Cambridge, UK: Cambridge University Press.
Widdows, Heather. 2005. *The Moral Vision of Iris Murdoch.* Hampshire, UK: Ashgate.
Williams, Kathryn, and Harvey, David. 2001. "Transcendent Experience in Forest Environments." *Journal of Environmental Psychology* 21: 249–260.
Wittgenstein, Ludwig. 1998. *Philosophical Investigations.* Translated by G.E.M. Anscombe. Oxford, UK: Blackwell.

Wittgenstein, Ludwig. 1999. *Tractatus Logico-Philosophicus*. Translated by C.K. Ogden. Mineola, NY: Dover.
Woolf, Virginia. 1985. *Moments of Being: A Collection of Autobiographical Writing*. Edited by Jeanne Schulkind. New York: Harcourt.
Woolf, Virginia. 2005. *Mrs. Dalloway*. Edited by Mark Hussey. Orlando, FL: Harcourt.
Wordsworth, William. 2008. *The Major Works*. Edited by Stephen Gill. New York: Oxford University Press.
Wright, Robert. 2017. *Why Buddhism Is True*. New York: Simon & Schuster.
Yates, Richard. 2000. *Revolutionary Road*. New York: Vintage Books.
Young, Julian. 2005. *Schopenhauer*. New York: Routledge.
Zhang, Jia Wei, Paul K. Piff, Ravi Iyer, Spassena Koleva, and Dacher Keltner. 2014. "An Occasion for Unselfing: Beautiful Nature Leads to Prosociality." *Journal of Environmental Psychology* 37: 61–72.
Zimmerman, Michael E. 1993. "Heidegger, Buddhism, and Deep Ecology." In *The Cambridge Companion to Heidegger*, edited by Charles Guignon, 240–269. Cambridge, UK: Cambridge University Press.

Index

Acceptance Commitment Therapy (ACT), 171–73, 195n.6
addiction, 142, 143–44, 194n.7
agoraphobia, 7, 41–42, 56, 149–50, 174–75, 195n.10, 196n.9
alarm response, 12
alcohol, 44–45, 69–70, 142, 143–44, 194n.7
Alessandri, Mariana, 17, 187n.4
American Pragmatism, xi, 47–48, 52, 60
anguish, xii, 5–6, 28, 47, 57, 63, 119–20
anxiety, 4–5, 13–15, 18–19, 23, 25–26, 27–34, 40–44, 49, 52–53, 58, 67, 71–72, 80–84, 116, 123–24, 138
   differentiated from fear, 4, 12–13, 25–26, 28, 82, 138, 185n.10
   heterogeneity of, 4, 5–7, 11–12
   non-human animals and, 20–21, 165, 184n.5, 188n.8
   normativity of, 7, 10–11
   phenomenology of, 7, 9, 42–43, 65
   physical symptoms of, 13–14, 42–43, 62–63, 109–10, 151–52
   as selfish emotion, 27, 133, 137–38, 150–51
   tendency to avoid or flee from, 33–34, 84–85, 189–90n.9
   treatment for, 69–70, 127–28, 138–39, 142–44, 151–52, 164, 176–79, 180–81 (*see also* psychotherapy)
Arendt, Hannah, 74–75
Aristotle, 2, 178–79, 192n.7, 194n.8
art, 36, 130–31, 193n.1
attention, 66, 69, 84, 108, 127–28, 132–34, 138, 139–40, 150–51, 173, 177–78
Auden, W.H., 5–6
Augustine, St., 23, 185n.8, 186n.23
Aurelius, Marcus, 154–55, 157, 160, 161, 162–63, 165–67, 168–69, 170–71, 176. *See also* Stoicism

Auster, Paul, 56
awe, 127, 138–39, 145, 146–47, 149, 150–53, 196n.9

Barlow, David, 174–75, 195n.10, 196n.9
Barnes, Julian, 77–78, 79–80, 189n.6
Barrett, Lisa Feldman, 65–66, 151–53
Being and Time (Heidegger), 76, 86–87
Berlin, Isaiah, 50, 187n.3
Berry, Wendell, 41–42, 141
Brady, Michael S., ix, 7–8
Buddhism, 3–4, 71, 101, 105–6, 115, 116, 191n.4, 192n.8, 195n.1
   Four Noble Truths of, 105
Burton, Robert, 191n.5

cancer, 7, 49, 91–92
Carel, Havi, 87–88, 186n.21
Carlisle, Clare, 17, 18, 28–29, 32–33
Chopra, Samir, ix, 12–13
Christianity, 19–20, 23, 24, 25, 59–60, 155–56, 185n.8
Chrysippus, 155
Cleanthes, 155
Cognitive Behavioral Therapy (CBT), 171, 172–74, 177, 186n.24, 195n.6
compassion, 115–22, 123–24, 125

Darwin, Charles, 188n.8
death, xii, 3, 7, 24, 29, 52, 59–60, 83–84, 96–97, 107, 158–59
   Amélie Rorty on, 94–96
   and anxiety, 71–73, 76–77, 81, 84–85, 88–91, 105, 107–8, 167
   different attitudes toward, 84, 91–94
   inner and outer perspectives on, 77–80, 85–88
depression, 17, 39–41, 48–49, 191n.5, 196n.9
Descartes, Rene, 145–46

INDEX

de Sousa, Ronald, 7–8, 9, 90–91
Dewey, John, 60–61
Diagnostic and Statistical Manual of Mental Disorders (DSM), 5, 12, 56, 183n.2, 186n.20
Dickinson, Emily, 20–21, 31–32, 121, 122
Dowbiggin, Ian, ix, 196n.9
Du Bois, W.E.B., 47–48, 87
du Bos, Charles, 77–78

Emerson, Ralph Waldo, 48, 194n.8, 196n.9
emotions, 4, 31, 36–37, 46–47, 51, 62–63, 64–66, 145–46, 150–52, 161–62
    appropriateness of, 9–11, 183–84n.7
    belief-dependence of, 8–9, 183n.5
Epictetus, 155, 157–63, 172. *See also* Stoicism
Epicurus, 71, 88–89, 90–91, 94–95, 157
epistemic value of anxiety, 5
evolutionary psychology, 12, 149–50
existentialism, 3–4, 18, 26–27, 28, 53, 71, 82, 91–92, 129
exposure therapy, 92, 173–76, 177–78, 180

Fichte, Johann Gottlieb, 101
Flanagan, Owen, 194n.7
Foucault, Michel, 134
Foulkes, Lucy, 187n.4
freedom, xii, 2, 18, 21–23, 27–30, 35, 39–40, 92, 93, 185–86n.17, 186n.20
    anxiety and, 3, 18–19, 20–21, 42–45
    phenomenology of, 34–36
    "spontaneous" freedom (Gingerich), 36–39
Freud, Sigmund, 3–4, 5, 11–12, 13–14, 47–48, 71, 85–87, 125–26, 184n.5, 185n.10, 193n.2
    neurotic anxiety and, 25–26
future, 1, 4, 5, 18–19, 27–28, 31, 36, 37, 60, 83, 85–86, 87–88, 98, 107, 108, 112–13, 114, 137–38
    Stoic attitude towards, 165–71
    uncertainty regarding, 20–21, 23, 25–26, 28, 29–31, 43–44, 49, 52, 53–54

Geuss, Raymond, 37, 83–85
Gingerich, Jonathan, ix, 36–37
Greek philosophy, 85, 155–57, 160–61, 178–79
Griffiths, Paul E., 6–7

Hadot, Pierre, 154–55, 156–57, 164, 177–78
Hägglund, Martin, 12–13, 23, 184–85n.7
    the distinction between natural and spiritual freedom in, 21–22
Haig, Matt, 69–70, 148–49, 191n.5, 194n.6
Hanh, Thich Nhat, 115, 146–47
Harvey, Samantha, 108–9, 110, 163–64, 170–71
Hayes, Steven, ix, 172–73, 195n.6
Hegel, G.W.F., 101–2
Heidegger, Martin, 3–4, 71, 96–97, 129
    biography of, 73–76
    concept of "idle talk" in, 84
    concept of "uncanny" in, 80–81
    contemplation of death in, 72, 73, 85–89, 92–94
    on the mood of anxiety, 81–85
    Nazism, involvement with, 73–74, 189n.3
Hobbes, Thomas, 1, 2
Holloway, Richard, 77
Horwitz, Allan V., 54–56
Hume, David, 42–43

James, William, 3, 46–47, 49, 50–51, 52–53, 59–60, 143–44, 149–50, 185n.9, 194n.7
    biography of, 47–48
    conception of habit in, 61–63, 67–68, 69
    concept of meliorism in, 60–61
    concepts of "sick souls" in, 54–58, 69–70
    theory of emotion in, 62–67
    tragic sensibility of, 48–53

Kafka, Franz, 184n.2
Kant, Immanuel, 101

Kierkegaard, Soren, 3-4, 16-17, 18-19, 26-27, 28, 32-34, 49, 71, 82, 124, 129, 184n.4, 185n.10
on anxiety as "dizziness of freedom", 18, 22, 27-28, 29-31, 45
biography of, 17-18
and *The Concept of Anxiety*, 18-19
concept of despair in, 23, 24-26, 184-85n.7
on possibility, 18-21, 22, 27-28, 31-32
Kurth, Charlie, ix, 10-11, 30-31, 53-54
on anxiety as "problematic uncertainty", 5

Larkin, Philip, 89-90, 167-68, 188-89n.2, 190n.13, 190n.14
Law, Iain, 39-40
Lawrence, D.H., 109
LeDoux, Joseph, 63, 137-38, 185n.10
literature, 7-8, 130-31
Locke, John, 173-74
Lucretius, 71, 88-89, 90-91, 94-95

Maibom, Heidi, 186n.19
May, Rollo, 11-12
meditation, 69-70, 93, 113, 127-28, 141-42, 143-44, 165-66, 179-80
mental health, 5, 12, 44-45, 46, 62-63, 67-68, 99, 170-71, 179, 180, 196n.9
diagnostic criteria and, 54-56
midlife crisis, 106-8, 112
Montaigne, Michel de, 31, 71, 92, 93-94, 116, 159-60, 185n.13
moods, 4, 5-6, 18, 45, 72, 76-77, 80-82, 83-85, 123, 179-80
as differentiated from emotions, 183n.5
phenomenology of, 81-82
Muir Woods, 144-45
Murakami, Haruki, 142-43
Murdoch, Iris, 3, 127-28, 132-34, 136-37, 143-44, 151-53, 169-70
biography of, 128-31
concept of "unselfing" in, 132-33, 137-39, 140, 141, 142, 150-51, 153, 193n.1
moral realism of, 134-36

Nagel, Thomas, 89-90, 188-89n.2, 190n.12
natural kinds, 6-7, 183n.4
nature, therapeutic power of, 142, 144-45, 147-49, 152, 153, 177-78, 194n.8, 196n.9
Nielsen, Kai, 91-92
Nietzsche, Friedrich, 1-2, 35, 98, 100-1, 124, 125-26, 185-86n.17, 196n.9
Nozick, Robert, 144-45
Nussbaum, Martha, 183n.5

Oliver, Mary, 141-42

Padgett, Ron, 191n.6
pain, xii, 5, 22-23, 25-26, 31-32, 44-45, 47, 54-56, 57, 59-60, 72-73, 79, 94-95, 109-10, 118-19, 124, 160
panic attacks, xi, 13-14, 26-27, 41, 45, 56, 66-67, 78-79, 81, 174-75, 196n.9
parental modelling, 58-59
Parfit, Derek, 178-79
Pascal, Blaise, 71, 185n.15
phobias, 45, 56, 174-75
Plato, 2, 135-36, 178-79, 193n.1, 193n.2
Prinz, Jesse, ix, 4, 146-47
psychiatric diagnosis, 54-56
psychotherapy, 171-74
Putnam, Hilary, 51

Ramsey, Frank, 14
Ratcliffe, Matthew, 5, 40-41, 63, 64-65, 80-81
recalcitrant emotions, 9-10, 11
Roberts, Robert C., 67
Roosevelt, Theodore, 47-48
Rorty, Amélie, 87, 94-96, 183n.4
Rorty, Richard, 72, 73-74, 189n.3, 193n.15
Rousseau, Jean-Jacques, 71

Sacks, Oliver, 147-48
Sartre, Jean-Paul, 3-4, 28, 39, 71, 129, 183n.1

INDEX

Schopenhauer, Arthur, 3, 98, 101, 106, 111–12, 119–22
  biography of, 99–103
  on compassion and ethics, 115, 116–19, 121–22, 192n.9
  influence of Indian philosophy on, 3–4, 101, 115, 116, 192n.9
  on the striving of the will, 103–5
  the unavoidability of suffering and, 105
self, 18, 19–20, 72–73, 134, 135, 136–37, 139–40, 150–52
  anxiety and, 137–38, 142–44, 150–53
  Cartesian notion of, 133–34
  Iris Murdoch on, 132, 133, 134, 135, 136–37, 193n.2
self-effacing goods, 178–79, 180
self-help, 2–3, 14, 58, 154–55, 177, 179–80
Seneca, 89, 155, 157, 159–60, 161–62, 165–66, 170–71, 172–79. *See also* Stoicism
Setiya, Kieran, 90–91, 106–8, 183n.1
  on telic and atelic activities, 111–15
Sickness Unto Death, The (Kierkegaard), 16, 19–20
Smith, Adam, 146–47
Smith, Daniel, 16–17, 58–59, 123–24
Socrates, 6–7, 32–33, 155, 156–57
Solomon, Andrew, 42–43, 44–45, 106, 123, 191n.5
Solomon, Robert C., 4, 8–9, 72–73, 87
Sorabji, Richard, 13–14, 163–65
Spinoza, Baruch, 93–94, 190n.16
Stoicism, 3, 71, 154–56, 159, 161–63, 164–65, 171, 173–74, 195n.1
  anti-anxiety techniques of, 157–58, 160, 164–65, 168–69, 171–74, 176–79
  concept of *apatheia* in, 154–55, 158–59, 180–81, 195n.3
  the distinction between *prohairetic* and *aprohairetic* in, 157–61, 162–63
  history of, 154–57
Stossel, Scott, 12–13, 184n.5
Strawson, Galen, 35
suffering, 12–13, 22–23, 25–26, 29–30, 31–32, 44–45, 47, 59–60, 79, 98, 99, 103–5, 111, 116, 117–18, 119–20, 121–26

Tappolet, Christine, 183–84n.7
Taylor, Charles, 134–35
Tillich, Paul, 71, 90–91

value pluralism, 187n.3
Varieties of Religious Experience, The (James), 46, 49, 54, 187–88n.7
Vazard, Juliette, ix
Virgil, 170–71
virtues and anxiety, 93, 125

Weekes, Claire, 196n.8
wellness industry, 179–80
Wittgenstein, Ludwig, xi, 14, 51, 85–86
wonder, 127, 138–40, 144–48, 149, 150–53, 183n.1
Woolf, Virginia, 38–40
Wordsworth, William, 139

Zeno, of Citium, 155